COMMUNICATING CLIMATE RISK: A TOOLKIT

Written by
Jo Lindsay Walton and Polina Levontin
With additional contributions from

Martine J. Barons, Dilman Dila, Jana Kleineberg, Erik Mackie, Maurice Ssebisubi, and Mark Workman

Layout and design by
Jana Kleineberg, kleineberg.co.uk/

Published by the Sussex Digital Humanities Lab (SHL Digital), Brighton, UK. This Toolkit is licensed under a CC BY-NC-SA 4.0 licence.
3RD EDITION, April 2024

ISBN:
978-1-912802-06-7   Communicating Climate Risk: A toolkit (1st edition)
978-1-912802-07-4   Communicating Climate Risk: A toolkit 2 (digital)
978-1-912802-08-1   Communicating Climate Risk: A toolkit 3 (print)
978-1-912802-09-8   Communicating Climate Risk: A toolkit 3 (digital)

DOI: doi.org/10.33774/coe-2021-mrx1f
Also: bit.ly/CommunicatingClimateRisk

Copyright and licence
Copyrights are held by contributing authors. This publication is licensed under a Creative Commons Attribution-NonCommercial-ShareAlike 4.0 International Licence (CC BY-NC-SA 4.0).

Recommended citation
Walton, J.L., Levontin, P., Barons, M.J., Dila, D., Kleineberg, J., Mackie, E., Ssebisubi, M., and Workman, M. *Communicating Climate Risk: A Toolkit* (Brighton, UK: Sussex Digital Humanities Lab, 2024).

Disclaimer
The opinions expressed in this publication are those of the authors.
They do not purport to reflect the opinions or views of the UK Universities Climate Network.

This page was intentionally left blank.

COMMUNICATING CLIMATE RISK:
A TOOLKIT

THIRD EDITION

TABLE OF CONTENTS

Copyright /Impressum
Executive summary 6
Key messages 7

CHAPTER 1. Introduction
Jo Lindsay Walton, Martine J. Barons, Polina Levontin, and Mark Workman

    Overview 10
    Uncertainty and climate risk communication 11
    The IPCC and the AR6 13
    Budgets, bombs, and uncertainty about uncertainty:
        an example of climate risk communication 13
    Uncertainty rebranded? 15
    Zeroing in on zero 16
    Risk vs. uncertainty 18
    References 19

CHAPTER 2. Understanding Audiences
Jo Lindsay Walton, Mark Workman, Martine J. Barons, and Polina Levontin

    Who are the experts, the decision-makers,
        and the stakeholders? 19
    The decision value chain 21
    Uncertainty and the decision value chain:
        eight recommendations 23
    Decision analysis: an interdisciplinary field,
        rooted in economics and statistics 23
    Storytelling vs. decision support: a checklist 25
    Funding climate storytelling in the media 25
    References 27

CHAPTER 3. Communicating around Tipping Points
Jo Lindsay Walton, Polina Levontin, and Erik Mackie

    What are tipping points 29
    The many emotions of apocalypse 33
    What's wrong with a little apocalypse 35
    Where do we talk about climate risks such as tipping points? 36
    Tipping points and the IPCC model ensemble 38
    Communicating around deep uncertainty 39
    "Participatory uncertainty" 41
    Visualising deep uncertainty 42
    References 44

CHAPTER 4. AR6 and modelling uncertainty
Jo Lindsay Walton, Polina Levontin, and Jana Kleineberg

    Introduction 46
    Sources of uncertainty in modelling 48
    The AR6 50 model ensemble 50
    Regional distribution of modelling 51
    Evaluating models 52
    Language to describe uncertainty in AR6 WGI 54

Visualisations of uncertainties	55
Visualising precipitation trends	56
Climatic impact drivers (CIDs) in SPM	58
The AR6 WGI Interactive Atlas	60
Seven recommendations for the IPCC and the modelling community	61
References	64

CHAPTER 5. **Climate Finance and Climate Risk**
Jo Lindsay Walton and Polina Levontin

Introduction	65
The climate finance gap	66
Challenges to reallocating capital	68
The major players in global finance	70
Climate finance key terms	73
An anatomy of climate risk	77
Unlocking private sector climate finance	78
Who benefits from framing climate change in terms of financial risk?	80
Improving climate-related reporting	81
Climate-related reporting in context	82
Scenario analysis and stress testing	82
Who is on the frontline of climate risk?	83
Challenges for scenario analysis	84
Emerging trends in scenario modelling	85
Climate risk at the enterprise scale	86
Climate risk into financial risk	87
Stranded assets and impairment	88
Double materiality	89
Dynamic materiality	92
Scoping the policy space	94
Acknowledgements	98
References	98

CHAPTER 6. **Communicating Climate Risk in Education**
Jo Lindsay Walton, Polina Levontin, Maurice Ssebisubi, Dilman Dila, and Jana Kleineberg

Introduction	101
Addressing eco-anxiety as an educator	102
Case study: Ugandan climate futures	105

CHAPTER 7. **Hacks, Insights, and Resources**
Jo Lindsay Walton and Polina Levontin

Introduction	113
5 tips for using data visualisations (…)	114
5 tips for using photo resources (…)	115
10 tips for dialogue with policymakers	116
Conversations at the COP26 UN's Climate Risk Summit	117
Definitions of risk, uncertainty, and related terms from the IPCC	119
Classifying uncertainty	121
Tools and resources	122

ENDMATTER Authors, contributing experts, and acknowledgements ... 124
The story behind the cover ... 125

EXECUTIVE SUMMARY

The 2020s are the decade of delivery for climate transition. Unless net emissions now fall rapidly, the 1.5 degree target will be missed. Global adaptation targets also appear elusive. This **Communicating Climate Risk Toolkit** ('the Toolkit'), from the UK Universities Climate Network (UUCN) seeks to narrow the gap between climate science and climate action, and support dialogue between climate experts, decision-makers, and diverse communities and stakeholders.

The Intergovernmental Panel on Climate Change (IPCC), the world's scientific authority on climate change science, has long been committed to **quantifying and communicating uncertainty** to inform robust decision-making. The IPCC's most recent reporting cycle (AR6) also includes greater emphasis on deep uncertainty, e.g. in domains such as tipping points and cascade risks. **Risk assessment and risk management** are also assumed in AR6 as key frameworks that underpin global mitigation and adaptation efforts. However, more needs to be done to connect scientific understandings of uncertainty to risk-based decision-making, and other forms of decision-making, across policy, business, finance, and broader societal contexts.

Key concepts and methodologies differ across and within different domains, creating the potential for information to be lost or misinterpreted. Even **risk** and **uncertainty** are not consistently used terms. **Deep uncertainty** is challenging to communicate and typically not well-integrated into standard risk management practices. **Model uncertainty** also presents significant challenges to communication, and even decision-makers who are highly risk literate may find it difficult to use such information. There is growing demand for data to better manage climate risk and opportunities, especially in the financial sector, but climate transition will be jeopardised unless there is a deepened understanding of the nature of such data and its uncertainties — of what such data can realistically do or not do.

Communication is about power, not just storytelling. What may appear as solely or primarily "problems of communication" are often actually rooted in economic, political, and cultural power. The study and practice of climate communication must therefore expand beyond its heartlands of storytelling and psychology, to integrate insights from the political economy of climate change. This Toolkit aims to introduce key themes to a wide set of interested audiences, and to identify open problems for further research and debate. Topics covered include varying conceptions of uncertainty and risk, best practice in visualising uncertainty data, case studies on tipping points and model uncertainty, and an introduction to climate finance.

The original edition of this Toolkit was developed as part of the COP26 Universities Network Climate Risk project in 2021. All editions of the Toolkit can usefully be read in conjunction with the project's other outputs: *Climate Action Unit's Communicating Climate Risk: A Handbook*, and the COP Conversations series.

The Toolkit is also complemented by *Decision Support Tools for Complex Decisions Under Uncertainty* and *Visualising Uncertainty: A Short Introduction*.

COMMUNICATING CLIMATE RISK: KEY MESSAGES

CLIMATE RISK MANAGEMENT

1. The communication of climate science into climate action can be improved. **Uncertainty** and **risk** are key terms. An effective approach to climate decision-making means **connecting scientific practices around uncertainty** to **risk management practices** across policy, business, finance, the third sector, and communities affected by climate risk.

2. However, as an overarching framework, **risk management has limitations when it comes to communicating decision-relevant climate information, and driving necessary transformations**. Limitations can be addressed by (a) adapting and evolving new risk management practices, (b) using risk management practices in reflexive and critical ways, and (c) knowing when to step outside of risk management frameworks altogether.

3. Narrative framings of climate transition must be clear that **risk management is only one part of transition governance,** alongside more mission-led approaches, participatory governance, and broader equity and justice considerations. Climate risk management plays an important but complex role: e.g. "good" climate risk management at the entity level may sometimes be misaligned with net zero and/or maladaptive at the global level.

4. **Key frameworks, standards, metrics, and concepts are in flux,** including ongoing work by the International Sustainability Standards Board, development of the Sustainability Disclosure Requirements (SDR) in the UK, the expanding work of the Science Based Targets initiative, and attempts to address shortcomings in ESG financial product labels. More broadly, there is support particularly in the European context for wider use of complementary Beyond GDP metrics, yet as yet little serious challenge to the centrality of GDP, while understandings of degrowth and post-growth remain fragmented across policy and wider social discourse. Beyond ESG has yet to gain significant traction.

CLIMATE COMMUNICATION AND BEHAVIOUR CHANGE

5. Sharing **positive stories** that normalise behaviour change can be effective. As well as **closing information gaps and raising awareness**, communications to support behaviour change must be attentive to the **emotive, rhetorical, and narrative aspects** of communication. Realistic but hopeful messaging is usually preferable to attempts to drive behaviour change through fear.

6. Behaviour change should be supported by **sharing many models for positive action, across many contexts,** rather than focusing solely on a limited cast of climate actors (i.e. beyond consumers, policymakers, corporate leaders, and activists), and a limited set of contexts (i.e. beyond climate-centred interventions and into cultural production at large).

7. Fostering behaviour change goes well beyond effective communication. **Institutional and economic incentives must transform in order for behaviour change to scale in time to meet climate targets.** Benefits from interventions that are not structurally supported have been shown to be short-lived.

8. **Overreliance on individual responsibility to limit emissions places timely transition to net zero in jeopardy**, providing cover for delay to urgent legal, institutional, and economic reforms. However, there are opportunities to foster cultures of individual responsibility which **reimagine individual responsibility in more realistic and innovative ways** i.e. considering individual responsibility to identify necessary institutional and systemic changes, rather than expecting individuals to act in ways that are not institutionally and systemically supported.

CLIMATE COMMUNICATION AND SCIENTIFIC UNCERTAINTY

9. The IPCC has long been committed to **quantifying and communicating uncertainty** to inform robust decision-making. The IPCC's most recent reporting cycle (AR6) also includes greater emphasis on deep uncertainty, e.g. in domains such as tipping points and cascade risks. Risk assessment and risk management are also assumed in AR6 as key frameworks that underpin global mitigation and adaptation efforts. However, **more needs to be done to connect scientific understandings of uncertainty to risk-based decision-making** across policy, business, and broader societal contexts. Key concepts and methodologies differ across and within different domains, creating the potential for information to be lost or misinterpreted. Deep uncertainty is challenging to communicate and typically not well-integrated into standard

risk management practices. There is growing demand across policy, business and finance for data to better manage climate risk and opportunities, but climate transition will be jeopardised unless there is a deepened understanding of the nature of such data and its uncertainties — of what such data can realistically do or not do.

10. Narratives and communicative practices around **model uncertainty** need to be strengthened, and lack of diversity in the modelling community needs to be addressed. **Regional disparities in modelling are also problematic.**

11. **When uncertainty is appropriately quantified and communicated, it can deepen collaboration between experts, decision-makers, and other stakeholders.** Many key frameworks, framings, and tools for transition governance do not yet adequately reflect uncertainty information in IPCC reporting. However, many kinds of uncertainty are challenging to quantify and/or communicate. Quantifying uncertainty is not always possible, e.g. where there is deep uncertainty or data poverty. When uncertainty is quantified, it is always from a specific perspective and according to specific assumptions, meaning that some things will be left out.

12. **Attempting to quantify uncertainty is not ethically and politically "neutral,"** and may sometimes be undesirable, e.g. incompatible with the goals of transparency, inclusion and justice, or unduly disadvantaging to particular stakeholder groups.

13. **Proportionality** should always be considered when communicating uncertainty. Including all the available uncertainty information does not necessarily lead to better decision-making, greater transparency, or more participatory and democratic processes. Discretion must be used. Comprehensive and prominent uncertainty information will be appropriate for some contexts but not all contexts.

CLIMATE COMMUNICATION AND THE CONSULTING INDUSTRY

14. There is a developing consensus on the importance of creating **practical models** for climate action, ideally customised for different contexts using participatory approaches. However, what counts as effective climate action varies considerably across different contexts, and **climate decision support is unevenly distributed,** with some actors much better served than others by models for action, evidence, tools, and infrastructure. Many organisations have ambitious net zero targets but are without detailed strategies for delivering them. **Climate consulting industry is rapidly expanding, and specialising, in order to address these gaps.**

15. **Tighter regulation** of net zero consulting and other climate consulting should be explored. **Innovative models** for less well-resourced organisations to access expertise should be developed.

16. The climate consulting industry has complex origins, but many legal structures, norms, and methods are derived from traditional management consulting. Advice is typically supplied on a commercial basis, and often in connection with proprietary tools and resources. The nature of these climate advisory services raises **questions as to whether these are adequately affordable, independent, transformative, and transparent**.

17. To improve **transparency**, where knowledge around achieving net zero is generated, it is crucial that this knowledge be shared rapidly within the sector. If knowledge is primarily being generated, retained and applied by external consultants, there is a risk that this will impede timely dissemination.

CLIMATE COMMUNICATION AND ARTIFICIAL INTELLIGENCE

18. Recent advances in **generative AI**, exemplified by the well-known chatbot ChatGPT, suggest potential to transform climate communication. However, **AI is also carbon intensive.** There are considerable carbon costs attached to training and deploying Machine Learning models. The current rush to embed generative AI into day-to-day digital communications is a cause for concern and deserves immediate further research and potential policy interventions.

19. **Innovative uses of AI and automation** may help to address the challenges of providing **cost-effective net zero decision support at scale**. Developing such systems effectively means taking a holistic approach, with a strong orientation to climate justice, and a pragmatic understanding of the scale and rapidity of transformation necessary to meet climate targets even under an orderly transition scenario.

CLIMATE COMMUNICATION AND PARTICIPATORY DEMOCRACY

20. The 2020s is the decade of delivery for climate transition, and unless net emissions fall rapidly, the 1.5 degree target will be missed. Adaptation targets are also extremely challenging. Even given this urgency, **much more can be done to deepen the participatory character of climate transition**. Attempting rapid transition without societal buy-in risks backlashes and delays.

21. Public consultations and stakeholder engagement exercises are important tools, but participatory approaches can go much deeper, e.g. **participatory budgeting** in climate reparation contexts. **Real transfers of money and decision-making power are yet to commence.**

22. **Comparative studies** and peer-to-peer learning allow different countries and localities to benefit from one another's experiences of strengthening participatory action.

23. **Stakeholder mapping and engagement** must adapt to accommodate the complex and interconnected nature of climate change. Well-established terminology for communication roles such as stakeholder, expert, decision-maker, community, and public, remains useful, but better attention can be paid to such terms' presuppositions and their potential to limit inclusivity and participation.

24. **Participatory processes are never free of value judgments or power dynamics.** Such processes are inherently concerned with the representation and weighting of the voices of diverse societal stakeholders. They are always embedded in broader dynamics of equity and inclusivity across society.

COMMUNICATING SCIENCE INTO POLICY

25. **Policymakers face challenges of fragmented climate policymaking.** Climate cuts across all policy areas, yet individual departments or policy teams often find they must pursue objectives, manage risks, and respond to budgetary and other constraints, in ways that do not reflect the wider systems-level picture. There is widespread support for more coordinated climate policy-making, but not yet a clear sense of how to address this fragmentation, beyond strengthening accountability and increasing budgets. Sectoral framings are inevitable and often useful, but also contribute to fragmentation and the challenge of holistic policymaking. In the UK context specifically, the new Department for Energy Security and Net Zero may provide important big picture oversight, although of course cross-departmental collaboration will remain key, as no one ministerial department can nor should be responsible for all aspects of climate transition.

26. Scientific and other academic research into climate risk embraces a degree of complexity and uncertainty that is extremely challenging to communicate into policymaking. **The interface between policymakers and a variety of experts can be improved.** Policymakers currently lack decision support tools, frameworks, and ways of working that to access decision-relevant syntheses of expertise, in formats that accommodate political realities. Local knowledge distributed across diverse communities is often even less available.

27. **Policymakers' time is a very scarce resource.** As a pragmatic reality, climate experts must make the best use of limited time. They must communicate succinctly and clearly, and must use language and concepts that relate to existing concerns (e.g. economic risks and opportunities). They must respond to windows of opportunity (e.g. natural disasters, economic crises, and other current events). However, it should not be accepted as inevitable that policymakers do not have adequate time to devote to expert advice on climate risk—this is a significant weakness within the decision value chain, and should be further studied and addressed. **The working conditions of policymakers in the 2020s are pertinent to the future of the planet for centuries to come.**

INTERDISCIPLINARY APPROACHES TO CLIMATE COMMUNICATION AND EDUCATION

28. Climate communication and education is a field with many open problems, and **there is clear value to interdisciplinary collaboration** across science, social science, and arts (e.g. graphic design) and humanities (e.g. environmental humanities). However such collaborations also demand significant time and energy, and in most national contexts **the pace of academic funding, research and impact is unsuited to the urgency of climate risk**.

29. **Communication is about power, not just storytelling.** What may appear as solely or primarily "problems of communication" are often actually rooted in economic, political, and cultural power. The study and practice of climate communication must expand beyond its heartlands of storytelling and psychology, to integrate insights from the political economy of climate change.

30. **Climate communication studies should be reflexive.** In other words, this research should recognise that it is not separate from the phenomena it studies. Researchers and practitioners should consider questions such as, "Why has a particular situation become framed as a problem of communication in the first place? What are the impacts of framing it this way? How else might it be framed?"

*What if those who are most willing to listen are **not** those who most need to hear?*

Chapter 1 — INTRODUCTION

OVERVIEW
What you'll find in this toolkit (and what you won't)

This Toolkit aims to improve the communication of climate risks. It has been guided by a few principles:

- The need to **improve dialogue between climate scientists, policymakers, business and finance, and other stakeholders**, to phase out fossil fuels, to remove and safely store greenhouse gases, and to build resilience to climate risks.
- The fact that climate risks are faced across society and around the globe, and the need for **holistic and participatory** approaches to communication, with strong regard for equity, inclusion, and justice.
- The many **uncertainties** associated with climate risks and climate action, and the need for robust understandings of and communication about those uncertainties.
- The **urgency** of climate change, and the need for immediate action of unprecedented type and scale, even given imperfect information, tools, experience, and terminology.

Where policy and climate science intersect, things can get complicated fast. The UK Government Office for Science (GO-Science) recommends policymakers adopt a joined-up and participatory approach to integrating scientific and other expert advice into policy. GO-Science advises that issues which need input from experts and communities should be identified early. Policymakers should seek advice from a wide range of experts; the more uncertainty there is, the stronger the rationale for widening the variety of experts consulted. These processes should be made as transparent and participatory as possible, to permit scrutiny by key stakeholders and the public (The Government Chief Scientific and Adviser 2010; Garb, Pulver, and VanDeveer 2008).

These are all sensible principles from GO-Science. In practice they imply **a lot of dialogue involving a lot of different participants. These participants** don't just bring their own expertise and values to these dialogues. They also bring their own ways of talking and thinking about the issues. For example, key terms like *uncertainty* and *risk* often come with different associations. These terms might even be considered examples of the "imperfect terminology" mentioned in the four principles above. What's more, participants bring their own norms about what counts as acceptable or good communicative practice.

Because these conversations are about climate change — or "everything change", as the speculative fiction author Margaret Atwood aptly put it — they need to include an

---

Subsections

Overview

Uncertainty and climate risk communication

The IPCC and the AR6

Budgets, bombs, and uncertainty about uncertainty: an example of climate risk communication

Uncertainty rebranded?

Risk vs. uncertainty

References

unprecedented variety of participants. That means that effective communication is more challenging than ever. The scope for **misinterpretation and information loss** is vast. Sometimes, participants may even struggle to find the right kinds of questions to ask. At other times, participants may leave feeling satisfied, without recognising they have been speaking at cross-purposes. Even communications among roughly the same type of actor — for example, different organisations within a sector trying to benchmark their decarbonisation progress — are prone to go wrong in these ways.

There is also scope for **disengagement,** and disintegration of the spaces where dialogue might occur. Policymakers tend to have many pressures on their time. A policymaker may sense that an expert has something important to tell them — about extreme weather events, about knock-on effects, about the uncertainty in upscaling novel technology, about the lived experiences of their community — yet not be able to connect it to their everyday decision-making. The policymaker may suppose the expert has good reasons for saying 'extreme precipitation' rather than 'floods,' or for saying 'it is unequivocal' rather than 'we are completely certain.' But the policymaker may not understand what those reasons are, and may not have the capacity to figure it out in the time available.

And of course, it's not just science that has its own technical vocabulary and norms. The wider world of policy and industry can present as opaque and inaccessible to scientific experts. Despite the extensive resources devoted to realising policy impact, many scientific experts still lack the necessary knowledge of policymaking to communicate in ways that make it "harder for climate policymakers to evade the practical consequences of the knowledge base they already accept" (Geden 2018). Because climate risk is so ubiquitous, and involves impacts that can cascade right through society, experts even face challenges in prioritising *which* decision-makers to seek out — let alone learning to speak their languages. What if those who are most willing to listen are *not* those who most need to hear?

To effectively address climate risk, we need to communicate effectively about climate risk. This Toolkit has been assembled by experts from decision science, statistics, modelling, neuroscience, the environmental humanities, and climate journalism backgrounds. It contains recommendations and insights for improving dialogue between scientific experts and the many decision-makers dealing with climate risks. It also hopes to support more broadly the needs of anyone who needs to communicate around climate risk and climate action. We don't have all the answers — the Toolkit also identifies challenges and open problems, and provides case studies to inspire you to form your own views. The Toolkit won't tell you exactly what word or what visual to use in every context to get your point across. But it will help us all to start asking one another the right questions.

> *To effectively address climate risk, we need to communicate effectively about climate risk.*

UNCERTAINTY AND CLIMATE RISK COMMUNICATION
Why it's hard to talk about uncertainty, and why we should talk about uncertainty

▶▶▶ *"I was telling a client that the likelihood had been estimated as one in fifty. But then the scientists said, 'That doesn't mean anything without the uncertainty.' I asked them, 'What do you mean, uncertainty? I thought one in fifty was already uncertain?'"*
(Interview Respondent, September 2021)

It is not enough to understand what is happening to our planet. Climate experts need to communicate what they know to non-experts — to people with power to do things about it. This means climate experts often need to communicate what they know about what they *don't* know. In other words, **climate experts need to communicate the *uncertainty* that is an inherent part of scientific expertise.**

To someone from a non-scientific background, the word *uncertainty* is associated with hesitancy, doubts, and indecisiveness. When a person from a non-scientific background tells you they are uncertain about something, they are usually implying, "I'm not really the right person to ask. Don't rely too heavily on my advice." But to scientists, uncertainty means something different. Uncertainty isn't just an absence of information: often uncertainty is its own kind of information, and it can be useful for making better decisions (Morgan 2009).

When uncertainty is carefully quantified and communicated, it can deepen understanding and strengthen collaborations between experts, decision-makers, and other stakeholders.

Nonetheless, when it comes to climate risk, it can be hard to talk about uncertainty. When uncertainty is mentioned, experts may be seen as lacking faith in their own science. They may be suspected of merely trying to save face, in case they turn out to be wrong about something. Or they may be perceived as being too wrapped up in the details, too out of touch with reality to ever give a straight answer, or the type of answer that is being sought.

Uncertainty may also send the message that we should wait until we can be more certain. This can be exacerbated by the continued spread of climate change disinformation, by powerful incumbent interests or by malicious rogue actors (Boykoff 2008; Supran and Oreskes 2017; McCright and Dunlap 2003). As Maxwell Boykoff puts it, "Uncertainty can be reframed as scientific incompetence" (in Liverman et al. 2008).

Quantifying uncertainty is not always possible (see **Chapter 3: Communicating around tipping points**) or desirable. For example, relying on quantitative forms of risk assessment might be incompatible with the goals of transparency and inclusion, in some cases disadvantageing indigenous voices and other relevant epistemologies and methodologies (Russill and Nyssa 2009).

For all these reasons and more, it can be hard to talk about uncertainty. But sometimes we need to talk about uncertainty. Climate action means vast numbers of people and organisations are shifting to new practices and new technologies. But they may not be doing what they claim to do. They may not be doing what they think they are doing. What they are doing may not have the intended consequences. Unless these and many other uncertainties are continually and carefully addressed, climate action will fall short. Climate change itself is characterised by

> *multiple intersecting and uncertain future hazards to natural and human systems, that are expected to unfold over a very large range of spatial and temporal scales, and whose probabilities may be difficult, or in some cases impossible, to quantify precisely (because of intrinsic and/or irreducible uncertainties about the future). It is a risk multiplier that interacts with other stressors to create new or alter existing risks[.]*
> (Weaver et al. 2017)

Uncertainty can be "represented by quantitative measures (e.g. a probability density function) or by qualitative statements (e.g. reflecting the judgement of a team of experts)" (AR6 WGI 2021). When uncertainty is carefully quantified and communicated, it can deepen understanding and strengthen collaborations between experts, decision-makers, and other stakeholders. **Uncertainty communication can underpin more robust decisions,** decisions that make sense across the whole range of possible futures — not simply the future that is most likely, or the one that strikes the imagination most forcefully. Scientists who communicate uncertainty can also "demonstrate the trustworthiness of their science by showing a commitment to transparency" (Padilla et al. 2021).

Uncertainty is also significant in **interdisciplinary collaboration.** Experts in the social sciences and humanities sometimes criticise physical scientists rather sweepingly for "scientism," a dangerous conviction in their own objectivity and comprehensiveness of scientific knowledge; better communication of uncertainty can enhance interdisciplinary understanding of existing scientific practices of self-reflection and self-governance, and explore concrete opportunities for improvement.

Finally, uncertainty is important for **participatory decision-making,** since areas of uncertainty can be areas where parties with different interests or perspectives can find space for mutually acceptable solutions[1]. Even more broadly, by embracing uncertainty, we also remind ourselves that the future is still open, and can still be fundamentally shaped by the choices we make today.

Just as there is equivocation on the word *uncertainty*, so too is there equivocation on the word *risk*. What does the word *risk* mean to you? Does *risk* mean the same thing to those with whom you are communicating, or those whose lives you seek through your research, decision-making, and/or advocacy? How confident are you that you know these answers? This topic is explored in greater depth later in this chapter.

---

[1] It has been argued that "most policymakers and political leaders are not keen to reduce uncertainties and overcome ambiguities — these are a source of political flexibility" (Geden 2018).

THE IPCC AND THE AR6
How the global scientific authority on climate talks about uncertainty and risk

The Intergovernmental Panel on Climate Change (IPCC) is an intergovernmental body of the United Nations, which for over thirty years has worked to assess the drivers and impacts of climate change and to formulate policy options. It is the global authority on climate science. The IPCC does not exist to conduct original research, but rather to review and communicate the current state of global climate research. At the time of writing, the IPCC is reaching the end of its sixth assessment cycle (2015-2022), and in the midst of publishing its sixth major report (AR6). At present the first part of this report, *AR6 Working Group I* (AR WGI), focusing on the physical science basis, is available in a near-final form (AR6 WGI 2021).

The IPCC tends to carefully avoid normative language. It tries not to tell us what we 'should' do. Nonetheless, the headline message of AR6 WGI is crystal clear: **we need to cut emissions rapidly, and we need to safely store more carbon;** we need to do this while **shoring up against floods, droughts, heatwaves, wildfires, and many more impacts;** these impacts are happening already, and will get worse. While there have been many advances in science in recent years, the AR6 results are broadly consistent with every Assessment Report ever issued by the IPCC. The greatest difference is that time is more short than ever.

In order to mitigate and adapt to climate change, scientific expertise must feed transformations in policy and strategy at many different levels and scales throughout society. AR6 WGI continues to demonstrate the IPCC's commitment to **quantifying and communicating uncertainty** in order to support transparency in science and inform robust decision-making. AR6 WGI also includes greater emphasis on deep uncertainty, e.g. in domains such as tipping points and cascade risks (see Chapter 4). Furthermore, **risk assessment and risk management** are assumed in AR6 WGI as key frameworks that underpin global mitigation and adaptation efforts. For more information, see 'Risk vs. uncertainty' below, and 'Some IPCC Definitions' (in Chapter 6).

However, **more needs to be done to connect scientific understandings of uncertainty to risk-based decision-making** by policymakers, NGOs, industry, and other actors spanning diverse epistemological, cultural and social contexts. Many kinds of uncertainty such as model uncertainty and deep uncertainty are challenging to communicate and are typically not well-understood by decision-makers, even those who are risk-literate. Key concepts and methodologies differ across and within different domains of science and policy, creating the potential for information to be lost or misinterpreted.

Moreover, to those unfamiliar with climate science and policy, the emphasis on *uncertainty* and *risk* can be perplexing. As described in the last subsection, the everyday meanings of these words may be associated with reluctance to give advice or to take action. For a **lay audience,** references to uncertainty and risk may weaken the cognitive or emotional impact of climate information. **Participation may also be disincentivised**, if stakeholders are made to feel they must acquire technical understandings of uncertainty and risk, in order to legitimately engage with climate science or with the policy it informs. Finally, some realities are very challenging to translate into terms of risk, and experts should also keep an open mind about whether or not a risk management framework is really the best way to understand a given aspect of climate change and climate action.

BUDGETS, BOMBS, AND UNCERTAINTY ABOUT UNCERTAINTY: AN EXAMPLE OF CLIMATE RISK COMMUNICATION
Should we always talk about uncertainty?
This mini-case study reveals there are arguments on both sides...

There are many "pragmatic and ethical reasons why communicating uncertainty is critical" (Padilla et al. 2021), and many organisations, including the IPCC, strongly advocate for communicating uncertainty about climate risk (IPCC WGI et al. 2021). There is also evidence that in many contexts uncertainty is currently not being appropriately communicated (van der Bles et al. 2019; Budescu, Por, and Broomell 2012). But are there times where experts simply *shouldn't* talk about uncertainty, or at least not about all uncertainties? For example, Climate Action Unit suggest that attempts to communicate uncertainty all the way down the decision chain may have "hindered rather than helped policy formulation and decision making" (CAU 2021).

This Toolkit focuses on providing decision-makers with climate risk information, including uncertainty. However, that does not mean we think it appropriate always to fully convey all known uncertainties within any given communication. We recommend that the audience, the aim, the available resources, the opportunity cost, and other relevant factors should all be weighed up, and that **proportionate attempts should be made to convey uncertainty.**

There can be no rigid formula for determining what is proportionate. We also emphasise the strong ethical aspect to such judgments: **"proportionality" should never be used as an excuse to evade obligations to transparency.** However, two sections in the next chapter provide some support for making such judgments: the decision value chain, and the communicating for decision support vs. communicating for storytelling checklist. The decision value chain is there to invite you to think holistically about how beliefs about uncertainty propagate through networks of actors. The communicating for decision support vs. communicating for storytelling checklist recommends that communicators can use an "opt in vs. opt out" framework to uncertainty.

Let's now look at an example of what is arguably very effective climate risk communication, the Mercator Research Institute on Global Commons and Climate Change (MCC) Carbon Clock (mcc-berlin.net/en/research/co2-budget.html). This **miniature case study** brings out some of the complexity around deciding whether to include uncertainty information in the first place.

The **MCC Carbon Clock** is a simple animation of our world, as a spinning blue marble suspended in space, with white text superimposed. At the top the text gives a figure for CO_2 emissions in tonnes per second, and at the bottom, CO_2 budget[2] remaining, also in tonnes. In the top corners, you can toggle between a 1.5 degrees scenario and a 2.0 degrees scenario. In the middle is a set of **rapidly counting down figures** — years, months, days, hours, minutes, seconds — representing the estimated time till we exhaust our carbon budget.

The MCC Carbon Clock effectively conveys a sense of urgency. It takes a subject matter that may feel remote and complex, and it portrays it as a ticking time bomb. At the time of writing, under the 1.5 degree scenario, the Carbon Clock unequivocally tells its audience: we only have seven years and nine months left. Whereas climate science often speaks about the decades or centuries ahead, the Carbon Clock presents a far more relatable timescale. You probably have items of clothing that are older than seven years. A Facebook algorithm might decide to resurface a photograph of you and your friends seven years previously. How time flies: look at him, he looks just the same! The planet doesn't.

Although it aims to convey urgency, MCC Clock also seeks to be transparent in its methodology. It describes the Clock as follows (emphasis in the original), prominently including a link to a key table in the AR6 WGI Summary for Policymakers (SPM) on which it is based:

> **The MCC Carbon Clock shows how much CO_2 can be released into the atmosphere to limit global warming to a maximum of 1.5°C and 2°C, respectively. With just a few clicks, you can compare the estimates for both temperature targets and see how much time is left in each scenario.**

As to the scientific basis of the carbon clock, we exclusively draw on data from the Intergovernmental Panel on Climate Change (IPCC), which represents the verified state of research. The IPCC last updated its estimate of the remaining carbon budget in summer 2021, with the presentation of the first part of its Sixth Assessment Report.

According to a report (see here, table SMP.2), on the 1.5 degree Celsius target, the atmosphere can absorb, calculated from the beginning of 2020, no more than 400 gigatonnes (Gt) of CO_2 if we are to stay below the 1.5°C threshold. Annual emissions of CO_2 — from burning fossil fuels, industrial processes and land-use change — are estimated to be 42.2 Gt per year, the equivalent of 1,337 tonnes per second. With emissions at a constant level, the budget would be expected to be used up in less than eight years from now. The budget for staying below the 2°C threshold, for its part, of 1,150 Gt, would be exhausted in about 25 years. The budgets are calculated in such a way that it is highly likely that the respective temperature target will be met, that is in two thirds of the climate scenarios examined.

The MCC offers further qualifications and invitations to explore, including this note on uncertainties:

While the Carbon Clock appears to be a precise measurement of the time left to ensure climate protection, many uncertainty factors remain, such as different definitions of the 1.5°C target as well as different assumptions about the climate sensitivity, the actually attained degree of global warming, and the future development of other greenhouse gases. Furthermore, for the time being, the

---

2 IPCC AR6 "suggests a remaining budget of about 420 $GtCO_2$ for a two-thirds chance of limiting warming to 1.5°C, and of about 580 $GtCO_2$ for an even chance (medium confidence). The remaining carbon budget is defined here as cumulative CO_2 emissions from the start of 2018 until the time of net zero"(IPCC WGI et al. 2021)

calculation is based on the assumption that annual emissions, after a dip in the pandemic year of 2020, will remain at the 2019 level from 2021 onwards.

Nevertheless, the MCC Carbon Clock can be criticised in at least two ways. First, **the Clock relies on metaphors which can be misinterpreted.** For example, in movies featuring tense countdowns, the hero often snips the wire at the last second — and saves the day, with no harm done at all. Bombs in blockbusters do not gradually explode as their timers tick down. Insofar as these cultural associations may be active in the MCC Carbon Clock, the Clock could convey the sense that sudden, drastic action after about seven years' delay will be adequate to limit global warming to below 1.5 degrees. More subtly, the Clock may carry traces of the 'population time bomb' concept that has thankfully has now largely fallen out of favour. This involved an estimated planetary carrying capacity expressed in terms of global population. (Given different demographic dynamics globally, such anxiety around population growth often had racist undertones).

Furthermore, by bringing vividly to life the carbon budget framework, the MCC Carbon Clock exacerbates the inadequacies of the 'budget' analogy. Financial budgets are for spending; for some budget holders, failing to spend a budget by a particular date means needing to return the unspent funds, and even the threat of a reduced budget the following year. There may also be the implication that the carbon budget is 'what we can safely get away with,' an interpretation which is at odds with the literature on tipping points, for example. From paleoclimate records we know that tipping points exist — profound and irreversible changes in major Earth systems — and there are concerns that several tipping points may be approaching or have already been crossed (see Chapter 3). The less CO_2 is emitted, the less likely we are to cross any tipping points which we have not already crossed. Reasoning about probabilities that are largely unknown, as in the case of tipping points, should be very different than contemplating if we want to avoid 1.5 degrees warming with a probability of 0.67 or 0.83.

Although it does seem to be implied that the Clock will be regularly updated to reflect the current rate of emissions, there is no detail about this prominently presented. It may therefore be misconstrued that the Clock is a model offering a *prediction*, i.e. that it *expects* emissions to remain constant because of a failure of mitigation (reducing energy demand, scaling up renewable sources, storing more carbon).

Second, the Clock presupposes the **collapsing or even suppression of uncertainty.** Carbon budget calculations depend on model projections and change as models evolve. The calculated budget is higher in the AR6 than it was in AR5. The budget will be recalculated in AR7 and may be higher or lower depending on new model runs, that will reflect changes in science that moves at a brisk pace, bringing new knowledge and reducing some aspects of uncertainty. Modelling uncertainty is not fully included in budget calculations; for example, one of the largest sources of uncertainty is to do with land fluxes — models disagree at scales that are bigger than the carbon budget — the budget was calculated

UNCERTAINTY REBRANDED?
IS THE TERM UNCERTAINTY FIT-FOR-PURPOSE?

THE TERM 'UNCERTAINTY' IS DEEPLY EMBEDDED IN SCIENTIFIC DISCOURSE. BUT IS IT FIT-FOR-PURPOSE?

Whether or not it is, it is unlikely to be going anywhere soon. Nevertheless, in light of the many misleading associations the term can give rise to among non-scientific audiences, it is worth exploring alternative vocabulary for conveying the same information, as a workaround for situations where extensive dialogue to inform such audiences is not feasible. In some contexts it may be more illuminating to use words like "reliability" to qualify forecasts. But could we go even further in creating more accessible language to talk about scientific uncertainty?

using median land model projections. There is further uncertainty in translating the current budget into country-level reductions; differences in accounting for land-based emissions between scientific communities imply that the AR6 carbon budget should be 120-192 Gt lower before it is used to set mitigation expectations in the form of national targets or NDCs (Grassi et al. 2021).

Saying that the budget runs out after seven years implies that the probability of meeting 1.5 degrees becomes zero. In fact, continuing emissions at the current level for twice as long (fourteen years), according to the same set of projections by the IPCC AR6 WGI, reduces the probability of meeting that target (from 67% to 17%), but does not make it impossible. Higher or lower reductions in non-CO2 emissions such as methane may also increase or decrease the values of the estimated carbon budgets by around 220 Gt (or give or take five years, at the current level of emissions).

Not disclosing that its calculations are based on explicitly probabilistic data, the Clock does not prominently mention, nor attempt to justify, basing its countdown on the IPCC table's 0.67 probability column. "Selecting a remaining carbon budget requires two normative choices as a minimum: the global warming level that is to be avoided, and the likelihood or chance with which this is achieved" (Rogelj 2021). The Clock does allow the user to set the level to either 1.5 or 2.0 degrees, but does not reveal anything about the likelihood or chance of achieving that limit, should net zero be reached before the estimated carbon budget is depleted.

The Clock illustrates some of the difficult trade-offs a communicator faces. By mobiling metaphors and by collapsing uncertainty — while also making efforts toward transparency — the Clock creates a sense of urgency without creating a sense of helplessness. But focusing exclusively on the relationship between current emission rates and current estimate carbon budgets creates opportunities for misunderstanding, and sidelines the systemic nature of climate risk — lower chance of staying under the selected target is associated with higher likelihood of extreme events, increasing chances of triggering tipping points, and unleashing cascades of socio-economic disruptions.

One can easily imagine an interactive tool which captures more uncertainty through customizable settings. The user might specify the probability at 0.17 and see the time remaining jump up. The user might set it at 0.83 and watch the time shrink to even less than seven years. Different scenarios for rate of CO2 emissions, and non-CO2 emissions, or for deployment of carbon sinks, could be overlaid. Playing with such a tool might shape an intuitive sense of the estimated carbon budgets and various sources of uncertainty. However, it would also be likely to undermine the urgency of the Clock's message. Global warming would be encountered as a relatively pliable phenomenon, something one can frighten oneself with for a thrill, and then push safely into the remote future with a few altered assumptions. In such interactions, the aggregates of many complex political, social, economic, and ecological processes would be modelled as though they were merely options available to the individual user. Could such a tool really be admired as 'more transparent' than the Clock, despite its greater fidelity to underlying assumptions?

Viewed from the perspective of speculative design, the MCC Carbon Clock is an impactful and worthwhile intervention. It demonstrates the challenges around how and whether to include uncertainty in climate communication when addressing different audiences. **Is the MCC Carbon Clock a proportionate attempt to convey uncertainty in climate risk communication**? We leave it to you to judge.

RISK VS. UNCERTAINTY
Despite some well-known definitions, meanings and nuances vary from context to context.

There are no universally accepted definitions of risk and uncertainty, and hence no universally accepted distinction between the two. For the purposes of this Toolkit, we avoid fixed definitions of risk and uncertainty. However, as background, we will briefly outline **some important definitions of risk**, and indicate some of their relations to **uncertainty**. We should also remember that definitions are not everything: informal understandings and use conventions are important too, and just because participants in a dialogue have agreed upon a definition of risk or uncertainty does not mean they will always stick to it.

In everyday speech, the word 'risk' often carries more negative connotations than 'uncertainty' does. This is formalised in the IPCC definition of risk as the potential for adverse consequences. More fully, risk is:

[t]he potential for adverse consequences for human or ecological systems, recognising the diversity of values and objectives associated with such systems. In the context of climate change, risks can arise from potential impacts of climate change as well as human responses to climate change. Relevant adverse consequences include those on lives, livelihoods, health and wellbeing, economic, social and cultural assets and investments, infrastructure, services (including ecosystem services), ecosystems and species.

(Reisinger et al. 2020)

For the IPCC, the uncertainty implied by the word *potential* "does not necessarily have to be quantified," but it is recommended that authors "provide some sense of the nature and degree of uncertainty to allow a meaningful risk assessment and risk management responses to be undertaken" (Reisinger et al. 2020). See 'Some IPCC Definitions' for more on the IPCC's approach to risk and uncertainty.

One important kind of risk is **disaster risk.** Disasters are adverse impacts such as floods, wildfires, droughts, hurricanes, pandemics, armed conflicts, and so on, which are seen as 'extraordinary.' In disaster risk management, a risk is usually broken down into the hazard itself, the exposure to that hazard, and the vulnerability of those who are exposed. Communication is a crucial part of disaster preparedness and response.[3]

Another important category of potential adverse impact is **transition risk.** This refers to financial and other risks associated with the shift to net zero, and the many changes in policy and practice which this shift implies. For organisations, both disaster risks and transition risks may also be associated with **liability risk**, including legal action because of a failure to prepare appropriately. Where climate is concerned, organisations and investors should consider not only the risks to which their assets and activities may be exposed, but also the risks they may be contributing to.

In the contexts described so far, the word 'risk' has a fairly negative association (even though approaching risk wisely can lead to good things). In other contexts, however, it means the probability of an event occurring multiplied by the magnitude of its impact, regardless of whether this is positive or negative.

Within finance and some business contexts, a mention of 'risk' may conjure up the association of the risk-return spectrum (also known as the risk-reward spectrum). Very crudely, the higher the return that is sought, the more risk must be accepted. In this respect, the connotations of 'risk' can be exciting, and perhaps positive. An organisation that is 'hungry for risk' may be trying out innovative activities, with a relatively high chance of failure, but also a relatively large pay-off. Risk in this usage is something that should be managed, but not all risks should be avoided or minimised. Sometimes risk will be deliberately incurred.

In yet another approach, 'risk' describes conditions where the probabilities of different outcomes are known, and 'uncertainty' (or 'ambiguity') describes conditions where this probability distribution is not known (Knight 1921). Again, the connotations of risk are not entirely negative. Roughly speaking, you don't know what is going to happen, but you know what *might* happen and how likely it is, so you can choose and prepare accordingly. For people using this convention, the notion of 'quantifying uncertainty' may be a contradiction in terms.

Universal convergence on a standard vocabulary of risk and uncertainty does not appear feasible, especially not on the urgent timescales required by climate action. Efforts to create greater consistency within a given organisation, project, partnership, network, sector, etc. may be of value. The IPCC definitions provide obvious reference points to which many different actors might align their usage (see also Chapter 5). However, in this respect the Toolkit's key recommendation is: **understandings of risk and uncertainty may vary, and clarity should be sought through dialogue on a case-by-case basis.**

---

[3] "Risk communication is a complex cross-disciplinary field that involves reaching different audiences to make risk comprehensible, understanding and respecting audience values, predicting the audience's response to the communication, and improving awareness and collective and individual decision making [...] Risk communication failures have been revealed in past disasters, such as Hurricane Katrina in 2005 or the Pakistan floods in 2010 [...] Particularly, the loss of trust in official institutions responsible for early warning and disaster management were a key factor that contributed to the increasing disaster risk. Effective and people-centered risk communication is therefore a key to improve vulnerability and risk reduction in the context of extreme events" (Field et al. 2012).

AUTHOR CONTRIBUTIONS
Conceptualization: JLW, MJB, PL, and MW;
Research: JLW, PL, MJB, and MW; **Writing:** *JLW, MJB, and PL.*

REFERENCES

Climate Action Unit (CAU), 2021. 'Goodybag' of climate risk communication resources provided to participants in Climate Risk Summit (COP26 Universities Network), 1 October 2021.

Bingler, Julia Anna, and Chiara Colesanti Senni. 2020. 'Taming the Green Swan: How to Improve Climate-Related Financial Risk Assessments'. *SSRN Electronic Journal.* doi.org/10.2139/ssrn.3795360

Bles, Anne Marthe van der, Sander van der Linden, Alexandra L. J. Freeman, James Mitchell, Ana B. Galvao, Lisa Zaval, and David J. Spiegelhalter. 2019. 'Communicating Uncertainty about Facts, Numbers and Science'. *Royal Society Open Science* 6 (5): 181870. doi.org/10.1098/rsos.181870

Boykoff, Maxwell T. 2008. 'Media and Scientific Communication: A Case of Climate Change'. *Geological Society, London, Special Publications* 305 (1): 11–18. doi.org/10.1144/SP305.3

Budescu, David V., Han-Hui Por, and Stephen B. Broomell. 2012. 'Effective Communication of Uncertainty in the IPCC Reports'. *Climatic Change* 113 (2): 181–200.

Garb, Yaakov, Simone Pulver, and Stacy D. VanDeveer. 2008. 'Scenarios in Society, Society in Scenarios: Toward a Social Scientific Analysis of Storyline-Driven Environmental Modeling'. *Environmental Research Letters* 3 (4): 045015. doi.org/10.1088/1748-9326/3/4/045015

Geden, Oliver. 2018. 'Politically Informed Advice for Climate Action'. *Nature Geoscience* 11 (6): 380–83. doi.org/10.1038/s41561-018-0143-3

Grassi, Giacomo, Elke Stehfest, Joeri Rogelj, Detlef van Vuuren, Alessandro Cescatti, Jo House, Gert-Jan Nabuurs, et al. 2021. 'Critical Adjustment of Land Mitigation Pathways for Assessing Countries' Climate Progress'. *Nature Climate Change* 11 (5): 425–34. doi.org/10.1038/s41558-021-01033-6

IPCC WGI, P. Zhai, A. Pirani, S. L. Connors, and WGI. 2021. 'IPCC, 2021: Summary for Policymakers'. *In Climate Change 2021: The Physical Science Basis. Contribution of Working Group I to the Sixth Assessment Report of the Intergovernmental Panel on Climate Change.* Cambridge University Press.

Jones, C. D., P. Ciais, S. J. Davis, P. Friedlingstein, T. Gasser, G. P. Peters, J. Rogelj, et al. 2016. 'Simulating the Earth System Response to Negative Emissions'. *Environmental Research Letters* 11 (9): 095012. doi.org/10.1088/1748-9326/11/9/095012

Knight, Frank H. 1921. 'Risk, Uncertainty and Profit'. SSRN Scholarly Paper ID 1496192. Rochester, NY: Social Science Research Network. papers.ssrn.com/abstract=1496192

Liverman, D. G. E., C. P. G. Pereira, Brian Marker, and Geological Society of London, eds. 2008. *Communicating Environmental Geoscience.* Geological Society Special Publication, no. 305. London: Geological Society.

Masson-Delmotte, V., P. Zhai, A. Pirani, and S. L. Connors. 2021. 'Climate Change 2021: The Physical Science Basis. Contribution of Working Group I to the Sixth Assessment Report of the Intergovernmental Panel on Climate Change'. Cambridge University Press.

McCright, Aaron M., and Riley E. Dunlap. 2003. 'Defeating Kyoto: The Conservative Movement's Impact on U.S. Climate Change Policy'. *Social Problems* 50 (3): 348–73. doi.org/10.1525/sp.2003.50.3.348

Morgan, M Granger. 2009. *Best Practice Approaches for Characterizing, Communicating and Incorporating Scientific Uncertainty in Climate Decision Making.* DIANE publishing.

Padilla, Lace, Sarah Dryhurst, Helia Hosseinpour, and Andrew Kruczkiewicz. 2021. 'Multiple Hazard Uncertainty Visualization Challenges and Paths Forward'. *Frontiers in Psychology* 12: 1993. doi.org/10.3389/fpsyg.2021.579207

Reisinger, Andy, Mark Howden, Carolina Vera, et al. 2020. 'The Concept of Risk in the IPCC Sixth Assessment Report: A Summary of Cross-Working Group Discussions'. Intergovernmental Panel on Climate Change.

'Remaining Carbon Budget - Mercator Research Institute on Global Commons and Climate Change (MCC)'. n.d. Accessed 8 October 2021. mcc-berlin.net/en/research/co2-budget.html

Rogelj, Joeri. 2021. 'RealClimate: A Deep Dive into the IPCC's Updated Carbon Budget Numbers'. 2021. realclimate.org/index.php/archives/2021/08/a-deep-dive-into-the-ipccs-updated-carbon-budget-numbers/

Russill, Chris, and Zoe Nyssa. 2009. 'The Tipping Point Trend in Climate Change Communication'. *Global Environmental Change* 19 (3): 336–44. doi.org/10.1016/j.gloenvcha.2009.04.001

Supran, Geoffrey, and Naomi Oreskes. 2017. 'Assessing ExxonMobil's Climate Change Communications (1977–2014)'. *Environmental Research Letters* 12 (8): 084019. doi.org/10.1088/1748-9326/aa815f

The Government Chief Scientific Adviser. 2010. 'Guidelines on the Use of Scientific and Engineering Advice in Policy Making'. Department for Business, Innovation and Skills.

Weaver, C. P., R. H. Moss, K. L. Ebi, P. H. Gleick, P. C. Stern, C. Tebaldi, R. S. Wilson, and J. L. Arvai. 2017. 'Reframing Climate Change Assessments around Risk: Recommendations for the US National Climate Assessment'. *Environmental Research Letters* 12 (8): 080201. doi.org/10.1088/1748-9326/aa7494

There need to be structural changes in society that allow for easier access to participatory forms of communication.

Chapter 2: UNDERSTANDING AUDIENCES

WHO ARE THE EXPERTS, THE DECISION-MAKERS, AND THE STAKEHOLDERS?
For mainstreaming more participatory approaches, these concepts are indispensable. But who might they leave out?

This chapter shifts the focus to *who* is communicating with *whom*. As Evans et al. (2018) describe,

> there need to be structural changes in society that allow for easier access to participatory forms of communication that enable the ordinary citizens, governments and the business sector to discuss and debate issues pertaining to climate change. Climate change communication is central to effective and sustainable mainstreaming of climate change in development policies, mitigation and adaptation policies, collective behavioural change, and more specifically attitudes towards climate change mitigation for improved efforts towards reducing greenhouse gas emissions. (108)

Within climate communication research, recipients of information are typically imagined as **decision-makers** and **stakeholders,** as well as **policymakers, the public, communities, audiences,** or **individuals.** Sometimes **scientists** and other **experts** are also characterised as recipients of climate information. More granular terms also sometimes appear.

These are all useful terms, and we use them in this Toolkit. Nonetheless these can also be slippery terms. So we open this chapter with some reflections on them. What might such terms presuppose? What do they invite us to imagine about these participants, which may not really be the case? For example, it has been suggested that "[w]hen thinking about the policy relevance of their work, climate researchers tend to address imagined rather than actual policymakers" (Geden 2018). Who concretely belongs to these categories? Who is capable of action that makes a communicator feel satisfied (rightly or wrongly) that they have consulted an expert, supported a decision-maker, engaged a stakeholder? And when participatory mechanisms are devised and implemented using them, do these really connect the lives that will be most affected?

The word *expert* is perhaps the most slippery of the entire list. Governments and organisations often aspire to evidence-based policy creation. This means **experts are routinely consulted for any number of problem-solving activities,** from government calls for evidence to consultancy toward bespoke solutions. Typically, expertise is taken into account in **informal or unstructured ways,** even though this type of practice is

Subsections
Who are the experts, the decision-makers, and the stakeholders?
The decision value chain
Decision analysis: an interdisciplinary field, rooted in economics and statistics
Sidebar: Funding climate storytelling in the media
Storytelling vs. decision support: a checklist
Sidebar: Funding climate storytelling in the media
References

Community members are experts in their own lives and the lived experiences of their environments.

open to well-known cognitive frailties (Kahneman, Slovic, and Tversky 1982; Burgman 2016), both within the consulted experts and among those who are synthesising their evidence in unstructured or informal ways (Sutherland and Burgman 2015). **Structured approaches** to eliciting expert judgements have been shown to ameliorate many cognitive biases. A broad range of expertise also provides more robust results (Hanea et al. 2018; Burgman 2016).

A strong understanding of the uncertainties within a system is important in generating evidence for policy decisions that are relevant and reliable. **Many uncertainties can be classified and quantified. Experts also develop intuitive understandings of uncertainties.** Relative to a 'well-calibrated' expert, an overconfident expert will tend to underestimate the uncertainties and an underconfident expert will overestimate the uncertainties. Experts become well-calibrated by having frequent feedback on the accuracy of their assessments, which is why surgeons are generally better calibrated than General Practitioners; in the latter case there are many reasons why a patient may not return besides the prescribed treatment being effective.

At what point does someone start being treated as an expert, and by whom? Expertise is often defined by credentials, but highly regarded experts can be no better than so-called novice experts in some situations. **Not all relevant expertise is accompanied by credentials.** Trained scientists are also members of communities, and some citizen groups can develop considerable scientific expertise (Oakden et al. 2021). Furthermore, the expertise of those with lived experience is increasingly being recognised, particularly with regard to social ills and impacts (Gallegos and Chilton 2019). Burgman (2016) recommends seeking broad-based expertise and taking measures to avoid groupthink: "Ideally, expert groups should be as diverse as possible, and systems for engagement should encourage people to listen and integrate information from as many sources as possible, and to explore competing explanations. The basic idea is that groups made up of individuals with diverse experiences, backgrounds and contexts will draw on different sources of information, form independent initial estimates and avoid shared professional myopia. They will not anchor on common points nor be motivated by common personal goals."

There are well-established ethical rationales for including the voices of communities in policy formation. This expertise also becomes vital at the point where policy implementation relies on the actions and choices of community members. These community members are experts in their own lives and the lived experiences of their environments. Successful policy implementation needs to mesh with the needs, aspirations and worldviews of those who will either ensure its success, or will game the system to meet their needs, thus undermining policy implementation.

There is not extensive literature on the structured elicitation of lived experience. However relevant insights are available under rubrics such as: stakeholder analysis and engagement, public engagement and citizen participation, participatory policymaking, participatory design, municipalism, participatory democracy, direct democracy, radical democracy. We highlight five points:

- A 'campaigning' mentality risks alienating people. **Genuinely participatory processes allow for emergent scope.** Taking time to understand the motivations and priorities of members of the community has been fruitful in aligning aspirations, for example harnessing rewilding to support tackling rural poverty in the UK.

- As is often the case in climate risk communication, **interdisciplinary collaboration** can yield better results. For example, the Affric Highlands Scheme employed a psychologist alongside conservationists for a rewilding scheme (Weston 2021).

- **More vulnerable groups and individuals may also be those less able to access participatory processes.** Participatory processes can replicate historical patterns of exclusion (McNulty 2019). Practical support should be offered, and more research is needed into eliciting community expertise, taking into account e.g. interactions between cognitive biases, asymmetries in lived experience, payoff structures and strategic interaction, power discrepancies, and cultural and psychological factors.

- **Stakeholder engagement is most effective when stakeholders acquire real influence on outcomes.** This may include joint projects and/or transfer of appropriate decision-making powers and resources to stakeholders; however where this is less than feasible, meaningful influence can still be achieved by 'full stack' stakeholder engagement integrated into the governance, strategy, and operations of relevant entities.

- **International comparative approaches** are invaluable; for example, other countries can learn from the experiences of several Latin American countries which in recent years have taken measures aimed at strengthening participatory governance.

A second slippery term is ***decision-maker***. It is widely used in decision theory, and it reflects the discipline's aspiration to be relevant to many different contexts. A decision-maker may be an actual person such as a senior executive, an elected official or a civil servant. Or a decision-maker may be an organisation or some other entity. **But despite this broadness, the term *decision-maker* may sometimes lead to overly narrow thinking.** For example, we may slide into thinking of a decision-maker as necessarily someone who wields significant political, social, or economic power. But as just touched on, many other categories of actors are constantly making decisions pertinent to the success, and the moral significance, of climate policy.

Furthermore, expecting to find a decision-maker may sometimes close down other possibilities, where agency to drive change does not map neatly onto any individual or organisational unit. Climate risk invites unprecedented depth and speed of organisational and cultural change, and so **the decisions that need to be made may be unlike any decisions made in the past.** To date, studies of decision-making under uncertainty "rarely speak to the organisational and political context in which triggers for evaluative action occur" (Sowell 2019). Within a given management system, the decisions that drive mitigation and adaptation *may* clearly sit with specific roles. But the network of actors best placed to recognise, legitimate, and enact appropriate action may also cut across disparate roles, areas of responsibility, forms of formal and informal power, and even organisations and sectors. Critical threshold may need to be reached where a decision becomes available to collectives that are not available to individuals. In communicating climate information to drive mitigation and resilience, it may not always be appropriate to focus exclusively on the decision-makers who most obviously have their hands on the levers. Especially where such decision-makers prove resistive, it is important to stay open-minded about the nature and origin of positive change within organisations and sectors.

Similarly, the term ***stakeholder*** reflects stakeholder theory and is widely used across government, industry, the third sector and other contexts. Typically a stakeholder is defined as anybody who can potentially impact or be impacted by a given policy, project, product, or other entity of interest. However, where climate policy is concerned, **the highly interconnected nature of climate risk means that it is difficult, and probably undesirable, to completely exclude anybody from stakeholder status.** Furthermore, taking a stakeholder analysis and engagement perspective can sometimes obscure the differences between different concrete individuals belonging to the same stakeholder category, especially when some individuals are more vocal than others. In this way, individuals may be permitted to speak on behalf of those whom they have no legitimate right to represent. Finally, terms like *public*, *community*, and (to a lesser extent) *audience* and *individuals*, can be used to conflate the membership of a population with whichever subset is most available for dialogue.

These concepts are imperfect but useful. Awareness of their limitations will be helpful in creating processes which are truly participatory, not only in name only. Decision-making in climate risk policy relies on a 'decision value chain' or cascade of information between those who undertake cutting-edge research, through policy design, to those whose everyday lives are affected by the resulting policies (Barons and Kleve 2021). The modes of communication which make this a successful enterprise need to take into account the language, culture, expectations and motivations of the actors involved (Yusha'u and Servaes 2021). Scenarios and storytelling can play a significant role in how information (including uncertainty) is lost, preserved, added, transformed, and/or re-prioritised as it moves through the chain. Ideally participants in this process will also regularly reflect on the limitations of their participatory concepts and mechanisms, draw lessons from historical and international counterparts, and seek options for improvement. We also recommend that where possible, narrower and more concrete terminology should be used to identify participants in dialogues.

THE DECISION VALUE CHAIN
The decision value chain is one way of thinking about evidence-based (or at least evidence-informed) policymaking

The last section indicated the complexity of communicating climate risk. But we also need frameworks for organising this complexity, even if they mean simplifying things more than we would ideally like. Ultimately, **closer engagement between analytical and policy communities will allow for a more critical interrogation of how**

decision support is brought into decision-making and policy design (Sutherland and Burgman 2015). To highlight the issues that need to be considered in the communication of climate risk, we offer the stylised 'decision value chain' (discussed in this section) as well as the 'storytelling vs. decision support' checklist (in the next section).

Communicating climate risk is an integral component to translating decision support into policy, creating traction with relevant audiences, and gaining societal buy-in. However, the extent of research in this area is limited and there is fragmentation amongst different ontologies. The concept of "policy paradigms" (Burns, Calvo, and Carson 2009) highlights that rather than a clear-cut distinction between analytical and decision-making functions in policy design, divergent interests, agendas and values shape policymaking. The role of co-production and boundary work around science and policy in conferring legitimacy on analytical policy inputs is well-documented (Beck and Mahony 2018). However, beyond the politics of climate policy, the psychology as to how decisions regarding policy are actually formulated, the role of detailed analysis and expertise in the process of policy development, and its role in final policy output and decision-making, are not well-understood (Conway and Gore 2019).

What is known is that heuristics and biases are prevalent, particularly around issues involving deep uncertainty. Moreover, dialogue between analytical and policymaking communities is marked by very different cultures, processes and lexica (Kahneman and Klein 2009; Kahneman, Slovic, and Tversky 1982; G. A. Klein 2013; Kahneman and Klein 2009; G. Klein et al. 2007). With so much translation going on, there are many opportunities for useful information to get lost in translation. Dubois et al. (2018) divide the flow from analysis through policy into five phases: **pre-existing knowledge, projection, impact assessment, adaptation strategy, and adaptation plan.** Using content analysis of relevant documents (focusing on uncertainty communication and visualisations), they confirm that "the richness and completeness of the information are reduced" as it moves along the chain.

Nevertheless we stress that the participation of multiple actors in policy formation is also an advantage, with the **potential to integrate plural forms of expertise** and to generate greater legitimacy and buy-in.

Below a circular 'decision value chain' is suggested as a way to schematise the flow of information, while thinking more inclusively about who applies expertise, and where important decisions occur. The decision value chain shows the pattern of information flow from discovery and foresight, to synthesis and insight, to design, to implementation, to impact, then informing later discovery and foresight.

Value in the form of expertise can be introduced all the way around the chain. We would not want to live in a world where scientists made all the decisions. Policymakers have experience and insight about policy levers and trends; communities and individuals have a wealth of lived experience and tacit knowledge, and so on. While climate information may degrade in certain respects as it transfers from one participant to the next, it can also be enriched by new expertise, and be subjected to diverse forms of scrutiny and validation.

Just as expertise can be added all the way around the chain, so too can **decisions occur all the way around the chain.** Many key decisions become 'finalised' in the diagram's lower left zone by policy designers, parliamentary counsel, politicians and civil servants (or local equivalents). However, decisions can also be made by other participants, either because there are formal participatory mechanisms to delegate decision-making power, or because participants find the power to take action in ways that are informal or unauthorised.

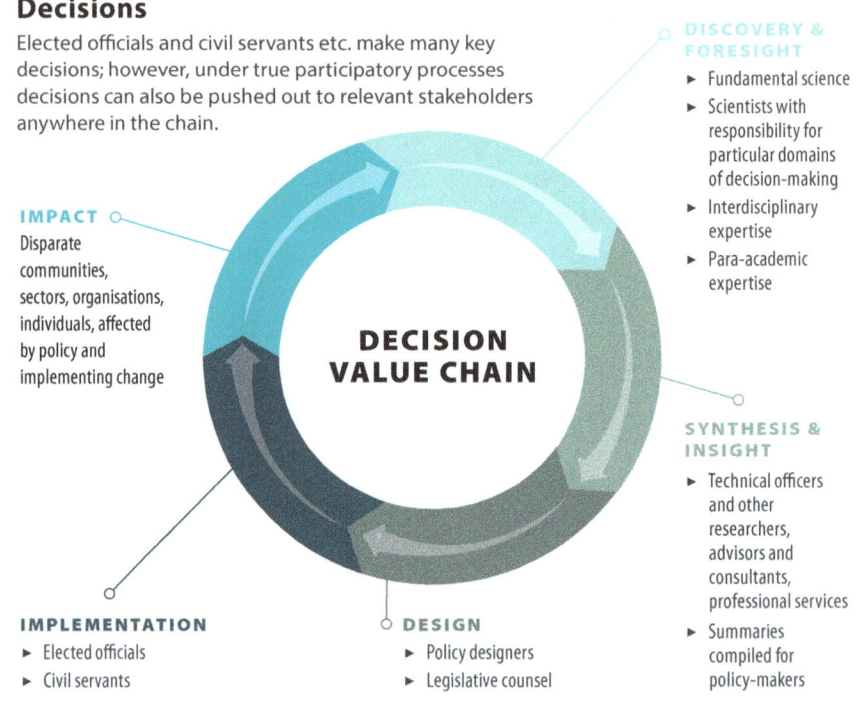

Figure 1. Decision value chain.

The sequence of the chain indicates only the broad direction of travel within a network where decision value can potentially also move between any of the participants (including 'upstream' or 'shortcut across' the central hub). Participants may join or leave the chain halfway through the process; the form of connection between them may alter (in terms of bandwidth, responsibilities, etc.); these transformations may be the result of internal evolutionary dynamics, external shocks, and/or deliberate redesign and reconfiguration. Indeed, exploring different connective configurations, giving careful regard to evidence from international comparative democratic politics, is key to strengthening participatory climate policy formation.

UNCERTAINTY AND THE DECISION VALUE CHAIN: EIGHT RECOMMENDATIONS

Dubois et al., focusing on **uncertainty,** make several recommendations for improving the transfer of uncertainty information from science into policy. These include:

1. Encouraging the actors involved in different phases to **work in parallel,** rather than sequentially.
2. Adopting more **participatory approaches,** such as **empowering societal stakeholders** in methodological choices.
3. **Adopting more consistent conventions** for uncertainty representation and the use of visualisations, by:
   a. developing best practice guidelines at the national, local, and/or sector-specific level;
   b. conducting more research into visualisation tools, since the drivers of their efficacy across different contexts are still not well-understood.
4. **Training end users to understand scientists better** (e.g. basics of climatology and decision theory).
5. **Training scientists to understand end users better** (e.g. communication, social and political context of climate policy).

DECISION ANALYSIS: *AN INTERDISCIPLINARY FIELD, ROOTED IN ECONOMICS AND STATISTICS*

IN THIS TOOLKIT, we frequently mention decisions, decision-making, and uncertainty. When we do so, we are speaking principally from within the field of decision analysis. In other words, we are particularly interested in how decisions can be formally modelled, for the purposes of evaluating alternative actions, and how competency in decision-making can be assessed. Decision analysis has its roots in economics and statistics. While it remains closely tied to these disciplines today, it is also an increasingly open and interdisciplinary field, drawing insight from across the sciences, social sciences, and arts and humanities. This rich interdisciplinarity is all the more important when we consider communication, a topic which necessarily includes themes such as authority, trust, interpretation, persuasion, and power.

Even mentioning uncertainty in the context of climate runs the risk, in some contexts, of undermining the confidence in robust scientific findings. Nonetheless, the IPCC has championed transparent approaches to communication of uncertainties, and strived to reflect degrees of confidence in discussing specific elements of assessments of climate risk both in text, graphically, and most recently in its interactive online Atlas. The confidence varies from virtually certain 'facts', that humans are responsible for climate change on a global scale, to high levels of uncertainty regarding specific regional future climate risks, tipping points or cascading risks.

These recommendations appear credible, and we broadly endorse them. This Toolkit may be seen as a small contribution toward the fourth and especially fifth recommendations. We propose three further recommendations to improve the flow of decision value.

6. **Placing participants outside their usual roles** to gain visibility and experience, both upstream and downstream. For example, funding more extended collaborations between scientists, technical officers, policy designers, communications experts from the social sciences (including experts in comparative democratic politics) and from the arts and humanities, and societal stakeholders. Such collaborations can embed a communications orientation from the very start (rather than as an afterthought), can contribute to forming new classes of multi-disciplinary experts, and can improve understandings and transparency on the political and ethical choices that decarbonisation entails. Placements could also contribute to international peer-to-peer collaboration and learning.

7. **Addressing substantive barriers and incentives to participation,** including socioeconomic inequality, linguistic and cultural factors, geographic distance, health and wellbeing inequalities, and traditional patterns of exclusion around gender, class, race, disability, and wealth. Measures to improve the participation of hard-to-reach groups should continue to be implemented, but the need for rapid action also means there may not always be time to wait for the results of such outreach. Where timescales dictate, innovative methods of eliciting community expertise and integrating it into the decision value chain should be explored, alongside more standard outreach.

8. **Multiplying channels for participation and cooperation** via which decision value may transfer among different participants, e.g. (a) public- and community-oriented institutions such as citizens assemblies, democratic engagement platforms, mandated participatory budgeting processes, national council systems, citizens enquiries, participatory planning and investment processes in local government, village committees, neighbourhood and employee councils, habitat and biodiversity conservation plans, trade unions, and innovative public fora based on models used in issue-specific strategic engagement, as well as (b) more targeted channels between specific segments of the value chain. We recommend bold and exploratory research into the range of connectivity mechanisms, especially around inclusion, equity, and translations of uncertainty and risk information across science, policy, and wider deliberative and participatory contexts.

At the same time, caution is also necessary. In following any of the eight recommendations above, we should be mindful of the following caveats.

- What is **timescale** appropriate? Is it necessary to find a more rapid workaround, perhaps in parallel with longer term structural change?

- What are the **opportunity costs**? Collaboration, translation, and working outside one's niche takes time, energy, and resources. Take the example of **training** (recommendations 4 and 5). What are the opportunity costs of training end users to think more like scientists, and/or scientists to think more like end users? If more time is devoted to training, is less time devoted to other activities? If more skills are added to a role, does it narrow the pool of potential candidates who can feasibly fill that role? If new content is added to a curriculum, what content is dislodged or de-emphasised? How does training also increase the influence of educators within the decision value chain — another set of actors with personal biases who may likewise adapt information, introduce new information, and summarise and synthesise information?

- Participatory approaches should be accompanied by careful attention to **how stakeholders are identified and mapped,** and who is empowered or disempowered by a given participatory process. Stakeholders include stakeholders who may be impacted by a policy, stakeholders who may influence its outcomes, stakeholders of potential alternative policies, stakeholders with whom there are existing or potential tensions, and stakeholders engaged to broaden diversity of perspectives, backgrounds, and lived experience. Other stakeholders include future generations and nonhuman actors. Where stakeholders have influence on one another this influence, including its type, should ideally be taken into account. **Ultimately where climate is concerned, there is nobody who is *not* a stakeholder.** See also above, the section 'Who are the experts, the decision-makers, and the stakeholders?' in this chapter.

- How might the measure be gamed, particularly by those with relatively extensive financial and/or ICT resources?

STORYTELLING VS. DECISION SUPPORT: A CHECKLIST

Popper (2019) draws a broad distinction between two cultures: the numerate, reductionist analytical community, rooted in deductive logic, and the culture of policy, which is more narrative based and framed in the logic of abductive reasoning. Following this distinction, we can think about climate risk communications in at least two ways. Climate risk experts can **support decisions.** At the same time, they can **tell stories,** transforming attitudes and behaviour in ways that are difficult to directly measure.

For the someone communicating climate risk, decision support and storytelling are not rigid and mutually exclusive categories. Instead they serve as 'lenses' through which you can reflect on and improve your practice. In particular, they can help you to decide how to present uncertainty. When deciding how to do this, consider your purpose and your intended (and unintended) audiences. You can start by answering the following ten questions.

1. Who is this communication for, e.g. what are their background, motivations, needs?
2. Who else might encounter this communication?
3. What are your criteria for successful communication?
4. Are there alternative ways the communication could make a positive impact?
5. Do you expect to receive information to evaluate its success? If so, how?
6. What concepts, frameworks, and methodologies (if any) could be used to talk about uncertainty, and how familiar do you expect your audience to be with these?
7. Can you give specific examples of behaviours, decisions, skills, and/or values you want to influence?
8. Can you give specific examples of how including or excluding uncertainty information (e.g. model uncertainty) could alter the results of your communication?
9. How do your recipients perceive you, and what do they expect from you (if anything) prior to the communication?
10. Do you think these perceptions may change, and if so how?

Remember, these questions are not designed to cover *everything* you might want to consider as someone who is communicating about climate risk. They are designed to serve a specific purpose: to help you think about your communication as decision support and as storytelling, and to **reflect on how to frame uncertainty in your communications,** to ensure it is understood accurately and constructively.

Once you have answered these questions, read through the two archetypes below and relate them to your situation. If you wish, you can assign each bolded statement a value between one and ten (1: strongly disagree, 5: neither agree nor disagree; 10: strongly agree).

In reality, **communications don't neatly fit into either archetype,** but always combine aspects of both. For example, scenarios play a prominent role in communication for decision support. Furthermore, even when you are not deliberately using scenario-based methods, your information will still 'tell a story' to the decision-makers who interpret it. On the flip side, any compelling narrative has the potential to influence our future decision-making.

FUNDING CLIMATE STORYTELLING IN THE MEDIA

WHILE CLIMATE-RELATED MEDIA are already being funded for purposes of education, training, and public awareness, there is scope to amplify impacts (Robinson, Hess, and Bui 2021). Areas where funding could realise impact include:

▶▶▶ More interventionist media-based initiatives to support climate action, e.g. on the model of shows like Shamba Shape Up (Kenya).

▶▶▶ More editorial and production support for shows that are not primarily climate themed, but want to review and improve the climate implications of their storytelling (e.g. Kampala Yénkya project described in this Toolkit).

▶▶▶ More media aimed at communities exposed to and/or impacted by climate risks, with a capacity building and decision support orientation.

▶▶▶ More investigative journalism, broadly construed, to improve public oversight of GHG emissions claims.

COMMUNICATING TO TELL A STORY

1) YOU ARE ENGAGING WITH AN AUDIENCE.

- You may already know who your audience are. Or you may be telling a story in hope of finding an audience.
- You may reach an audience who are mostly similar to one another. Or you may reach an audience with diverse interests, values, perspectives, motives, levels of engagement and agency, and so on.
- If you do reach a mixed audience, you may or may not have the chance to tailor your communications to each segment.

2) YOUR AUDIENCE MAY HAVE MULTIPLE DIFFERENT MOTIVES FOR ENGAGING YOU, SUCH AS:

- acquiring new skills, knowledge, and/or values;
- testing their existing skills, knowledge, and/or values;
- fulfilling their curiosity;
- entertaining themselves;
- acquiring evidence to progress agendas;
- fulfilling obligations to engage.

3) YOU MAY HAVE MULTIPLE MOTIVES FOR ENGAGING YOUR AUDIENCE, SUCH AS:

- raising awareness; seeking alternative perspectives to enhance your expertise;
- encouraging your audience to reassess the importance of the subject matter to themselves;
- encouraging your audience to change behaviours;
- confronting misinformation or common misconceptions about the subject matter;
- improving your audience's literacy for future communications about the subject matter;
- equipping your audience with the conceptual and emotional resources
- to engage with the subject matter in the future;
- giving your audience insights to pass on to their own audiences;
- trying out metaphors and analogies;
- supporting decision-making.

COMMUNICATING TO SUPPORT DECISIONS

1) YOU ARE ENGAGING WITH A DECISION-MAKER / DECISION-MAKERS.

- It is mostly clear who is in the decision-maker role. For example, this could be a particular person, or a decision-making process involving various stakeholders.

2) THEY ARE ENGAGING WITH YOU AS AN EXPERT.

- The decision-maker recognises you as an authority in the subject matter and is actively seeking your advice.
- The decision-maker may be relying on you exclusively. Or the decision-maker may be receiving input from other experts in the same domains and/or in different domains, and/or from other stakeholders.

3) THERE ARE MOSTLY GOOD CONDITIONS FOR ANALYSIS, COMMUNICATION, AND DECISION-MAKING.

- For example, it is clear what kinds of decisions are relevant. This may be a specific decision, or all the decisions pertaining to a particular area of responsibility or a particular policy aim.
- Experts and decision-makers have enough time and capacity to engage thoroughly in the process.
- There is typically a shared commitment to making the 'best' decision.
- The criteria for evaluating which decisions are the best may be fixed in advance. Such criteria may be transformed or developed in the course of the consultation/ co-production.

COMMUNICATING TO TELL A STORY	COMMUNICATING TO SUPPORT DECISIONS
4) IT MAY OR MAY NOT BE CLEAR WHICH OF YOUR MOTIVATIONS, AND/OR WHICH OF YOUR AUDIENCE'S MOTIVATIONS, MATTER THE MOST. ▶▶ You may or may not have clear criteria for what counts as 'successful' communication. ▶▶ Accountability is mostly informal.	**4) YOUR ENGAGEMENT MAY BE EMBEDDED IN BOTH INFORMAL AND FORMAL COMPLIANCE, ACCOUNTABILITY AND/OR REPORTING STRUCTURES.**
5) YOU LEAN TOWARD AN "OPT-IN" APPROACH TO UNCERTAINTY. ▶▶ In this context, you think transparency is best served by clear, straightforward messaging and opportunities for dialogue and further questioning. ▶▶ There are clear paths your audience can follow to deepen their understanding in various ways, including engaging in detail with uncertainty information, if they elect to do so.	**5) YOU LEAN TOWARD AN "OPT-OUT" APPROACH TO UNCERTAINTY.** ▶▶ You have integrated uncertainty thoroughly and clearly throughout your communication. ▶▶ Decision-makers are given support and encouragement to integrate uncertainty into their decision-making.

AUTHOR CONTRIBUTIONS

Conceptualization: JLW, MW, MJB, and PL; *Research:* JLW, MW, MJB and PL; *Writing:* JLW, MW, MJB, and PL.

REFERENCES

Barons, Martine J., and Sue Kleve. 2021. '"Mastering Another Language"—a Case Study in Interdisciplinary Teaching and Learning on Food Security across Two Countries and Two Universities'. *Warwick Journal of Education*, WJETT Education Conference Special Issue.

Beck, Silke, and Martin Mahony. 2018. 'The IPCC and the New Map of Science and Politics'. *WIREs Climate Change* 9 (6). doi.org/10.1002/wcc.547

Burgman, Mark A. 2016. *Trusting Judgements: How to Get the Best out of Experts.* Cambridge, United Kingdom: Cambridge University Press.

Burns, Tom R., Dolores Calvo, and Marcus Carson, eds. 2009. *Paradigms in Public Policy: Theory and Practice of Paradigm Shifts in the EU.* Frankfurt am Main ; New York: Peter Lang.

Conway, Gareth E., and Julie Gore. 2019. 'Framing and Translating Expertise for Government'. In *The Oxford Handbook of Expertise*, by Gareth E. Conway and Julie Gore, edited by Paul Ward, Jan Maarten Schraagen, Julie Gore, and Emilie M. Roth, 1131–52. Oxford University Press. doi.org/10.1093/oxfordhb/9780198795872.013.49

Dubois, Ghislain, Femke Stoverinck, and Bas Amelung. 2018. 'Communicating Climate Information: Traveling Through the Decision-Making Process'. In *Communicating Climate Change Information for Decision-Making*, edited by Silvia Serrao-Neumann, Anne Coudrain, and Liese Coulter, 119–37. Springer Climate. Cham: Springer International Publishing. doi.org/10.1007/978-3-319-74669-2_9

Evans, Henri-Count, Lauren Dyll, and Ruth Teer-Tomaselli. 2018. 'Communicating Climate Change: Theories and Perspectives'. In *Handbook of Climate Change Communication: Vol. 1*, edited by Walter Leal Filho, Evangelos Manolas, Anabela Marisa Azul, Ulisses M. Azeiteiro, and Henry McGhie, 107–22. Climate Change Management. Cham: Springer International Publishing. doi.org/10.1007/978-3-319-69838-0_7

Gallegos, Danielle, and Mariana Chilton. 2019. 'Re-Evaluating Expertise: Principles for Food and Nutrition Security Research, Advocacy and Solutions in High-Income Countries'. *International Journal of Environmental Research and Public Health* 16 (4): 561. doi.org/10.3390/ijerph16040561

Geden, Oliver. 2018. 'Politically Informed Advice for Climate Action'. *Nature Geoscience* 11 (6): 380–83. doi.org/10.1038/s41561-018-0143-3

Hanea, A.M., M.F. McBride, M.A. Burgman, and B.C. Wintle. 2018. 'Classical Meets Modern in the IDEA Protocol for Structured Expert Judgement'. *Journal of Risk Research* 21 (4): 417–33. doi.org/10.1080/13669877.2016.1215346

Kahneman, Daniel, and Gary Klein. 2009. 'Conditions for Intuitive Expertise: A Failure to Disagree.' *American Psychologist* 64 (6): 515–26. doi.org/10.1037/a0016755

Kahneman, Daniel, Paul Slovic, and Amos Tversky. 1982. *Judgment under Uncertainty : Heuristics and Biases / Edited by Daniel Kahneman, Paul Slovic, Amos Tversky*. Cambridge, United Kingdom: Cambridge University Press.

Klein, Gary A. 2013. *Seeing What Others Don't: The Remarkable Ways We Gain Insights.* First edition. New York: PublicAffairs.

Klein, Gary, Jennifer K. Phillips, Erica L. Rall, and Deborah A. Peluso. 2007. 'A Data-Frame Theory of Sensemaking.' In *Expertise out of Context: Proceedings of the Sixth International Conference on Naturalistic Decision Making*, 113–55. Mahwah, NJ, US: Lawrence Erlbaum Associates Publishers.

McNulty, Stephanie L. 2019. *Democracy from above?: The Unfulfilled Promise of Nationally Mandated Participatory Reforms.*

Oakden, Libby, Gemma Bridge, Beth Armstrong, Christian Reynolds, Changqiong Wang, Luca Panzone, Ximena Schmidt Rivera, et al. 2021. 'The Importance of Citizen Scientists in the Move Towards Sustainable Diets and a Sustainable Food System'. *Frontiers in Sustainable Food Systems* 5 (September): 596594. doi.org/10.3389/fsufs.2021.596594

Popper, Steven W. 2019. 'Reflections: DMDU and Public Policy for Uncertain Times'. In *Decision Making under Deep Uncertainty*, edited by Vincent A. W. J. Marchau, Warren E. Walker, Pieter J. T. M. Bloemen, and Steven W. Popper, 375–92. Cham: Springer International Publishing. doi.org/10.1007/978-3-030-05252-2_16

Robinson, Lisa, Janto S. Hess, and Thi Quynh Anh Bui. 2021. '… And Action! How Media Can Address Climate Change in Countries Most Affected'. BBC Media Action.

Sowell, Jesse. 2019. 'A Conceptual Model of Planned Adaptation'. In *Decision Making under Deep Uncertainty: From Theory to Practice*, edited by Vincent A. W. J. Marchau, Warren E. Walker, Pieter J. T. M. Bloemen, and Steven W. Popper. Cham: Springer International Publishing. doi.org/10.1007/978-3-030-05252-2

Sutherland, William J., and Mark Burgman. 2015. 'Policy Advice: Use Experts Wisely'. *Nature* 526 (7573): 317–18. doi.org/10.1038/526317a

Weston, Phoebe. 2021. 'Planting a vision: why the secret to rewilding success is about people, not trees'. *The Guardian*, 27 September 2021, sec. Environment. theguardian.com/environment/2021/sep/27/planting-a-vision-why-the-secret-to-rewilding-success-is-about-people-not-trees-aoe

Yusha'u, Muhammad Jameel, and Jan Servaes, eds. 2021. *The Palgrave Handbook of International Communication and Sustainable Development*. Cham, Switzerland: Palgrave Macmillan. doi.org/10.1007/978-3-030-69770-9

*'Look at the world around you,' Gladwell argues.
'It may seem like an immovable, implacable place. It is not.
With the slightest push — in just the right place — it can be tipped.'
(Gladwell 2015)*

Chapter 3: COMMUNICATING around TIPPING POINTS

WHAT ARE TIPPING POINTS? AND HOW SHOULD WE COMMUNICATE ABOUT THEM?

> [R]egardless of whether it is being communicated to policy makers or the public [...] [u]sing scientific terminology, such as 'tipping points' and 'feedback loops', is complex and can be difficult to grasp. When climate change is presented in the form of predictions and graphs it can also appear inaccessible, as too big, or disengaging, when not paired with solutions.
> (**Huxley** 2018).

In this chapter we examine some of the challenges of communicating around **tipping points,** an area often characterised by **deep uncertainty.** Googling 'tipping point' in October 2021, we found that our top results were all about the British game show *Tipping Point*. Could we take this as one small indication that the science about tipping points has not yet penetrated popular discourse to the extent that we would wish?

A tipping point is a critical threshold beyond which a system reorganises, often abruptly and/or irreversibly. For example, over two million cubic kilometres of ice locked in the Western Antarctic Ice Sheet could collapse and pour into the ocean, causing sea levels to soar by three metres or more. The IPCC believes with *medium confidence* that it won't collapse this century; Chris Rapley, formerly Director of the British Antarctic Survey, has already said of the Western Antarctic Ice Sheet, "I would argue that this is now an awakened giant" (Rapley et al. 2006).

The probability of triggering a tipping point may be low (or difficult or impossible to quantify) at a given level of global warming, yet with consequences that are catastrophic and far-reaching. Some potential tipping points of concern include:

Subsections
What are tipping points?
The many emotions of apocalypse
What's wrong with a little apocalypse?
Where do we talk about climate risks such as tipping points?
Tipping points and the IPCC model ensemble
Communicating around deep uncertainty
"Participatory uncertainty"
Visualising Deep Uncertainty
References

1. Collapse of the Western Antarctic Ice Sheet and/or other major ice formations (Arctic sea ice, Greenland ice sheet, Wilkes basin in East Antarctica), leading to much higher sea level rises.
2. Permafrost thaw releasing methane, a powerful greenhouse gas, accelerating global warming.[1]
3. Massive loss of forests including Boreal forests[2] and Amazon rainforest[3] — meaning not only profound loss of biodiversity, but also the release of vast amounts of extra greenhouse gases, accelerating global warming.
4. Mass extinctions of animals, plants and other life forms unable to adapt to rapid climate change (Barnosky et al. 2011).
5. A shutdown of a major system of ocean currents (AMOC) that conveys heat from the tropics into the Northern Hemisphere.
6. Increase in El Niño–Southern Oscillation (ENSO) leading to drought in South East Asia[4] (Lenton et al. 2008).
7. West African Monsoon shift and potential recurring droughts across Mauritania, Senegal, Burkina Faso, Mali, and Niger.
8. Greening of the Sahara leading to greater local biodiversity.[5]
9. Indian Monsoon shift and potential recurring droughts on the Indian subcontinent.
10. More generally, tipping points can occur at regional rather than global levels, and have severe local impacts.
11. Tipping points can also affect marine ecosystems; for example, abrupt West Tropical Indian Oceanic Bloom, caused by a sudden increase in deep water upwelling that brings nutrients to the upper layers of the ocean, leading to gains in productivity from microorganisms to fisheries (Drijfhout et al. 2015).
12. Disappearance of coral reefs, leading to the loss of biodiversity, habitats, greater coastal erosion as well as cultural and economic losses.

Many of these tipping points have implications for **food harvests** and for **extreme weather** such as floods, storms, and wildfires. Other effects could include disintegration of systems that produce and distribute goods and services; and destruction of infrastructures which supply people with energy, food, water, light, heating; infrastructures which store data and carry voices and images around the world; infrastructures which dispose safely of waste and sewage; they could include failures of healthcare, social care, security, finance, housing, transport, education, emergency services; and the unravelling of societies as homes, jobs, and communities are lost, populations are scattered, governance of organisations and institutions weakens or collapses, and wars and conflicts intensify and spread. For those who have been fortunate enough to live under conditions of relative peace, tipping points represent the tearing apart of our taken-for-granted world.[6]

Many tipping points also have implications for the **feasibility of achieving net zero GHG emissions.** For example, shrinking of the Amazon rainforest and Boreal forest through drying, forest fires, pests, habitat loss and other factors, could result in large, swift releases of GHGs.[7] Likewise, carbon release

---

1 IPCC AR6 WGI notes that it is *"very unlikely* that gas clathrates (mostly methane) in deeper terrestrial permafrost and subsea clathrates will lead to a detectable departure from the emissions trajectory during this century".

2 "Boreal forest dieback is not expected to change the atmospheric CO_2 concentration substantially because forest loss at the south is partly compensated by (i) temperate forest invasion into the previous boreal area and (ii) boreal forest gain at the north (Friend et al., 2014; Kicklighter et al., 2014; Schaphoff et al., 2016) *(medium confidence)*" (IPCC AR6 WGI).

3 IPCC AR6 WGI puts an upper limit of how much CO_2 can be released by Amazon forest dieback as 0.5ppm per year (the current concentration is 442 ppm): "This implies an upper limit to the release of tropical land carbon of <200 PgC over the 21st century (assuming tropical warming of <4oC, and no CO_2-fertilisation), which translates to $dCO_2/dt < 0.5$ ppm yr-1 (IPCC AR6 WGI)."

4 "Given also that past climate changes have been accompanied by changes in ENSO, we differ from IPCC and consider there to be a significant probability of a future increase in ENSO amplitude. The required warming can be accessed this century with the transition happening within a millennium, but the existence and location of any threshold is particularly uncertain" (Lenton et al. 2008).

5 "Such greening of the Sahara/Sahel is a rare example of a beneficial potential tipping element."(Lenton et al. 2008)

6 Human history is replete with evidence that dramatic shifts in societies can happen in response to relatively small environmental drivers, an idea popularised by Jared Diamond in *Collapse: How Societies Choose to Fail or Survive* (Diamond 2011). But social tipping points are also discussed in a positive context: Otto et al. (2020) describe the tipping points they identified that if triggered would enable a radical decarbonisation of society that is currently required.

7 IPCC AR6 WGI: "Based on the evidence presented in this section, we conclude that abrupt changes and tipping points in the biogeochemical cycles lead to additional uncertainty in 21st century GHG concentrations changes, but these are very likely to be small compared to the uncertainty associated with future anthropogenic emissions *(high confidence)*."

Figure 1. Conceptual model for tipping points.

(including methane release) from permafrost thaw may mean that remaining carbon "budgets" are smaller than we think (Comyn-Platt et al. 2018).[8] The range of socioeconomic risks mentioned in the previous paragraph also could deplete our capacity to mitigate GHGs, e.g. climate technologies may be more difficult to develop and deploy at scale in the midst of mass movements of populations, rolling pandemics, famines, wars, and so on. In this sense tipping points are closely associated with dynamics that have been variously imagined as domino effects, cascade risks, feedback loops, vicious circles, cliff edges, points of no return, situations spiralling out of control, runaway processes, and so on.

Now let's take a step back, and focus on **communication**. This list we've given above includes somewhat inadequate summaries of complex topics of interdisciplinary inquiry. It also veils numerous qualifications and interconnections: to take just one example, a warming climate could bring about droughts to the Sahel region of West Africa (#7), or could actually bring more rainfall to the Sahel and the growth of vegetation in southern parts of the Sahara (#8). The list scarcely reflects any disparities in climate vulnerabilities, for example the devastating impact of Amazon die-back on indigenous societies. Interactions between tipping elements are also a source of deep uncertainty: what is expected is that crossing any major tipping point threshold will have implications for other tipping

---

8 Recent releases of methane have been impossible to quantify due to the lack of large scale baseline data, and on a larger time scale "several independent lines of evidence indicate that permafrost thaw did not release vast quantities of fossil CH4 associated with the transient warming events of the LDT, suggesting that large emissions of CH4 from old carbon sources will not to occur in response to future warming *(medium confidence)*" (IPCC AR6 WGI 2021).

points, and that temporal sequence is important. Overall, the list above also includes some language that may strike many experts as somewhat loose and clumsy.

Despite these drawbacks, this list is also our attempt to **illustrate some good practice in communicating around tipping points.** Tipping points are characterised by complexity and uncertainty. It is easy for experts to become preoccupied with the puzzle of vividly communicating this uncertainty and complexity, and to overlook more basic problems of communication which might be more easily addressed. Audiences may not connect with terms like AMOC, monsoon shift, biome shift, die-back, food security, circulation shutdown. It can be helpful to add words like **rain, fire, snow, hunger, storms, winds, ocean currents, floods, droughts, famines, forests, animals, birds, plants,** and so on—words that connect to the imagination and the senses. Audiences may know that disappearing rainforest, weakening ocean currents, or sea level rises are undesirable, but could benefit from brief discreet reminders why.

Attention to the basics is certainly recommended in communications aimed at policymakers or the public. Furthermore, **experts could also challenge themselves to bring vividness to more technical communications too**, within the scientific community. There are three good reasons: (a) to practice these skills; (b) to uncover where experts may actually not share the understandings they assumed they did; (c) texts can often circulate beyond their intended audiences. Interdisciplinary and multi-professional collaboration is also always worth supporting and celebrating: not every scientist should be expected to be a poet as well, and the arts and humanities have much to contribute.

Visualising connections between tipping points might also help communicate complex interactions that increase systemic risks (Figure 1). Here again, experts are encouraged to cater for a wide audience where possible. They can consider visualising some more basic, "core" concepts in climate change, and/or to use visualisations that may allow audiences to connect climate risk with what they already care about or can already vividly imagine. Clear, accessible visualisation of GHG emissions and global warming, for example, can be framed as useful context for the narrower topic of tipping points.

Figure 1 shows an interconnected system of potential climate tipping that could have the property where small changes (even below 1.5 degree warming) can trigger outsized impacts that interactively propagate through the system, altering climate drastically and causing large-scale devastation. Such tipping points might have been triggered in the past simply by internal variability (called **noise-induced tipping**), but the risk is higher when external forcings such as human-cased GHG emissions are present. The interpretation of evidence for abrupt changes in Earth's historical record is now accompanied by a greater understanding of possible mechanisms by which a climate might respond to small stochastic variations not with gradual changes but sudden shifts (Wunderling et al. 2021). Further, once some threshold is crossed (in cases of **bifurcation tipping**) and changes are underway, stopping external forcing (e.g. achieving net zero GHG emissions or better) will not impede the transformation to a new state, and a reversal may be difficult or impossible: one term for this is "**hysteresis**."[9] Other tipping points, like the Arctic Sea Ice melt, could be reversible within decades (Masson-Delmotte et al. 2021).

One of the first triggers to be activated is thought to be AMOC, a major system of ocean currents that already has noticeably weakened. It is possible that AMOC is a self-reinforcing system that can switch from one state to another with a relatively small push (it is believed to be an example of noise-induced tipping, i.e. there is no explicit threshold to cross as in bifurcation). Weakening this global ocean circulatory pattern could have an effect of weakening it further, perhaps until the circulation functionally shuts down, as might have happened repeatedly throughout Earth's history. This in itself would be a disaster for agriculture, human health and biodiversity, due to loss of rainfall, rise in extreme cold and heat, and loss of entire habitats. One of the key centres of biodiversity that is especially threatened by AMOC shutdown is the Amazon rainforest (Cai, Lenton, and Lontzek 2016). The next domino to fall might be the West Antarctic and Greenland ice sheets[10], whose disintegration would unleash long-term irreversible sea level rises of several meters or more, drowning cities, coastlines and low-lying countries — China, United States, Japan and the Netherlands would be especially affected.

---

9   Regrettably recalling the word "hysteria," which Tasca et al. (2012), describe as "the first mental health disorder attributable to women," and which became a highly disciplinary and punitive diagnosis employed by patriarchal medicine in the 19th and 20th century (and also a locus of adaptation and resistance by women; cf. Showalter 1987).

10 Referring to repeated abrupt shifts, some associated with AMOC, throughout Earth's history, the IPCC AR6 WGI report notes that the sensitivity of the response to a rise in temperature is uncertain: "The paleoclimate record indicates that tipping elements exist in the climate system where processes undergo sudden shifts toward a different sensitivity to forcing, such as during a major deglaciation, where one degree of temperature change might correspond to a large or small ice sheet mass loss during different stages."

> *Apocalypses are about many more emotions than fear and hope. ...the end of the world can feel alluring.*

THE MANY EMOTIONS OF APOCALYPSE
The science of tipping points can lend itself to apocalyptic storytelling. What are some of the pros and cons?

▶▶▶ *"Are you getting this on camera, that this tornado just came and erased the Hollywood sign? The Hollywood sign is gone, it's just shredded."*
— Character in *The Day After Tomorrow* (2004)

From the perspective of climate risk communication, tipping points can be associated with **apocalyptic and cataclysmic narratives.** The tipping points session at the COP26 Universities Network Climate Risk Summit, late 2021, provides an illustration (Mackie 2021). The session opened with a slide alluding to the 2004 Hollywood blockbuster *The Day After Tomorrow*. Of course, this movie stretches science in ways that are regrettably familiar. "Scenarios that take place over a few days or weeks in the movie would actually require centuries to occur" (National Snow & Ice Data Center 2004). Nonetheless, *The Day After Tomorrow* does represent a real tipping element: the potential shutdown of AMOC, a large system of ocean currents that conveys warm water from the tropics northwards, which is responsible for the relative warmth of the North Hemisphere.

Movies like *The Day After Tomorrow* vividly communicate the fragility of human lives — as tornadoes tear apart the Los Angeles skyline and toss cars through the air, as New Yorkers scramble down narrow streets from oncoming tsunami-like waves — in ways that are not always captured by terminology such as "extreme weather events." In the broader context of climate action, is it useful to tug on the heartstrings in this way? Much of the literature on catastrophic narratives and climate storytelling focuses on a distinction between fear and hope. **An overreliance on fear has been quite widely criticised.**

> *[...] some studies suggest that there are better chances to engage an audience by including positive messages in film narratives about environmental risks, especially climate change, rather than adopting the strategy of fear, which would instead distance and disengage them, making them feel overwhelmed and helpless [...]*
>
> (Leal Filho et al. 2017)

However, one thing we should remember is that **apocalypses are about many more emotions than fear and hope.** A movie like *The Day After Tomorrow* showcases a range of emotions including exhilaration, confusion, companionship, desire, curiosity, anger, encounters with the sublime, and even moments of humour, both grim and sweet. As many scriptwriters will tell you, an immersive narrative needs emotional variety, or the audience will introduce variety of their own — they will daydream, feel bored, pick holes in the plot, or find their own things to laugh about. Apocalyptic hearts are full hearts: there is probably no human emotion that cannot find some niche in narratives of disaster and collapse. Indeed, the end of the world can feel alluring. The more dissatisfied people are with their existing lives, the more alluring it may feel. As the recent ASU Apocalyptic Narratives and Climate Change project describes (focusing on the US context):

> *From infectious disease to war, a broad swath of the public has long interpreted social and environmental crisis through the prism of apocalypse, casting potential catastrophes and their causes in religious and moral terms. These apocalyptic visions are often narrated from the point of view of the survivors (the "elect"), thus reinforcing a sense that the end times need to be survived by remaining among the elect, rather than prevented through pragmatic action.*
>
> (CSRC 2020)

Alternatively, an apocalyptic or eschatalogical idiom can sometimes make climate change feel like nothing special. When has the world *not* been ending? "For at least 3,000 years, a fluctuating proportion of the world's population has believed that the end of the world is imminent" (Garrard 2004). Insofar as apocalyptic framings feel extreme yet in a familiar way, they can be counter-productive, especially with audiences who are already wary. This includes those who are ready to view anthropogenic climate change as a left wing conspiracy (perpetrated by charlatan scientists to secure themselves power and funding, in cahoots with governments that aim to justify increasingly authoritarian, totalitarian, and unjust policies) or as a neocolonialist agenda (perpetrated by the rich countries of the world to impose new forms of domination, indebtedness, and exploitation on the Global South).

De Meyer et al. (2021) offer an intriguing spin on the respective merits of fear, hope, and other emotions: **they suggest that current debates on climate communication have exaggerated the role of emotions altogether.** Instead they advocate for a focus on **practice**, by storytelling (and doing other things) to create spaces where new audiences can experience agency in relation to the climate, at many different scales and in many different circumstances. People should be able to see what they can do.

> *Here, we propose that both place-based, localized action storytelling, and practice-based action storytelling have a role to play in expanding climate agency. As examples of the latter, for creative writers and journalists the required agency would be about knowing how to make action on climate change part of their stories; for architects, how to bring climate change into building design; for teachers, how to teach about climate action within the constraints of the curriculum; for fund managers, how to bring climate risk into their investment decisions; for health professionals, to support the creation of place-based community systems that respond to the health impacts of climate change. These examples of communities of practice provide different opportunities and challenges to expand the notions of climate action beyond the current notions of consumer choice and activism.*
>
> —*De Meyer et al. (2021)*

Let's summarise, then, some approaches to effective climate risk communication. One approach is to focus on **information**. How can information be clearly expressed and tailored for users to easily incorporate it into their decision-making? A second approach (partly in response to perceived shortcomings of the first) places more emphasis on **emotion**. What mixture of emotions should be appealed to in order to motivate action? This focus on emotion is also implicitly a focus on moral normativity, an appeal to the heart rather than the head (there is of course a great body of literature deriding this split between reason and emotion, which in reality are always mutually entangled). More recently we are seeing the emergence of a third approach, not strictly supplanting but rather complementing the other two, which focuses on **practice**.

The distinction between a "practice" focus vs. a focus on "informative and tailored stories" or "stories of hope not fear" is a bit subtle. Of course the three may often overlap. It may be helpful to think about what the "practice" focus means in the longer term. In the longer term, each new representational domain of climate agency will not emerge solely through hopeful portrayals of an agent (e.g. journalist, architect, teacher, fund manager) exemplifying an orthodox version of their role-specific climate action, however cognitively and affectively well-judged. Telling these stories may certainly be the priority in the short term. But what they should hope to kickstart are diverse stories filled with diverse agents, affects, and values: stories which superficially contradict each other in many ways, but whose deeper presuppositions mesh to create fields of imaginable action that can accommodate the particularity and the creativity of real people. "Environmental activist" is a social role that is available for real people to fill precisely because it can be filled in many ways (not just one way) and because it means many contradictory things (not just one thing). The same is true of the figure of the ethical consumer.

Audiences are more likely to engage with stories about the world they live in, than about who they must be in that world. Successful rapid mitigation and adaptation entails shifting to more participatory and equitable societies. Many audiences with centrist or conservative leanings may struggle to see themselves accepted within such societies. They may reject realistic climate narratives as hoaxes, or even welcome the end times: revel in fantasies of courage, ingenuity, largesse and revenge, set amid the ruins of civilisation. More can be done to create narratives that accommodate a range of self-reported aspirational virtues across the political spectrum, in ways that are cohesive with an overall just transition.[11] Storytelling that focuses on multiplying domains of agency also entails interventions beyond representational techniques altogether, transforming the material contexts in which people seek to exercise agency.

---

11 *Britain Talks COP26: New insights on what the UK public want from the climate summit* (Wang et al. 2021) is one small example of exploring (in the UK context) how climate risk communication might be diversified to appeal to myriad different political and ethical values. It does not (and we should not expect every such study to) engage with the challenging questions about which values fall beyond the scope of those that are compatible with a participatory and just transition.

Reducing emissions as rapidly as possible will make crossing tipping points less probable, and will make it more likely to stay under the 1.5 degrees threshold. But with regards to **storytelling,** *it may often feel simpler to give your audience one or the other to focus on.*

WHAT'S WRONG WITH A LITTLE APOCALYPSE?
Are experts sometimes overly wary of apocalyptic connotations?

For reasons described in the previous section, apocalyptic framing and imagery should be used with care. Moreover, it can be difficult to narratively reconcile tipping points with the Paris Agreement target of 1.5 degrees. As already mentioned, with regards to *action*, there is no contradiction at all. Reducing emissions as rapidly as possible will make crossing tipping points less probable, and will make it more likely to stay under the 1.5 degrees threshold. But with regards to *storytelling*, it may often feel simpler to give your audience one or the other to focus on.

However, experts can also stray into different problems when they are *too* averse to apocalyptic associations. Consider another example from the AR6 WG1 report that in trying to distance itself from apocalyptic storytelling, in style, gets semantically tangled up.

In summary, while there is a strong theoretical expectation that Amazon drying and deforestation can cause a rapid change in the regional water cycle, currently there is limited model evidence to verify this response, hence there is **low confidence** *that such a change will occur by 2100.*

(Masson-Delmotte et al. 2021)

Firstly, there is an ambiguity about the word 'change' in the last sentence: does it refer to Amazon deforestation on the whole, or to the regional water cycle (the two are also connected, so the uncertainty is not just linguistic but epistemological — would one cause another, and how to interpret 'a strong theoretical expectation' that it would, despite being told that such changes are implausible)? It seems that the epistemological uncertainty over the mechanism for change is low (the theoretical understanding of the process is solid) while modelling uncertainty is high and evidence is lacking, and as a result there is low confidence about the risk of a rapid undesirable change. And how to interpret this? How should we feel as a result of reading this sentence? What are the appropriate ethical or judgment responses?

It is also worth noting that cataclysmic storytelling around tipping points *preceded* their acceptance within academic circles. The narrative about tipping points within dominant climate science is relatively recent, emerging around 2005. Previously it was considered "too alarmist for proper scientific circles" (Russill and Nyssa 2009), although there was earlier scientific exploration of large-scale discontinuities, especially associated with warming in excess of 2 degrees. Russill and Nyssa (2009) found the timeline disconcerting, asking, "Should we draw any conclusions from the fact that popular discourse on tipping points precedes use of the concept in peer-reviewed climate change science?" But we might also then ask: should we be worried about travelling by air, or using touch screen devices, simply because these practices appeared in science fiction before they became reality? 'Tipping points' are an example of **diegetic prototyping** (Kirby 2010), whereby an idea arrives from the popular imagination to aid the development or articulation of technology or science — in this case, the science of climate risk modelling.

The tipping point metaphor is an example of the less common reverse journey, beginning as a rhetorical device to communicate the dangers of abrupt climate change to the public (in 2005–2007) and then developing into a theory-constitutive metaphor in the climate sciences (2007 onwards). While the exegetical function of the metaphor aims at explaining the underlying process to others, in the theory-constitutive phase, the metaphor starts shaping a subdomain of climate science.

(van der Hel, Hellsten, and Steen 2018)

Tipping points are now a lot more prominent in both popular and scientific cultures. The context in which we communicate changes rapidly; if it was perhaps true that in the early 2000s that "[t]he desire to increase public urgency is driving the mainstreaming of tipping points in climate change communication, not the reporting of peer-reviewed research" (Russill and Nyssa 2009), then the scientific research in the last decade has matured considerably. However, their research poses questions that are still relevant today, especially since 'climate anxiety' has entered mental health professionals' list of symptoms: "Do tipping points induce unwarranted anxiety and perhaps fatalism [...], or, on the other hand, do they help correct for the 'false sense of security' produced by smooth projections of change, which can lull society into inactivity?" (Clayton 2020; Thompson 2021).

WHERE DO WE TALK ABOUT CLIMATE RISKS SUCH AS TIPPING POINTS?
Climate storytelling tends to be siloed, which reduces its impact. How can we help to spread it more widely through our cultures?

Science fiction across various forms (literature, movies, games, etc.) has a long history with climate change themes, and provides one key cultural context for communicating climate risk. Here is a description of tipping points, from *Fifty Degrees Below*, a novel by Kim Stanley Robinson:

> *They had passed the point of criticality, they had tipped over the tipping point in the same way a kid running up a seesaw will get past the axis and somewhere beyond and above it plummet down on the falling board. They were in the next mode, and coming into the second winter of abrupt climate change.*
>
> (Robinson 2006)

This passage is also quoted by van der Hel, Hellsten, and Steen (2018) who are interested specifically in the physicality of the metaphor, noticing that the "image of the earth on the edge of a cliff, only inches away from tipping over and falling into the abyss" is pervasive in all forms of communication. The researchers combed through a vast array of scientific papers, popular media and journalism around tipping points, and found four linguistic and discursive archetypes:

> *"(1) In the climate sciences, the tipping point metaphor was first introduced from 2005 onwards as a rhetorical device, warning the public and scientific peers for abrupt and possibly irreversible changes in the climate system. This use of the metaphor is characterized by occasionally clearly deliberate metaphorical language use explaining tipping points as motion in space.*
>
> *(2) Meanwhile, journalists adopted and employed the notion of a tipping point in climate change as a metaphorical scientific concept with societal implications, also occasionally exhibiting features of deliberate metaphorical use.*
>
> *(3) From around 2007, the tipping point phrase becomes popular as a theory-constitutive metaphorical model for research in the climate sciences.*
>
> *(4) Finally, from around 2011, notions of tipping points in news media on climate change become used as conventionalized ideas and expressions for important impending change, no longer automatically drawing attention to the metaphorical status of the phrase."*
>
> (van der Hel, Hellsten, and Steen 2018)

There is a lack of consensus about the relative roles of metaphors, scientific information and narratives in terms of translating into actions, especially in the face of climate emergency (De Meyer et al. 2020). What is clearly significant in this respect is one's politics (Kahan 2012). Whether scientists like it or not, questions about politics and climate science will be asked. The inclusion of political considerations in discourse about effective climate communication partly reflects a frustration with the use of "the need for better public engagement" to distract from well-attested economic and political obstacles to effective climate action. Furthermore, the example, the extent to which political climate could influence science, especially modelling results (one may question on this basis the extremely low value for climate sensitivity in Russian models) and their interpretations, has to be addressed in some constructive way. The more limited the scientific evidence the greater is the potential for the social and political backgrounds to be reflected in the narrative about climate risks. Assessing that influence can be tricky, since "the standard ways of using probabilities to separate ethical and social values from scientific practice cannot be applied in a great deal of climate modeling, because the roles of values in creating the models cannot be discerned after the fact—the models are too complex and the result of too much distributed epistemic labor" (Winsberg 2012).

The production and circulation of this knowledge is also shaped by (among other things) structural power and by the counterpower of social movements, such as Black Lives Matter and many others, which critically foreground the historical, economic and cultural politics of climate change. In this way the cultural politics of climate change aspire to echo post-colonial discourse in "paying attention to histories of vulnerability and responsibility" (O'Riordan and Lenton 2013). Moreover, recent reframings of climate change in terms of extractivist and neocolonial histories have not yet translated into the effort to redress these historical injustices by cancelling debts, or providing proportionate level of support through grants for adaptation and mitigation in developing countries — or what is referred to be the "compensatory justice" or polluter-must-pay component of climate justice (Okereke 2010). The other important aspect of climate justice is "procedural justice":

> *Despite the elevation of certain 'methods and prescriptions in our epistemologies' and the increasingly 'scientized veneer' of modern climate debate, it is well known that*

> *The climate storytelling that does exist plays out against a background of intensive cultural production which undermines it and crowds out its perspectives and possibilities.*

decisions on targets, metrics, emission counting methodologies, and reporting systems all involve both technical and political considerations. Hence, figuring out how to ensure broad and effective participation of all countries in the decision-making process represents another important dimension of justice in the climate regime.
(Okereke 2010)

O'Riordan and Lenton (2013) propose that "six features—global pervasiveness, uncertainty, interdependency, the reverberations of history, interdisciplinarity, and temporality—form the cultural foundation on which media engagement with climate change has developed and will continue to unfold." Yet one perennial problem with climate risk communication is that it is usually so clearly identifiable as climate risk communication, or nearby discourses like apocalyptic or superdisaster narratives, or science fiction (especially subgenres such as cli-fi or solarpunk). Heavy-handed framing risks limiting the audiences who engage with it, limiting the variety of cognitive and affective resources with which climate risk is construed, and limiting the proliferation of action-based storytelling. At the same time, the climate storytelling that does exist plays out against a background of intensive cultural production which undermines it and crowds out its perspectives and possibilities. It is even tempting to indulge in dubious fantasies of controlling all the stories that are told, to ensure full-bandwidth climate messaging. Setting aside the ethically untenable presuppositions of such fantasies, they also miss the point: the aim should be to encourage climate action themes to spread throughout culture and to hybridise with its preexisting variety in ways that are surprising, generative, and perhaps sometimes discomfiting—even to lose control of the messages. In this spirit, there are strategies that policymakers, third sector, environmental activists and creators, and other stakeholders might explore to help break climate storytelling out of its traditional well-marked boxes.

But Okereke's procedural justice also requires representation not just in the decision-making process or the cultural contexts which broadly inform it, but also in the production of knowledge that feeds it, especially if the knowledge is deeply uncertain.[12] The next sections begin to explore how tipping points, and other kinds of deep uncertainty, tend to expose the polycentric character of knowledge. All knowledge is distributed across specific knowing persons (and the technological systems in which they are embedded). Knowledge about climate change, for example, is embedded across a vast variety of different perspectives, values, interests, and levels and forms of power, all of which inform the nature of that knowledge. So if deep uncertainty is understood as a lack of agreement about how to model a system, it raises the question of who has been invited to agree in the first place—the question of whose voices count.

TIPPING POINTS AND THE IPCC MODEL ENSEMBLE
Do tipping points come with cultural baggage that constrains their integration into climate policy?

Action is the focus with which Chatham House, the well-respected UK policy think tank, introduces tipping points in its 2021 Climate Change Risk Assessment (Quiggin et al. 2021). Overall, the briefing paper is an exemplary piece of communication, whose expression and organisation is lucid, detailed and punchy. However, the paper tends not to communicate uncertainty information. At least, it avoids using the

---

12 This is not to conclude that the tipping point discourse is always on the right side of anti-racist theory and practice. Consider the following passage that links tipping points to population growth (in Africa and Asia) and frantically calls for 'drastic action': "The Earth is within decades of reaching an irreversible tipping point that could result in 'planetary collapse,' scientists warned yesterday. They called for drastic action, such as rapid curbs on population growth, to prevent food supplies being threatened by major changes to farming caused by climate change. (Dalton, 2012)" in (van der Hel, Hellsten, and Steen 2018).

The IPCC definition of "low-likelihood, high-impact outcome" deserves to be closely examined. Might this term mislead non-experts?

word 'uncertainty,' except for a few occasions — and tipping points is not one of them.

> *Ice sheets are crucial for the stability of the climate system as a whole, and are already at risk of transgressing their temperature thresholds within the Paris range of 1.5°–2°C. A domino-like effect has recently been identified between various tipping points, which can lead to abrupt non-linear responses. Tipping point cascades (two or more tipping points being initiated for a given temperature level) have been identified in more than 60 percent of simulations, for which the initial trigger is likely to be polar ice sheet melting, with the Atlantic Meridional Overturning Circulation (AMOC) acting as a mediator transmitting cascades.*
>
> (Quiggin et al. 2021)

Notice the firm, guardedly urgent tone of phrases like "already at risk," "has recently been identified," and "identified in more than 60 per cent of simulations." There is some important *implied* uncertainty here, e.g. "60 percent of simulations" sounds like something to be worried about (especially given the magnitude of the impact), but it is nowhere near certitude. But what kind of uncertainty is it? Readers might reasonably mistake "60 percent of simulations" as referring to the main IPCC projections, e.g. those used to calculate the carbon budget. In reality tipping points occur in such projections rarely if at all.[13]

> *Processes that change on long timescales—particularly AMOC, ocean heat content, and ice sheets—require additional projections beyond the CMIP scenarios to explore longer term commitment, post-forcing recovery measured in centuries rather than years or decades, and potential tipping points and thresholds. There were only a few new studies focussed on longer timescales and none based on CMIP6 models.*
>
> (IPCC AR6 WGI)

The study (Wunderling et al. 2021) cited as a reference, by contrast, creates more space for considering uncertainty. It takes as its premise that these high-profile IPCC models are not able to adequately capture tipping point dynamics. Tipping point dynamics "cannot be fully analysed with state-of-the-art Earth system models due to computational constraints as well as some missing and uncertain process representations of certain tipping elements" (Wunderling et al. 2021). Due to this epistemological uncertainty, the study instead adopts a conceptual network model. This is constructed based on expert judgements about plausible interactions that might trigger tipping points. Such models are suitable for exploring consequences of different scientific beliefs that are not amenable to other methods.

This is not to say that the authors of the Chatham House article are sweeping anything under the carpet. But they have made the pragmatic decision not to lead with the distinction between tipping point conceptual network modelling (and its uncertainties) and other sorts of climate modelling (and their uncertainties). This communicative strategy can be read as symptomatic of the topic's lingering awkward associations, both in terms of the discursive shaping of tipping points within popular culture (see previous section), and the perceived authority of conceptual network models vs. Earth Systems Models (which in turn reflects a lack of strong narratives around model reliability, their groundness in data and experimental evidence; see next chapter).

It is worth exploring ways of conceptual model techniques much more richly into climate decision-making, especially as part of a shift toward more holistic and participatory frameworks. However, the IPCC has yet to figure out how to deal satisfactorily with the more speculative character of such approaches (for example, Wunderling et al. 2021 does not appear in the thousands of articles consulted and synthesised); the AR6 contents itself with describing evidence for tipping point as "limited" and "characterised by deep uncertainty":

---

13   IPCC AR6 WGI report notes that abrupt changes do show up in ensemble simulations but very rarely and correlate with less plausible scenarios and narrow regions of parameter space: "At the regional scale, abrupt changes and tipping points, such as Amazon forest dieback and permafrost collapse, have occurred in projections with Earth System Models (Drijfhout et al., 2015; Bathiany et al., 2020; Chapter 4, Section 4.7.3). In such simulations, tipping points occur in narrow regions of parameter space (e.g., CO2 concentration or temperature increase), and for specific climate background states. This makes them difficult to predict using ESMs relying on parameterizations of known processes."

There is limited evidence for low-likelihood, high-impact outcomes (resulting from ice sheet instability processes characterized by deep uncertainty and in some cases involving tipping points).
(IPCC WGI AR6 2021)

Excerpts from meeting notes on the approval of text for the IPCC AR6 WGI Summary for Policymakers offer insight into the politics of discussing deep-uncertainty events, as well as the limitations to the capacity of political forces to subvert a scientific process:

'*C.3: This subsection addresses low-likelihood outcomes. On the Headline Statement on low-likelihood outcomes being impossible to rule out and being part of risk assessment,* INDIA *objected to such* **speculative language.** SAUDI ARABIA *said the* **uncertainty was unhelpful.** DENMARK, *supported by* NORWAY, LUXEMBOURG, GERMANY, SAINT KITTS AND NEVIS, MEXICO, FRANCE, *and* SPAIN, *underscored that* **low-likelihood high-impact events are highly policy-relevant.** *Several countries requested specifying "tipping points," and* DENMARK, LUXEMBOURG, *and the* UK *requested further examples, such as Amazon diebacks.* JAPAN *preferred "risk to be considered" or "risk" over "risk assessment."*

'*C.3.2: On this paragraph dealing with occurrence of low-likelihood, high-impact outcomes in all GHG emissions scenarios,* **delegates called for: inclusion of quantitative information; more specificity regarding levels of probability in the different scenarios; and addition of levels of confidence.** *During discussion, the paragraph was revised to: note likelihood that, high-impact outcomes "could" occur, rather than "may;" specify the reference to tipping points "of the climate system"; and add forest dieback as another example of abrupt response. The paragraph was approved after* **the authors clarified that "cannot be ruled out" is the best estimate that can be given since no actual likelihood assessment can be made for issues with deep uncertainty** *such as a strongly increased Antarctic Ice Sheet melt.'*

(Bansard and Akanle Eni-ibukun, n.d.)

Several things can be inferred. Politics clearly is a factor. Uncertainty is disliked, at least in this case: it is found objectionable and unhelpful. Quantitative information is preferred, although the scientists can and do push back, refusing to produce numbers where only words are valid.

COMMUNICATING AROUND DEEP UNCERTAINTY
Tipping points pose special challenges for climate communication.
How do we address the deep uncertainty around tipping points?

The forecasting of tipping points, and even the observation of tipping points that may be underway, is associated with deep uncertainty. The IPCC state that "[e]stablishing links between specific GWLs (global warming levels) with tipping points and irreversible behaviour is challenging **due to model uncertainties and lack of observations, but their occurrence cannot be excluded,** and their likelihood of occurrence generally increases at greater warming levels" (IPCC AR6 WGI, 2021). They further emphasise that "[i]t is not currently possible to carry out a full assessment of proposed abrupt changes and tipping points in the biogeochemical cycles," and suggest that the potential for improving such assessments in the future is limited because "[t]he rare nature of such events and the limited availability of relevant data makes it difficult to estimate their occurrence probability" (IPCC AR6 WGI 2021).

The term **deep uncertainty** does not have a precise and universally accepted definition. It may be understood as characterising problems or situations whose uncertainty cannot be quantified, cannot be quantified *given available resources or data*, and/or whose quantification is not desirable. Under deep uncertainty, there is no authoritative model that captures all the relevant driving forces and their relationships — perhaps because there is not enough knowledge about the processes or parameters to build such a model, or perhaps because there are multiple inconsistent models (Lempert, Popper, and Bankes 2003).[14] Deep uncertainty is also intrinsically linked to themes of **participatory governance** and **just climate transition.**

Strictly speaking, a tipping point refers to a point at which a system reorganises, often abruptly and/or irreversibly. Low probability or deep uncertainty per se are not what characterise the tipping point concept (even though the major climate tipping points of concern have these features, in other areas of science such as epidemiology tipping points

---

14 In this sense, the concept of deep uncertainty overlaps somewhat with that of wicked problems (Rittel and Webber 1973).

Sometimes (a little paradoxically) uncertainty can simplify the task of communication.

are more predictable), but rather this dynamic of reorganisation which is rapid and/or irreversible. It is important to remember this, in order to appreciate the IPCC's approach to tipping points, especially **how tipping points overlap with what the IPCC calls 'low-likelihood, high-impact outcomes.'** Not all low-likelihood, high-impact outcomes involve tipping points, as this quotation demonstrates (our emphasis):

> *There is limited evidence for low-likelihood, high-impact outcomes (resulting from ice sheet instability processes characterized by deep uncertainty and in some cases involving tipping points) that would strongly increase ice loss from the Antarctic Ice Sheet for centuries under high GHG emissions scenarios.*[15]
>
> (AR6 WGI 2021)

The IPCC definition of **"low-likelihood, high-impact outcome"** deserves to be closely examined. Might this term mislead non-experts? Might it distort the discourse around tipping points? According to the IPCC, the term "low-likelihood high-impact" should be used of events or outcomes whose *probability of occurrence is **low or not well known** (as in the context of deep uncertainty) but whose potential impacts on society and ecosystems could be high.*
(AR6 WGI Annex VII, emphasis added).

When asked the probability that a low-likelihood high-impact event will occur, a reasonable respondent might well answer, "Obviously the probability is low!" They may add that it's still worth worrying about. By contrast, what reasonable person would guess that the probability of a "low-likelihood high impact" event occurring is not actually "low"—but rather "low or not well-known"! A closely-related slippage of meaning may also occur, especially when communicating with policymakers or the public: when an expert describes an event as being of low likelihood, audiences may reasonably infer that the expert is confident that an assessment of probability could be made.[16]

It is also important to recognise that the science and evidence around each different tipping element is very different, and undergoing evolution. It is true that the field as a whole offers many forms of deep uncertainty. But we should be careful not to conflate all these uncertainties, nor to forget where potential tipping points have been investigated and ruled out, rather than filed under "deeply uncertain." For example, consider the distinction the IPCC draws between Arctic and Antarctic ice: "There is no tipping point for this loss of Arctic summer sea ice *(high confidence)*" (AR6 WGI 2021), whereas Antarctic ice is considered a low-likelihood high-impact risk due to instability of the West Antarctic Ice Sheet.

Nor should we jump to conclusions about a given deep uncertainty being permanent; one relevant example here might be statistical time series analyses, which some research suggests may allow observational detection of "early warning signals," where a certain tipping element has lost stability and may be approaching a tipping point (Boers 2021).[17] The broad point here is that when we communicate about tipping points, conveying uncertainty must not mean downgrading them to speculative storytelling.

Standard Earth System Models can still be useful in identifying and investigating tipping points. The

---

15 We note the linguistic ambiguity of the phrase "there is limited evidence." Should reading such a sentence make one adjust one's perception of risk upward or downward? The intended sense in the quoted passage is that you should adjust it upward slightly: there is evidence for x, although this evidence is limited. But an alternative interpretation might be that the statement is a tacit refutation of x, loosely speaking: "Given the large efforts made to show that x is the case, and the still small amount of evidence in favor of x, in our opinion x is probably not the case."

16 The tipping points explored in this chapter thus fall into the category of 'unknown risks'—risks that are undertaken involuntarily, whose consequences are delayed, and which seem not fully known to science—factors that have been shown to increase risk sensitivity (Fischhoff et al. 1978).

17 However, other studies have indicated that due to the stochastic behaviour of tipping points, such as AMOC, detection of warning signs is not possible (Ditlevsen and Johnsen 2010).

models that were downweighted in the CMIP6 50 model ensemble, because they appear to be less plausible, can actually be useful in constructing narratives around tipping points:

> *A real-world ECS higher than the assessed very likely range (2°C–5°C) would require a strong historical aerosol cooling and/or a trend towards stronger warming from positive feedbacks linked to changes in SST patterns (pattern effects), combined with a strong positive cloud feedback and substantial biases in paleoclimate reconstructions — each of which is assessed as either unlikely or very unlikely, but not ruled out. Since CMIP6 contains several ESMs that exceed the upper bound of the assessed very likely range in future surface warming, these models can be used to develop low-likelihood, high warming storylines to explore risks and vulnerabilities, even in the absence of a quantitative assessment of likelihood*
>
> (IPCC AR WGI 2021).

Because of their complexity and deep uncertainty, tipping points pose special challenges for communication. Yet at the same time, **tipping points give us some of the most straightforward messages we are likely to find anywhere in climate science.** We must reduce net carbon emissions to zero as rapidly as possible. We must build resilience around the world as rapidly as possible. Sometimes (a little paradoxically) uncertainty can simplify the task of communication. Because trigger thresholds usually cannot be known with confidence, and because the impacts would be catastrophic, deciding what to do using cost-benefit logic becomes crystal clear: *as much as we can, with everything we have.* In some respects, we are saved the complexity of the question: *but will it be enough?*

"PARTICIPATORY UNCERTAINTY"
Low-likelihood high-impact outcomes deserve further study, but our best response is a just and participatory transition

There are many good reasons to change how we think, and how we communicate, about low-likelihood high-impact events. We can reject the priority of quantitative reasoning over qualitative, emphasise conceptual models over Earth Systems Models, and emphasise participatory decision-making under conditions of deep uncertainty. These considerations are relevant throughout this Toolkit, but especially when it comes to tipping points.

> *Deep uncertainty has been used to describe situations where "analysts do not know, or the parties to a decision cannot agree on, (1) the appropriate conceptual models that describe the relationships among the key driving forces that will shape the long-term future, (2) the probability distributions used to represent uncertainty about key variables and parameters in the mathematical representations of these conceptual models, and/or (3) how to value the desirability of alternative outcomes"*

(Lempert, Popper, and Bankes 2003).

This definition has the benefit of clarifying what deep uncertainty is. However, it does make it **impossible to definitively say where deep uncertainty begins and ends**. Deep uncertainty tends to draw in other forms of uncertainty. For example, ambiguity may also be relevant, insofar as parties might believe themselves to agree or to disagree, but be mistaken about the state of consensus. Currency may also be relevant, insofar as values and beliefs change over time. Even if everyone who is involved can agree today, beliefs can diverge tomorrow.

More loosely speaking, when we take the perspective of deep uncertainty, we are reminding ourselves to have epistemological humility. We are recognising that, however good we get at thinking about uncertainty, reality is full of surprises: "the long-term future may be dominated by factors that are very different from the current drivers and hard to imagine based on today's experiences" (Lempert, Popper, and Bankes 2003).

So for almost any domain (perhaps any domain), deep uncertainty becomes a lens which may be used. When some decision seems to be demurely contained within neat models to everybody's satisfaction and delight, it is simple to reintroduce deep uncertainty merely by expanding the scope of 'everybody' — to include, for example, the participation of those with profoundly different political or ethical views. But for some domains, including tipping points, deep uncertainty is something else: a lens which cannot reasonably be refused. And for such domains, we might speak of "operating under conditions of deep uncertainty."

Deep uncertainty resists quantification and any type of modelling, even loose conceptual modelling. However, **many measures have been suggested to accommodate deep uncertainty.** Among the most important are:

Deep uncertainty has been used to describe situations where "analysts do not know, or the parties to a decision cannot agree on, (1) the appropriate conceptual models that describe the relationships among the key driving forces that will shape the long-term future, (2) the probability distributions used to represent uncertainty about key variables and parameters in the mathematical representations of these conceptual models, and/or (3) how to value the desirability of alternative outcomes" (Lempert, Popper, and Bankes 2003).

- improving the participatory, deliberative, and democratic qualities of decision-making processes[18];
- improving equity to build generic resilience;
- exploring ways to make decisions more flexible to adapt to new information as it arises; and
- finding ways to challenge our presuppositions about the parameters of the decision space, and to discover new potential pathways.

These are overlapping and mutually reinforcing. They further imply that **quantification can still be helpful under conditions of deep uncertainty, so long as it is exploratory,** and used to clarify reasoning and keep questions open — not shut them down or put precise price tags on uncertainties. In this way, deep uncertainty has inspired new ways of using probability theory in decision support, such as the Robust Decision Making model (RDM) approach. This can include the deliberative integration of multiple plausible probability distributions, based on expert, stakeholder, and/or group judgments.

There are at least four broad rationales to address deep uncertainty by improving participatory decision-making: informational (participatory processes acknowledge that expertise may be generated not only by accredited experts but by all); behavioral (participatory processes improve societal buy-in and mitigate against societal backlash); anticipatory (participatory processes go hand-in-hand with broader socioeconomic equity that has been shown as a form of resilience in its own right); and existential (participatory processes can distribute more widely the moral responsibility for actions whose outcomes are deeply uncertain).

VISUALISING DEEP UNCERTAINTY
Can deep uncertainty be visualised, or perhaps perceptualised in innovative ways?

One of the promising options to communicate the systemic risks potentially hidden at the tails of the distributions is Figure 2. Here the low risk does not fade to the safety of zero but turns into something potentially worse, a whiteness that feels hot and dangerous, perhaps because it invokes a semantic metaphor for lightning — white hot explosion of plasma that reaches 27,000°C, hotter than the sun. That is the region where risk is labeled 'undetectable' invoking the concept of deep uncertainty (van der Hel, Hellsten, and Steen 2018).

More commonly, deep uncertainty resists visualisation just as much as it resists quantification and modelling. Visualisation is often used in science communication to convey uncertainty

---

18   We would also add a less-well-known term, "agonistic." Agonism is used by democratic theorists to describe participatory processes that express (or "sublimate") real social conflicts, rather than disguise those conflicts under a pretense of rational representative and/or participatory consensus. However, agonism also requires that adversaries are not merely competitors, but deeply and materially acknowledge and support one another's legitimacy in the participatory process, implying strong limits as to how far they would go to score a political win. "While antagonism is a we/they relation in which the two sides are enemies who do not share any common ground, agonism is a we/they relation where the conflicting parties, although acknowledging that there is no rational solution to their conflict, nevertheless recognize the legitimacy of their opponents. They are 'adversaries' not enemies" (Mouffe 2005).

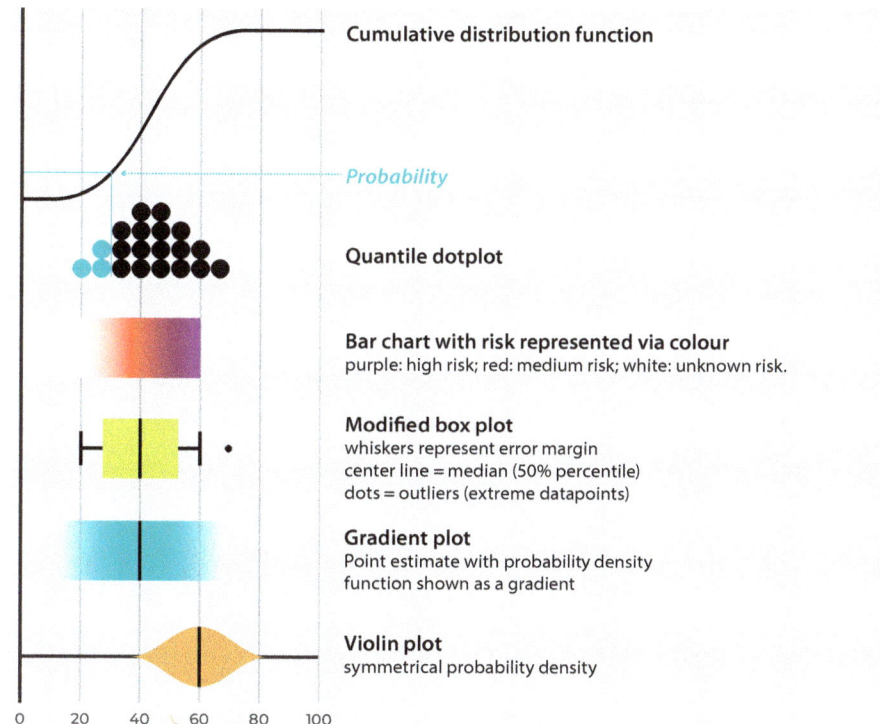

Figure 2. Visualising probabilities and risk.

information. There is evidence that visualisation of uncertainty affects many aspects of decision-making; for example, choices about the graphical presentation of hurricane forecasts have been shown to influence people's decisions on whether or not to follow evacuation orders. Even when graphics are not used, a user's reasoning around a subject may nonetheless be influenced by both the visual presentation of the information, and the kinds of imagery invoked in the user (whether deliberately or not). In this sense, the visual character of uncertainty can be key to interpretation, decision-making, and action. But deep uncertainty offers serious challenges to visualisation:

> First, it is assumed that uncertainty, or at least uncertainty of interest, is both knowable and identifiable. Similarly, to be visualized, uncertainty must be quantifiable, such as through statistical estimates, quantitative ranges, or qualitative statements (e.g., less or more uncertain). Moreover, evaluations define effectiveness as an ability to identify specific uncertainty values, which assumes that identifying specific uncertainty values is useful to decision-makers and that the values of interest can be quantified. Lastly, there is an assumption that the quantification of uncertainty is beneficial, applicable to the decision task, and usable by the decision-maker, even if users do not currently work with uncertainty in that way. These assumptions pose a challenge for visualizing uncertainty to support decision making under deep uncertainty, where quantification of uncertainty is not possible or necessarily desirable. In this way, current approaches to uncertainty visualization are more normative in nature, reflecting what researchers think decision-makers need to know about uncertainty.
>
> (Deitrick and Wentz 2015)

Dynamic visualisations and interactive media may be promising, insofar as interactive media can incorporate their own nonlinear dynamics suggestive of the deep uncertainties of climate risk, and can also act as aids in participatory processes involving many different stakeholders. The development and use of such tools do bring their own special considerations vis-a-vis equity and a just transition to sustainable society. Challenges around filtering and prioritising climate risk communications are pertinent, as communication is likely to multiply and diversify in the years ahead, as transition becomes more central to more societies. Exploring these issues in any detail is outside of the scope of this Toolkit, but we suggest that useful perspectives may be discovered in the literature on structured elicitation as well as in the fields of the philosophy of science and technology and critical data studies, particularly work on metric power and algorithmic governmentality. Democratic theory, e.g. high level conceptualisations of deliberative vs. agonistic democracy (Mouffe 2005), is another important source.

AUTHOR CONTRIBUTIONS

*Conceptualization: JLW, PL, and EM; **Research**: PL, JLW and EM;*
***Writing**: JLW and PL; **Figures**: JK and PL.*

REFERENCES

Bansard, Jennifer, and Tomilola Akanle Eni-ibukun. n.d. 'Summary of the 54th Session of the Intergovernmental Panel on Climate Change and the 14th Session of Working Group I: 26 July - 6 August 2021'. *Earth Negotiations Bulletin.* enb.iisd.org/climate/IPCC/IPCC-54-WGI-14/summary

Barnosky, Anthony D., Nicholas Matzke, Susumu Tomiya, Guinevere O. U. Wogan, Brian Swartz, Tiago B. Quental, Charles Marshall, et al. 2011. 'Has the Earth's Sixth Mass Extinction Already Arrived?' *Nature* 471 (7336): 51–57. doi.org/10.1038/nature09678

Boers, Niklas. 2021. 'Observation-Based Early-Warning Signals for a Collapse of the Atlantic Meridional Overturning Circulation'. *Nature Climate Change* 11 (8): 680–88. doi.org/10.1038/s41558-021-01097-4

Cai, Yongyang, Timothy M. Lenton, and Thomas S. Lontzek. 2016. 'Risk of Multiple Interacting Tipping Points Should Encourage Rapid CO2 Emission Reduction'. *Nature Climate Change* 6 (5): 520–25. doi.org/10.1038/nclimate2964

Clayton, Susan. 2020. 'Climate Anxiety: Psychological Responses to Climate Change'. *Journal of Anxiety Disorders* 74 (August): 102263. doi.org/10.1016/j.janxdis.2020.102263

Comyn-Platt, Edward, Garry Hayman, Chris Huntingford, Sarah E. Chadburn, Eleanor J. Burke, Anna B. Harper, William J. Collins, et al. 2018. 'Carbon Budgets for 1.5 and 2 °C Targets Lowered by Natural Wetland and Permafrost Feedbacks'. *Nature Geoscience* 11 (8): 568–73. doi.org/10.1038/s41561-018-0174-9

CSRC. 2020. 'Apocalyptic Narratives & Climate Change | Center for the Study of Religion and Conflict'. 2020. csrc.asu.edu/apocalypticnarrativescalimatechange

De Meyer, Kris, Emily Coren, Mark McCaffrey, and Cheryl Slean. 2020. 'Transforming the Stories We Tell About Climate Change: From "Issue" to "Action"'. *Environmental Research Letters* 16 (1): 015002. doi.org/10.1088/1748-9326/abcd5a

Deitrick, Stephanie, and Elizabeth A. Wentz. 2015. 'Developing Implicit Uncertainty Visualization Methods Motivated by Theories in Decision Science'. *Annals of the Association of American Geographers* 105 (3): 531–51. doi.org/10.1080/00045608.2015.1012635

Diamond, Jared M. 2011. *Collapse: How Societies Choose to Fail or Survive.* New York, NY: Penguin Books.

Ditlevsen, Peter D., and Sigfus J. Johnsen. 2010. 'Tipping Points: Early Warning and Wishful Thinking: TIPPING POINTS-EARLY WARNING'. *Geophysical Research Letters* 37 (19): n/a-n/a. doi.org/10.1029/2010GL044486

Drijfhout, Sybren, Sebastian Bathiany, Claudie Beaulieu, Victor Brovkin, Martin Claussen, Chris Huntingford, Marten Scheffer, Giovanni Sgubin, and Didier Swingedouw. 2015. 'Catalogue of Abrupt Shifts in Intergovernmental Panel on Climate Change Climate Models'. *Proceedings of the National Academy of Sciences* 112 (43): E5777–86. doi.org/10.1073/pnas.1511451112

Fischhoff, Baruch, Paul Slovic, Sarah Lichtenstein, Stephen Read, and Barbara Combs. 1978. 'How Safe Is Safe Enough? A Psychometric Study of Attitudes towards Technological Risks and Benefits'. *Policy Sciences* 9 (2): 127–52. doi.org/10.1007/BF00143739

Garrard, Greg. 2004. *Ecocriticism.* London: Routledge.

Gladwell, Malcolm. 2015. *The Tipping Point: How Little Things Can Make a Big Difference.* Paperback edition. London: Abacus.

Hel, Sandra van der, Iina Hellsten, and Gerard Steen. 2018. 'Tipping Points and Climate Change: Metaphor Between Science and the Media'. *Environmental Communication* 12 (5): 605–20. doi.org/10.1080/17524032.2017.1410198

Huxley, Anna. 2018. 'Communicating Climate Change Through Narratives: A Cross Pollination of Science and Theology'. In *Handbook of Climate Change Communication: Vol. 1,* edited by Walter Leal Filho, Evangelos Manolas, Anabela Marisa Azul, Ulisses M. Azeiteiro, and Henry McGhie, 201–14. Climate Change Management. Cham: Springer International Publishing. doi.org/10.1007/978-3-319-69838-0_13

Kahan, Dan M. 2012. 'Ideology, Motivated Reasoning, and Cognitive Reflection: An Experimental Study'. *SSRN Electronic Journal.* doi.org/10.2139/ssrn.2182588

Kirby, David. 2010. 'The Future Is Now: Diegetic Prototypes and the Role of Popular Films in Generating Real-World Technological Development'. *Social Studies of Science* 40 (1): 41–70. doi.org/10.1177/0306312709338325

Leal Filho, Walter, Evangelos Manolas, Anabela Marisa Azul, Ulisses M. Azeiteiro, and Henry McGhie, eds. 2017. *Handbook of Climate Change Communication.* Vol. Vol. 1. New York, NY: Springer Berlin Heidelberg.

Lempert, Robert J., Steven W. Popper, and Steven C. Bankes. 2003. *Shaping the Next One Hundred Years: New Methods for Quantitative, Long-Term Policy Analysis.* Santa Monica, CA: RAND.

Lenton, T. M., H. Held, E. Kriegler, J. W. Hall, W. Lucht, S. Rahmstorf, and H. J. Schellnhuber. 2008. 'Tipping Elements in the Earth's Climate System'. *Proceedings of the National Academy of Sciences* 105 (6): 1786–93. doi.org/10.1073/pnas.0705414105

Mackie, Erik. 2021. 'COP26 Universities Climate Risk Summit Blog: "When Is the Day After Tomorrow?": Tipping Points and Abrupt Climate Responses | Www.Zero.Cam.Ac.Uk'. 2021. zero.cam.ac.uk/who-we-are/blog/cop26-universities-climate-risk-summit-blog-when-day-after-tomorrow-tipping-points

Masson-Delmotte, V., P. Zhai, A. Pirani, and S. L. Connors. 2021. 'Climate Change 2021: The Physical Science Basis. Contribution of Working Group I to the Sixth Assessment Report of the Intergovernmental Panel on Climate Change'. Cambridge University Press.

Mouffe, Chantal. 2005. *On the Political.* Thinking in Action. London ; New York: Routledge.

National Snow & Ice Data Center. 2004. '"The Day After Tomorrow" Q&A Response'. nsidc.org/cryosphere/day-after-response

Okereke, Chukwumerije. 2010. 'Climate Justice and the International Regime: Climate Justice and the International Regime'. *Wiley Interdisciplinary Reviews: Climate Change* 1 (3): 462–74. doi.org/10.1002/wcc.52

O'Riordan, Timothy, and Timothy Lenton, eds. 2013. *Addressing Tipping Points for a Precarious Future.* British Academy. doi.org/10.5871/bacad/9780197265536.001.0001

Otto, Ilona M., Jonathan F. Donges, Roger Cremades, Avit Bhowmik, Richard J. Hewitt, Wolfgang Lucht, Johan Rockström, et al. 2020. 'Social Tipping Dynamics for Stabilizing Earth's Climate by 2050'. *Proceedings of the National Academy of Sciences* 117 (5): 2354–65. doi.org/10.1073/pnas.1900577117

Quiggin, Daniel, Kris De Meyer, Lucy Hubble-Rose, and Antony Froggatt. 2021. 'Climate Change Risk Assessment'. Chatham House. https://www.chathamhouse.org/2021/09/climate-change-risk-assessment-2021.

Rapley et al., Chris. 2006. 'West Antarctic Ice Sheet: Waking the Sleeping Giant?' *British Antarctic Survey* (blog). 2006. bas.ac.uk/media-post/west-antarctic-ice-sheet-waking-the-sleeping-giant/

Rittel, Horst W. J., and Melvin M. Webber. 1973. 'Dilemmas in a General Theory of Planning'. *Policy Sciences* 4 (2): 155–69. doi.org/10.1007/BF01405730

Robinson, Kim Stanley. 2006. *Fifty Degrees Below.* London: HarperCollins.

Russill, Chris, and Zoe Nyssa. 2009. 'The Tipping Point Trend in Climate Change Communication'. *Global Environmental Change* 19 (3): 336–44. doi.org/10.1016/j.gloenvcha.2009.04.001

Showalter, Elaine. 2011. The *Female Malady: Women, Madness and English Culture, 1830-1980.* Reprint. London: Virago Pr.

Thompson, Tosin. 2021. 'Young People's Climate Anxiety Revealed in Landmark Survey'. *Nature*, 22 September 2021. nature.com/articles/d41586-021-02582-8

Winsberg, Eric. 2012. 'Values and Uncertainties in the Predictions of Global Climate Models'. *Kennedy Institute of Ethics Journal* 22 (2): 111–37. doi.org/10.1353/ken.2012.0008

Wunderling, Nico, Jonathan F. Donges, Jürgen Kurths, and Ricarda Winkelmann. 2021. 'Interacting Tipping Elements Increase Risk of Climate Domino Effects under Global Warming'. *Earth System Dynamics* 12 (2): 601–19. doi.org/10.5194/esd-12-601-2021

Decision-makers without an understanding of the uncertainty in a forecast may be underinformed, placing undue levels of confidence in a forecast.

Chapter 4 — AR6 AND MODELLING UNCERTAINTY

INTRODUCTION

The IPCC AR6 WGI report represents an extraordinary challenge for climate risk communication.

Three working groups are responsible for AR6, each looking at a different aspect of climate change: The Physical Science Basis (AR6 WGI); Impacts, Adaptation, and Vulnerability (AR6 WGII); and Mitigation of Climate Change (AR6 WGIII). There is also a Task Force on National Greenhouse Gas Inventories. In this case study we look at The Physical Science Basis (AR6 WGI) (AR6 WGI 2021). Specifically, we dive into the Summary for Policymakers (SPM) (IPCC WGI et al. 2021), and the new online visualisation tool — the IPCC WGI Interactive Atlas — that offers novel ways to explore climate change projections on flexible spatial and temporal scales (Iturbide, Maialen et al. 2021).

The SPM represents an extraordinary challenge for high-level climate risk communication. The complete AR6 WGI report is based on an assessment of over 14,000 scientific publications on topics like greenhouse gases and aerosols in the atmosphere; temperature changes in air, land, and ocean; the hydrological cycle and changing patterns of rain and snow; extreme weather events; the behaviours of glaciers and ice sheets; oceans and sea level rise; biogeochemistry and the carbon cycle; and climate sensitivity. The report runs to nearly 4,000 pages, which the SPM shrinks to just forty.

In this chapter we look at the principles, strengths and weaknesses of how the new IPCC report communicates uncertainty, with some focus on the SPM. Expressions of confidence are attached to many kinds of statements in AR6 WGI, but since the vast majority of findings relate to modelling, **we focus here on model uncertainty.** The next section outlines three major sources of uncertainty in model-

Subsections

Introduction
Sources of uncertainty in modelling
The AR6 50 model ensemble
Regional distribution of modelling
Evaluating models
Language to describe uncertainty in AR6 WGI
Visualisations of uncertainties
Visualising precipitation trends
Climatic impact drivers (CIDs) in SPM
The AR6 WGI Interactive Atlas
Seven recommendations for the IPCC and the modelling community
References

based projections. Another motivation for engaging with model uncertainty is that public discourse on this topic is relatively weak. It is a difficult subject (despite being now a bit more familiar to the public, because of recent coverage of epidemiological models by the mainstream media), and is relatively easily exploited by climate deniers. So it is essential to consider ways we can build a narrative about model uncertainty in order to sustain credibility, trust, and action on climate. We will hone in on model uncertainty, exploring a range of models in the AR6 ensemble; how they and other models are evaluated (and the challenges in doing so); and a range of interrelated geographical and socio-economic disparities.

Then we turn to strategies of communication, including language choice, visualisation, and the interactive tools of the AR6. The IPCC is known for its efforts to encourage communication of uncertainty, including standardised terminology (although not yet for modelling), and consistent visualisation conventions (although only in the more widely-read sections). Challenges clearly remain (Budescu, Por, and Broomell 2012; van der Bles et al. 2019; Dieckmann et al. 2017). For example, a look at some of the figures deep in the AR6 WGI report makes it clear that not all authors have followed good practice on visualisations. There are other inconsistencies and choices in design 'language' that are problematic.

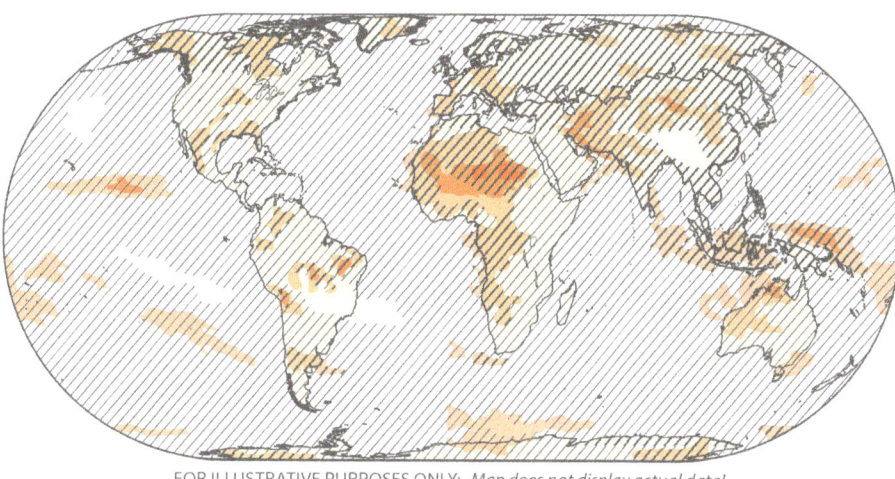

FOR ILLUSTRATIVE PURPOSES ONLY: *Map does not display actual data!*

Figure 1. Representing modelling uncertainty as hatched lines overlaid on top of the model-based predictions that are in colour makes it tricky to see where the modelling predictions are reliable and where they are not, as areas free of hatched lines are hard to notice. However, this type of representation of modelling uncertainty is the default option in the AR6 WGI report (print version).

For example, in some figures in the AR6 WGI report, hatched lines indicating model disagreement are overlaid on top of colour-coded values *(Figure 1)*. However, at other times the areas that are uncertain are left colour-free *(Figure 2)*. This invites different interpretations: in the colour version, the results might be interpreted as informative but uncertain, whereas entirely removing the colour conveys that reliable regional predictions cannot be made. The lack of a consistent visual vocabulary is not helpful to the audiences that need to relearn graphical conventions for different figures. Visually, the colour-free option is also more legible *(Figure 2)*. Overlaying the lines on the colour background make it very difficult to distinguish areas where the models agree from areas where they don't *(Figure 1)*. The interactive Atlas (mostly) wisely opts for the blank background option.

Trust in climate models is also not independent of trust in other models; comparisons (fair or not) between complex climate models and complex economic models are often made. The inability of mainstream economic and financial modelling to predict the 2008 economic crisis was damaging to the trust people placed in models. Government decisions informed by epidemiological modelling during the Covid-19 pandemic reinforced perceptions of a lack of independence between politics and modelling.

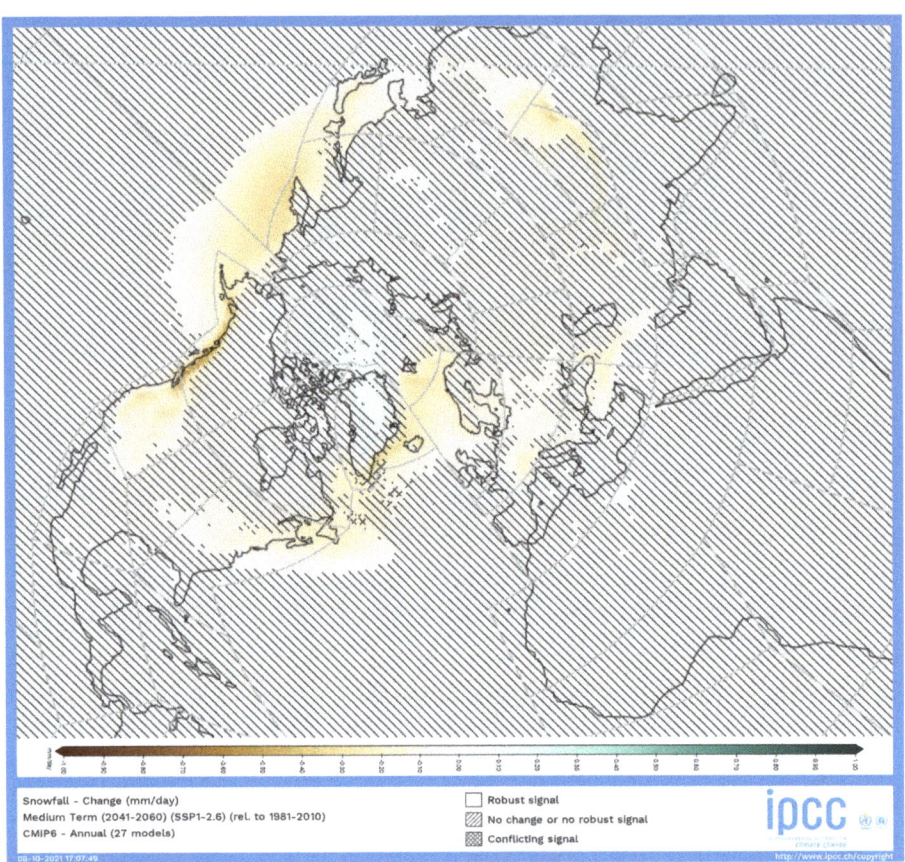

*Figure 2. Interactive Atlas example, representing modelling uncertainty.
Source: the "Medium Term (2041-2060) SSP1 2.6 (rel. to 1981-2010)-Annual (27 models)" scenario. The darkest colour denotes a change of about -0.5mm per day.*

Consistency is clearly to be preferred, all else being equal. Of course, there may sometimes be a rationale for tailoring conventions. The type of uncertainty representation chosen should also take account of the expected size it would be viewed as. Representations of modelling uncertainty are clearer in the interactive online Atlas which, unlike the PDFs, is more likely to be viewed on smaller screens or mobile phones, *Figure 2*.

Beyond the observations of our case study here, research is needed to test the effectiveness of the IPCC's strategies to improve communication of uncertainty. For example, are authors really using uncertainty language consistently? How are such communications being received by different users, and how easily can they translate their information into their own familiar frameworks (e.g. in risk management)? How effectively is uncertainty being communicated in visualisations and interactive tools? Do the conventions that have been devised and discussed with respect to a given data set behave the same when the data changes? Greater consistency and more testing would likely improve user comprehension of these visualisations.

The deeper question remains: how to translate these visualisations into meaningful information about the world? What would it feel like, for example, to live in the world predicted by these snow projections *(Figure 2)*? What would a ½ mm decrease in daily snow precipitation mean for my grandchildren as far as cross-country skiing or snow fights go? Would there be fewer days when they could make snow angels, would they miss a climate they did not know?

SOURCES OF UNCERTAINTY IN MODELLING
There are at least three major types of uncertainty in model-based projection

There are many types of models in the AR6 WGI report. We first consider those in the ensemble—a set of Earth System Models that are run in parallel—to produce key projections for future climate under different emissions scenarios. **Uncertainty in model based projections** is described in the AR6 WGI as arising from three main sources:

- model uncertainty,
- internal variability, and
- scenario uncertainty.

Model uncertainty is also sometimes known as structural model uncertainty or scientific uncertainty. Knowledge may be lacking to choose between different theories of how something works, so different models reflect different understandings of the world. Different Equilibrium Climate Sensitivity (ECS) values emerge as a result of epistemological uncertainties. Model uncertainty is related to model weighting; **some models are downgraded for not performing well according to some criteria, usually in confrontations with observational data.** Ideas of how to weigh models vary. One of the ways to filter models could be to require them to reproduce specific features that are related to risk, such as the weakening

Typical relative contributions of three sources of uncertainty to the variability in forecasts

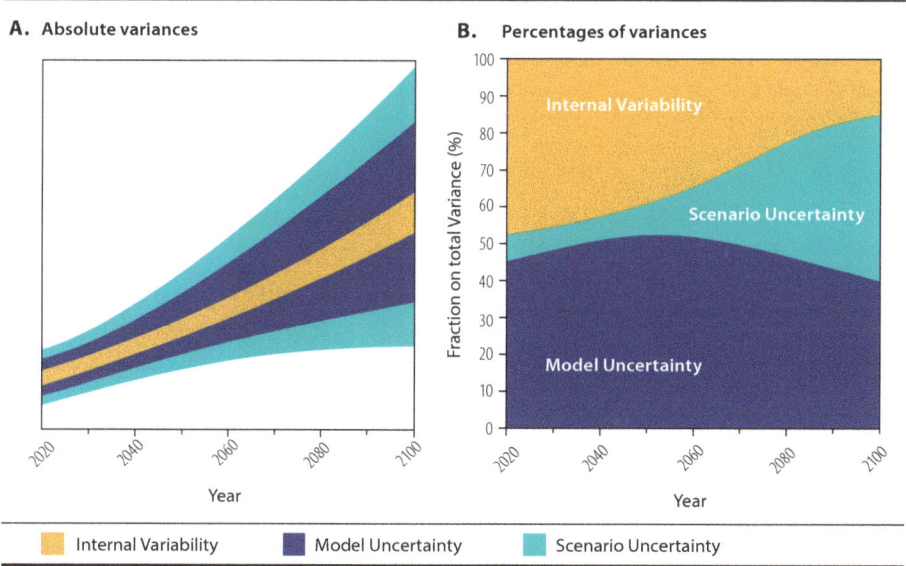

Figure 3. *The relative roles of different sources of uncertainty in projections.*

of the Atlantic Meridional Overturning Circulation system of currents (AMOC) that has been detected and that might be implicated in triggering tipping points. Models that don't reproduce these observations could be argued to be unsuitable for assessing future risk of climate change as they are likely to underestimate them.

Internal variability, by contrast, refers to modelled variability in climate behaviour (for example, the Atlantic Multi-decadal Oscillation (AMO), El Niño-Southern Oscillation (ENSO) or The Pacific Decadal Oscillation (PDO)). Other sources of variations might be traceable to exogenous events such as volcanic eruptions (if modelled) or fluctuations in energy received from the sun. Internal variability should mimic natural variability — climate is a complex stochastic system and many perturbations would still be there regardless of how much data we collect and how much better we are able to understand and model various processes.

Finally, **scenario uncertainty** refers to all the uncertainties connected with future human action on mitigation. Additionally, many other sources of uncertainty that don't fall into either of these three categories (e.g. some of those indicated in Chapter 5) may also be relevant.

The impact of these three forms of uncertainty on variability in projections depends on how far along into the future we are looking, on what spatial scale, and also what we are projecting (e.g. the hydrological cycle is an example where the influence of internal variability on the total uncertainty extends to long-term projections, whereas usually internal variability is more influential on the spread in near-term).[1]

Very generally:

- Internal variability and initial conditions account for most of the uncertainty near the start of the forecast and persist throughout projections as an irreducible source of uncertainty. However, it diminishes over time, in most cases, *as a proportion* of the whole variability range, due to the growing prevalence of other sources of uncertainty.
- Model uncertainty is important at all temporal scales, and generally grows over time.
- Scenario uncertainty has little influence at the beginning of the time series, but accounts for a substantial proportion of the variability in the long term.

Two types of visualisations are helpful to communicate relative influence of these main types of uncertainty *(Figure 3)*.

---

1   As stated in the AR6 WGI: "Internal variability is an irreducible source of uncertainty for mid-to-long-term projections with an amplitude that typically decreases with increasing spatial scale and lead time (Section 1.4.3; Section 4.2.1). However, regional-scale studies show that both large- and local scale internal variability together can still represent a substantial fraction of the total uncertainty related to hydrological cycle variables, even at the end of the 21st century (Lafaysse et al., 2014; Vidal et al., 2016; Aalbers et al., 2018; Gu et al., 2018)" (AR6 WGI 2021).

THE AR6 50 MODEL ENSEMBLE
We should always keep in mind not just what we are communicating, but who is producing the knowledge we communicate ...

The AR6 uses an ensemble of 50 main models, each of which imagines temperature responses to an increase in GHGs rather differently. They differ in spatial resolution: climate models divide the world into grid cells, the size of the cell can be coarse (100km length) or very fine (1km length). They differ with respect to exactly what and how they model. They differ with respect to who runs them, and on what computers. Some models describe climates very sensitive to doubling CO_2, others less so.

Not all models are treated as equally plausible, so the more extreme versions are given less of a say in the overall results. *Figure 3* shows a histogram of equilibrium climate sensitivity (ECS) values from the 50 model ensemble (data available from Mark Zelinka). These values correspond to how much warming each model would predict in a long-term equilibrium if CO_2 doubles.[2] The optimistic low values on the left are two Russian models (Schmidt 2021), see also *Figure 4*. The 66% 'likely' interval bar, above the histogram in Figure 4, refers to the integrated ECS distribution of all 50 models (IPCC WGI et al. 2021). It shows the impact of downweighting extreme models, as it clearly has lower variability than the histogram where all models have equal weight. If IPCC AR6 had treated all models as equally likely (i.e. had not used any model weighting) in its ensemble, its projections (as well as carbon budget calculations) would have come out much more uncertain.

The models are not strictly speaking independent; some of the models have many components in common, share chunks of code, are based around the same theoretical understanding of various processes shaping climates, or use the same assumptions (Abramowitz et al. 2019). There are clusters — some models are more similar than others. All this complicates interpreting the ensemble model mean, and raises concern that all models might be similarly biased.

It is important to keep in mind not only **who we are communicating with** but also **who is producing the knowledge that is being communicated** (van der Bles et al. 2019). The institutes that have produced the 50 models are clustered in Europe, North America, and East Asia (see *Figure 5*). Location is significant, as the next section explores. The regional disparity within the ensemble also exists in the larger set of models used across the whole of AR6 WGI.

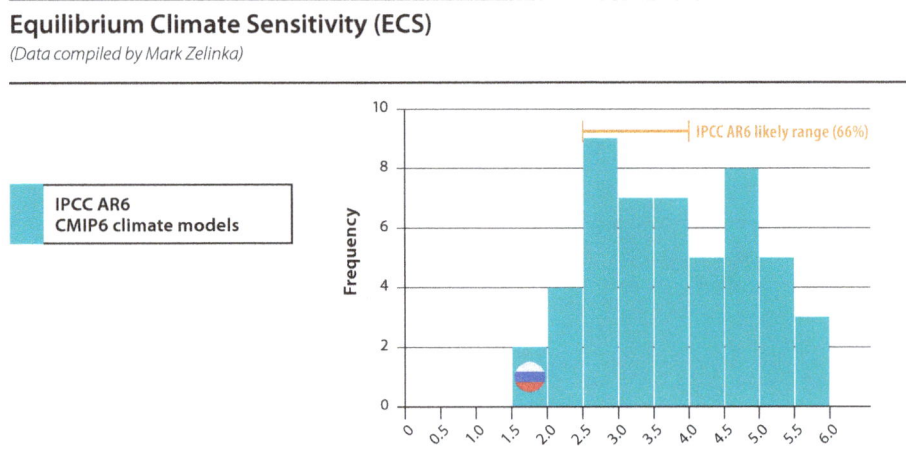

Figure 4. The 50 AR6 ensemble models are characterised by the equilibrium climate sensitivity parameter (ECS).

It is important to keep in mind not only who we are communicating with but also who is producing the knowledge that is being communicated.

---

2   The equilibrium values (ECS) are higher than the transient climate response (TCR) expected under the same models at the time of CO_2 doubling (as opposed to after climate reaches a new equilibrium); for TCR, the upper value estimated is 3°C as opposed to 5.6°C for ECS (see ECS values in *Figure 4*). From a policy perspective, if we are thinking decades ahead then the TCR is more relevant, if centuries then the ECS might be a better guide (Meehl et al. 2020).

REGIONAL DISTRIBUTION OF MODELLING

If you're modelling the whole world, does it matter where in the world you do it? It might ...

More research institutions are developing and running climate models than was the case for AR5, but they are not representative. The world is large and detailed, and scientists are relatively few, fewer in some places than in others. Inequities in the distribution of funds available for research, training and data collection contribute to these regional disparities. Despite the fact that nearly 40% of the global population is expected to live in Africa by 2100 (INED 2019), there is a striking lack of models in the ensemble from African research centers. There are not only regional inequalities in the location of CMIP6 institutions *(Figures 5 and 6)*, but also in the availability of data, the scope for evaluating different models, and how informative modelling is for different regions.

Model development has advanced in the world, but Africa still lags as a focus and in its contribution (James et al., 2018). None of the current generation of general circulation models (GCMs) was developed in Africa (Watterson et al., 2014), and the relevant processes in the continent have not been the priority for model development but treated in a one-size-fit-all approach (James

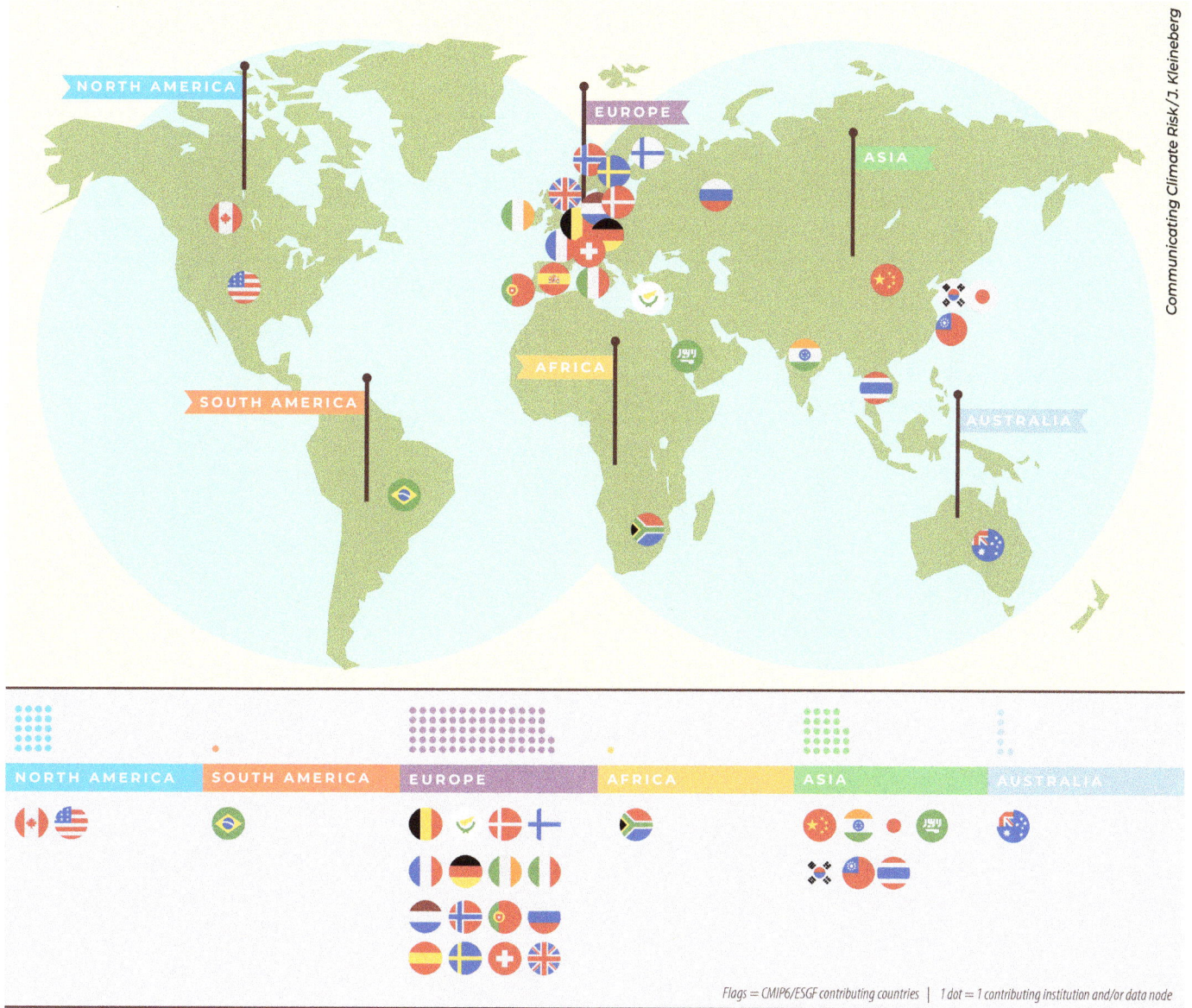

Figure 5. Locations of the institutes contributing to the CMIP6 modelling ensemble that produce projections for IPCC AR6 (data source).

et al., 2018) except for a few studies that focused on convective-permitting climate projections (Stratton et al., 2018; Kendon et al., 2019). However, there are growing efforts to boost African climate science by running and evaluating climate models over Africa (Endris et al., 2013; Kalognomou et al., 2013; Gbobaniyi et al., 2014; Engelbrecht et al., 2015; Klutse et al., 2016; Gibba et al., 2019).

(AR6 WGI 2021)

Decision-makers are often interested in predictions for specific regions and for specific climate features. **Data and research-poor regions are often the ones for which predictions are least informative. Yet these same regions are often the most vulnerable,** while lacking both forecasts that could support decision making or means to implement adaptation and risk mitigation measures. Such regions, Central Africa for example, are also the one with the least responsibility for the climate crisis. A lack of well-distributed models also poses the serious risk that some countries will encounter climate mitigation and climate adaptation as an externally-imposed agenda, an agenda freighted with neocolonial significance.

Efforts, such as downscaling, are under way to improve regional forecasts. The new set of models used in AR6 is believed to be more robust in assessing future global surface temperature, ocean warming, and sea-level rise. **In model evaluations, the new ensemble does better than the previous one on many criteria, but not on all.** What does this mean for a more general audience? How do we synthesise and interpret the information on model performance when scientists themselves don't interpret performance metrics in the same way, or always agree on assessments of model skill? If a model seems to perform well in some places but not in others, would the perceived importance (data richness) of one region over another influence our judgment of the overall model's fitness? How can we strengthen narratives and communicative practices around uncertainty in model-based projections? And given that uncertainty can reflect many viewpoints and plausible interpretations of the evidence being brought together, can we recognise the value of increasing uncertainty in some contexts?

Model evaluation, explored in more detail in the next section, is the practice of testing how well a model is performing. **The challenges of model evaluation also vary region by region, in ways which also reflect colonial histories and existing socioeconomic inequalities.** Padilla et al. (2021) imply that the need to communicate the reliability of modelling may be especially strong where there are large humanitarian needs:

> *…the humanitarian sector is increasingly developing standard operating procedures for anticipatory action (Pichon, 2019), including impact-based risk assessments that require policymakers to understand both geophysical and socioeconomic uncertainty (WMO, 2015; Forzieri et al., 2016; Taylor et al., 2021). Decision-makers without an understanding of the uncertainty in a forecast may be underinformed, placing undue levels of confidence in a forecast (Fischhoff, 2012; Fischhoff and Davis, 2014).*

(Padilla et al. 2021)

EVALUATING MODELS
Climate models are complex, so they are also complex to evaluate

Lots of data means that the models will fit some historical observations and not others, at some geographical scales but not at others, sometimes preserving the expected patterns of correlations between observations and sometimes not.[3] Given that the observations themselves are uncertain and potentially conflicting (or missing), we should not really expect good models to fit all the data well.

If a model does fit the historical data really well, it may sometimes have no real predictive power. Usually this happens when a model is overparameterized—many parameters enable the fit, but can result in too much noise to make meaningful forecasts.[4] Or it can happen because the processes that shape climate are themselves non-stationary, and structural assumptions are either inconsistent with historical data or invalid for the future. Getting around the fact

---

[3] "In fact, when using observations for model evaluation, there are multiple examples where inter-observational uncertainty is as large as the inter-model variability" (AR6 WGI 2021).

[4] "There is high confidence that an ensemble of multiple observational references at a regional scale is fundamental for model performance assessment" (AR6 WGI 2021).

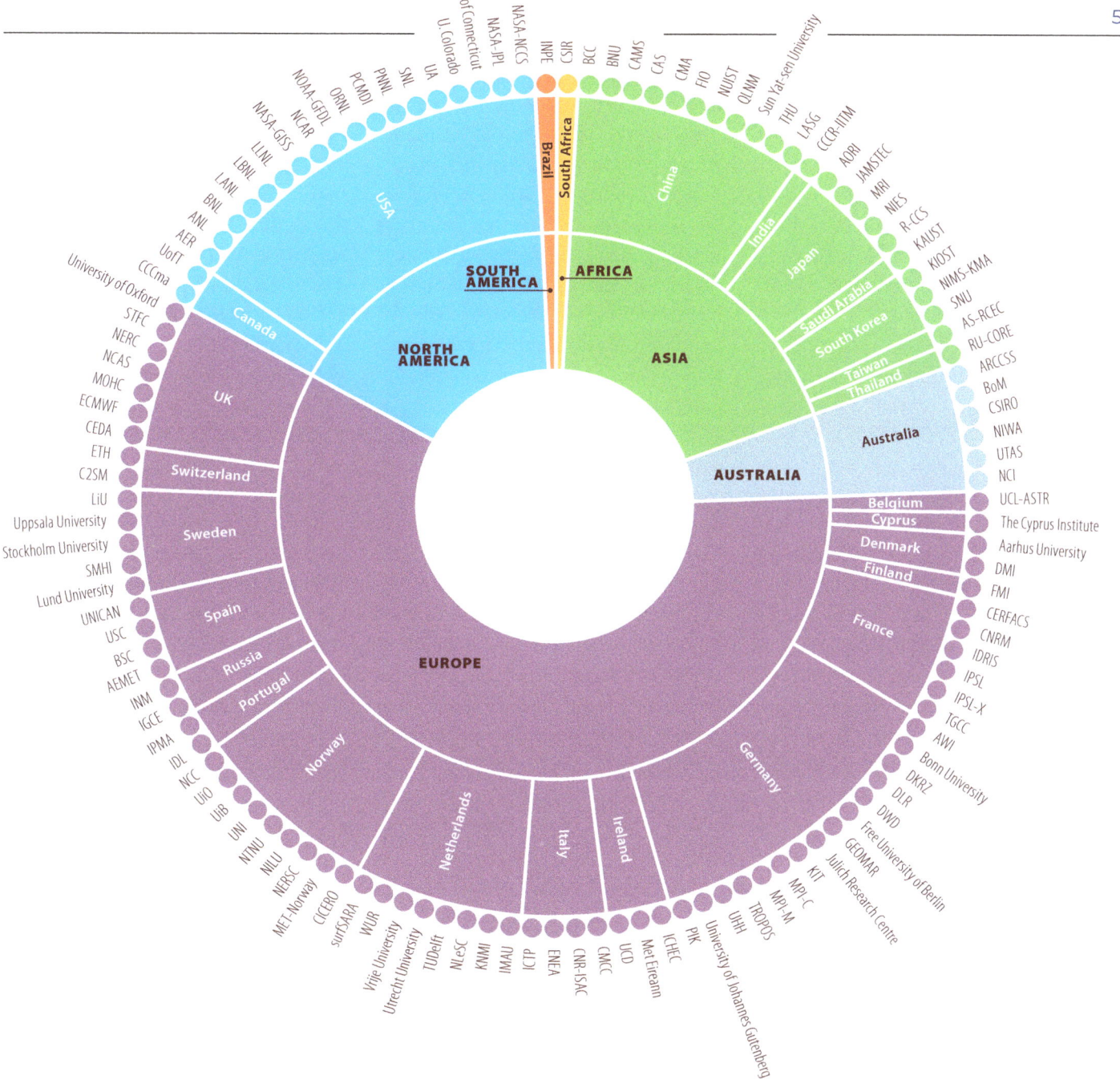

Figure 6. Earth System Grid Federation (ESGF) data nodes and modelling centers contributing to AR6 WGI simulations (data source).

that external data is lacking when your model makes forecasts on a 100 year scale is not easy: the only option is pretty much to substitute another model for the real world to simulate 'external' data for validation (which is an actual part of some model evaluation protocols). Furthermore, what it means for data to fit a model 'well' is rarely well-defined, although in weighting different models within an ensemble, the weighting procedure selected depends on explicit fitness criteria.

There should be different approaches to evaluating models, but having a unifying framework would be useful. Although there are efforts to have a generic open-source framework for evaluating climate models such as ESMValTool, neither methodologies nor terminology on model evaluation are standardised. In various chapters of the AR6 WGI report, the authors speak of model skill, model performance, fitness for purpose, plausibility, Type 1 and Type 2 errors, biases, and so on. Some terms, more common in modelling in other fields, such as 'model validation' or 'hindcasting'—where some historical data is taken away from the model so it can try to predict it—rarely appear in the AR6 WGI report, and various synonyms are used instead.

A key problem with using historical data to assess models are uncertainties in data, especially at regional scales. "The evaluation of model performance at historical variability and long-term changes provides further relevant information (Flato et al.,

2014). Trend evaluation may provide very useful insight, but has limitations in particular at the regional scale, mainly due to multi-decadal internal climate variability (Section 10.3.3.8), observational uncertainty (in both driving reanalysis and local trends; Section 10.2), and the fact that often not all regional forcings are known, and that past trends may be driven by forcings other than those driving future trends (Sections 10.4.1 and 10.6.3)" (AR6 WGI 2021).

It is far easier to improve models that make predictions that can be tested often, e.g. weather models. The scarce opportunities for climate models to be confronted with external data presents further challenges. In particular, when they do occur and appear not to go well (e.g. 'hiatus'[5]), trust in climate modelling gets damaged. **Trust in climate models is also not independent of trust in other models;** comparisons (fair or not) between complex climate models and complex economic models are often made. The inability of mainstream economic and financial modelling to predict the 2008 economic crisis was damaging to the trust people placed in models. Government decisions informed by epidemiological modelling during the Covid-19 pandemic reinforced perceptions of a lack of independence between politics and modelling.

Evaluation of models is also uneven across regions, often following the same geographical patterns as data availability and reliability of predictions. For example, there are relatively few studies examining model performance over Southwest Asia.[6] Sometimes it is Catch-22: to assess if a model is fit-for-purpose demands a more detailed model that is harder to parameterise in data-poor regions.

Within a given geographical region, model performance may also depend on the aspect of the climate being modelled. For example, in Africa some features of current climate are captured by some of the climate models while others (such as rainfall over Uganda) are not (Kisembe et al. 2019). Some regions (e.g. Central Africa) might lack historical observations, not only leading to poor quality predictions, but also making it difficult to assess if the model is fit-for-purpose as such evaluations sometimes must rely on more detailed models (that require higher resolution data and longer time series data to be properly conditioned). "Fitness-for-purpose can also be assessed by comparing the simulated response of a model with simulations of higher resolution models that better represent relevant processes (Baumberger et al., 2017)" (AR6 WGI 2021).

LANGUAGE TO DESCRIBE UNCERTAINTY IN AR6 WGI
Efforts have been made to improve the consistency of uncertainty language, but there is more work to be done when it comes to model uncertainty

The IPCC has held workshops, issued guidance, and held discussions on how to reduce linguistic uncertainty and judgment uncertainties (see Box 1.1, Figure 1 in AR6 WGI). The aim was to have a standardised language to describe uncertainty, so that at least the report is internally consistent when it comes to expressions of confidence and likelihood, terms known to have very subjective meanings. In 'Confident, likely, or both? The implementation of the uncertainty language framework in IPCC special reports,' Janzwood reports on the results of interviews with many of the scientists involved in the IPCC. Despite available guidance, these terms remain stubbornly hard to apply consistently across various contexts in the special reports, and subjectivity remains hard to subdue (Janzwood 2020). For example, they find that "high confidence" can mean either subjective belief about a level of agreement among experts, perception by the author of the state of existing literature, interpretations of agreement between models, relativist perceptions on the abundance and quality of evidence/data, and so forth. Lower gradings could easily fail to differentiate between shortcomings in data, knowledge, model agreement, consensus among experts, etc. (Janzwood 2020).

---

5   Trust is easy to lose, and hard to regain. Making bad predictions can damage perception. Negative confrontation with data tends to receive more attention and stick in the public imagination: "One of the topics widely discussed even outside of the climate science community was the apparent 'failure' of the CMIP5 models to reproduce the warming hiatus seen in observations of the global mean warming rates from 1998 to 2013. Because of the high attention this topic received, there were even potential implications on the public perception of the trustworthiness of climate models and climate projections in general. It has been shown that the hiatus was likely predominantly a result of internal climate variability with the phase of the IPO playing an important role" (Bock et al. 2020).

6   "There is limited evidence about the performance of GCMs and RCMs in representing the current climate of southwest Asia due to very few studies evaluating models over this region, but literature is now emerging particularly on CMIP5/CMIP6 and CORDEX simulations" (AR6 WGI 2021).

The term 'virtually certain' is used in the AR6 WGI relatively infrequently but sometimes crucially: "It is virtually certain that global surface temperature rise and associated changes can be limited through rapid and substantial reductions in global GHG emissions."

The term 'virtually certain' is used in the AR6 WGI relatively infrequently but sometimes crucially: "It is *virtually certain* that global surface temperature rise and associated changes can be limited through rapid and substantial reductions in global GHG emissions."

There is a category above 'virtually certain' that is called 'fact' in the report. Table TS.1 names two facts: the world has warmed and we caused it (AR6 WGI 2021). The report is *virtually certain* that extreme warming events will increase in frequency as the climate continues to warm.[7] It is *virtually certain* that the Northern Hemisphere will see less snow. It is *virtually certain* about ocean acidification and changes in stratification. However, the likelihood and the direction of changes is often insufficient for decision-makers who want to know the magnitude, location and time period (and the relevant uncertainties).

While there was investment in harmonising the process by which authors report on uncertainty in general, there is less consistency about the language used to describe uncertainty related to modelling. While generic tools are being developed to test models, appraisals of models' predictive skills and comparisons between relative reliability of models are not transparent.

It is difficult to find uniformly described information in the AR6 WGI report (or elsewhere) about what uncertainties are important in what models and why, which uncertainties the modellers were able to account for and which ones they could not, how the models were validated, tested or evaluated, what appears to be the main concerns in terms of sensitivity of the results, and so forth. How were these uncertainties elicited in the first place? Was there an assessment of consensus among the experts? Greater transparency about uncertainties in modelling and their fitness for purpose in various relevant decision-making contexts is required.

VISUALISATIONS OF UNCERTAINTIES
Here's our verdict on two visualisations from the SPM

There are two general categories of uncertainty visualisation:

- Intrinsic representation techniques integrate uncertainty by varying the appearance of the variable being visualised (e.g. shape, texture, brightness, opacity, hue)
- Extrinsic representation techniques involve addition of geometry to describe uncertainty (e.g. arrows, error bars, charts, glyphs)

AR6 WGI uses both techniques, sometimes in the same figure, for example AR6 WGI Figure SPM.3 (partly reproduced below as *Figure 7*). Ideally uncertainty visualisations are evaluated through testing, using robust methodology that does not only rely on self-reporting. In this chapter we make do with close interpretative readings, guided by principles such as the principle of appropriate knowledge and the semantic principle (see Chapter 7, 'Hacks, Insights, and Resources').

---

7 "Each finding is grounded in an evaluation of underlying evidence and agreement. A level of confidence is expressed using five qualifiers: very low, low, medium, high and very high, and typeset in italics, for example, medium confidence. The following terms have been used to indicate the assessed likelihood of an outcome or a result: virtually certain 99–100% probability, very likely 90–100%, likely 66–100%, about as likely as not 33–66%, unlikely 0–33%, very unlikely 0–10%, exceptionally unlikely 0–1%. Additional terms (extremely likely 95–100%, more likely than not >50–100%, and extremely unlikely 0–5%) may also be used when appropriate. Assessed likelihood is typeset in italics, for example, very likely. This is consistent with AR5. In this Report, unless stated otherwise, square brackets [x to y] are used to provide the assessed very likely range, or 90% interval" (AR6 WGI 2021).

VISUALISING PRECIPITATION TRENDS

Figure 7 shows part of Figure SPM.3, which visualises observed change in precipitation worldwide and the confidence with which it can be attributed to human-caused climate change. We also present a slightly modified version *(Figure 8)* to aid in the discussion.

Several sources of uncertainty related to attribution are aggregated into one measure called "Confidence in human contribution." Confidence in attributions has three levels (high, medium, low), and four options (high, medium, low due to limited agreement, low due to limited data). For this Toolkit, we have not been able to run objective tests on comprehension of these visualisations, but we invite readers to consider several questions to evaluate them informally. For example: Do they communicate effectively to core users? Do they provide accessible pathways for audiences who are not core users, but are nonetheless interested? Do they capture the attention of people who really should be core users, whether they know it or not? How easy is it to find the relevant information? Are these figures aesthetically expressive? Will the conventions chosen reinforce, rather than undermine, what the figures need to communicate? Are there potential unintended associations, such as grey diagonal stripes representing rain, or the 'blank' interior of Africa invoking neocolonial imaginaries (see **the semantic principle** in Chapter 7, 'Hacks, Insights, and Resources')?

For many audiences, the most striking message of *Figure 7* will be that **so many parts of South America and Africa are characterised by "limited data and/or literature"** on observed change (with North America, Australasia, and the South Pacific also patchy, containing several regions characterised by "low agreement in the type of change"). Part of the explanatory text reads:

> The IPCC AR6 WGI inhabited regions are displayed as hexagons [grouped in an anthropocentric way to reflect where people live, described elsewhere in the report] with identical size in their approximate geographical location (see legend for regional acronyms). All assessments are made for each region as a whole and for the 1950s to the present. Assessments made on different time scales or more local spatial scales might differ from what is shown in the figure.

The last bit involved some controversy during the SPM approval process. A number of delegates, especially from Global South countries, objected to their regions being characterised as having insufficient evidence.

> ANGOLA noted that for AR5, there was information on precipitation in Africa, generally indicating precipitation had decreased, but Figure SPM.3 contradicts AR5 in claiming insufficient evidence. The authors said the regions were aggregated at the subcontinental level to be large enough to generate a good evidence base from the modeling, to then be matched to evidence from the literature, and that much regional evidence is assessed in the underlying chapter but is insufficient to be aggregated to the scale of Figure SPM.3. (Bansard and Akanle Eni-ibukun, n.d.)

Trends detectable in one location do not necessarily translate into detectable trends on a larger scale, even if all local trends within a larger area show significant trends. This can happen if trends in adjacent areas are in conflict, when they should agree. Disagreement with geographically adjacent trends can be a sign

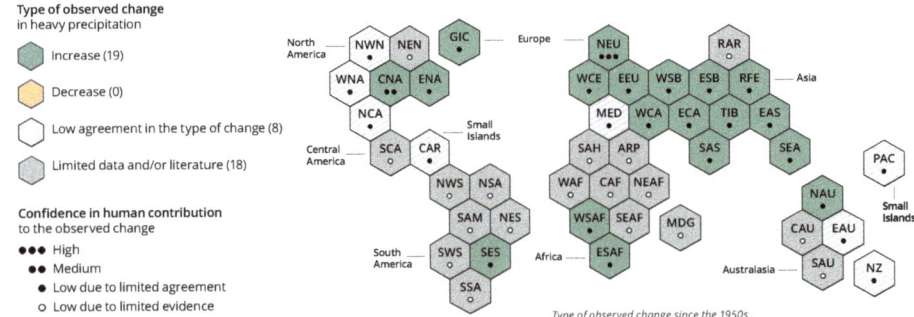

Figure 7. Part of IPCC WGI AR6 SPM.3, recreated.

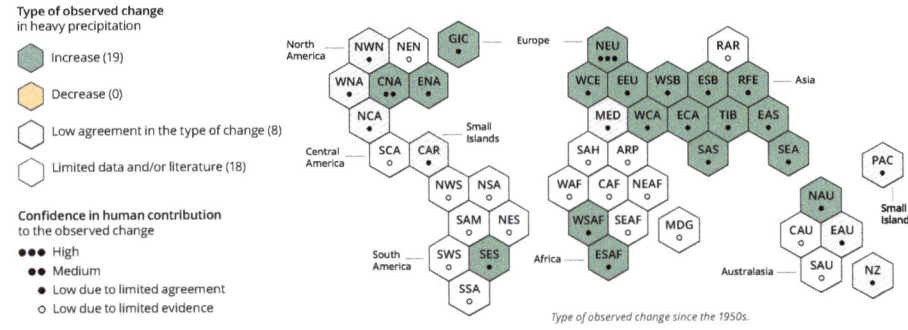

Figure 8. Suggestions for improving uncertainty visualisations for Figure SPM.3 (IPCC WGI et al. 2021).

that regional predictions are of poor quality and not fit for purpose. The delegates' discussion illustrates how **even experts are challenged by the fact that you may appear to know something at a smaller geographical scale only to see that knowledge questioned at a more aggregated level.** Usually it is the other way around—we can estimate global trends, e.g. temperature, more reliably than local ones. More generally, confusion over uncertainty at different spatial scales is a persistent problem for communicating climate risk:

There is no one-size-fits-all method for representing robustness or uncertainty in future climate projections from a multi-model ensemble. One of the main challenges is the dependence of the significance on the spatial scale of interest: while a significant trend may not be detected at every location, a fraction of locations showing significant trends can be sufficient to indicate a significant change over a region, particularly for extremes (e.g., it is likely that annual maximum 1-day precipitation has intensified over the land regions globally even though there are only about 10% of weather stations showing significant trends; Figure 11.13). The approach adopted in WGI works at a grid-box level and, therefore, is not informative for assessing climate change signals over larger spatial scales. For instance, an assessment of the amount of warming required for a robust climate change signal to emerge can strongly depend on the considered spatial scale. A robust change in the precipitation extremes averaged over a region or a number of grid-boxes emerge at a lower level of warming than at the grid-box level because of larger variability at the smaller scale (Cross-Chapter Box Atlas.1, Figure 2).

(AR6 WGI 2021)

The delegates eventually agreed amendments "to distinguish between low confidence [in human contribution] due to limited agreement and that due to limited evidence, as well as between low agreement in the type of change and limited data and/or literature"(Bansard and Akanle Eni-ibukun, n.d.). Presumably when there is low confidence in the type of change, there cannot be sufficient confidence in human contribution. The fact that there are no grey hexagons with black dots seems to confirm this. Of course, some redundancy is not necessarily a bad thing in data visualisation; however, these amendments do bear the hallmarks of the context of deliberation, politicking and compromise in which they arose. Is there any alternative? Perhaps a structured collaboration between scientists and graphic designers to refine visualisation problems, explore creative solutions, test graphics with audiences, and present options for review and approval.

The amendments also demonstrate the challenge of choosing the right level of detail in communicating uncertainty. Considering Angola's concerns (and setting aside the attribution aspect), the delegates' decision to differentiate "insufficient evidence" into "low agreement" and "limited data and/or literature" arguably only makes things worse.

Given the reasonable assumption that users will expect information about where heavy rain or snow may be increasing or decreasing, and given the fact the figure makes *some* differentiations between different forms of insufficient evidence, perhaps even more detail is necessary about why the figure does not provide trend information for some regions. Without more information, there is a risk of playing into a long history of colonial Western cartography, in which Africa has been shown as blank (Bassil 2011; Jarosz 1992).

For example, the summary could have mentioned that in some places the time-series data are shorter and hence noisier, obscuring trends (if that was the case). What this map does say is that we can already detect human-caused impacts of climate change on precipitation in two regions (Northern Europe (NEU) and Central North America (CNA)) with at least medium confidence. It would be unlikely for climate change to manifest uniformly across space and time, so there are likely natural reasons for these discrepancies also.

Another aspect of Figure 7 that is worthy of consideration is the use of colour to represent both the *assessed quantity* (increase or decrease in observed precipitation) and *reliability* of assessment.

> **The colours** in each panel represent the four outcomes of the assessment on observed changes. **White and light grey striped** hexagons are used where there is **low agreement** in the type of change for the region as a whole, and **grey hexagons** are used when there is **limited data and/or literature** that prevents an assessment of the region as a whole. Other colours indicate at least medium confidence in the observed change.

(AR6 WGI 2021)

Glyphs in terms of stripes represent model disagreement, but it might have been better to use blank space to denote limited evidence, especially because the colour grey being used to denote limited evidence has other semantic connotations in this context (grey skies filled with rain and snow). The use of stripes to represent disagreement in predictions is more or less consistent throughout the report as well as online (interactive-atlas. ipcc.ch/). Grey is not used as a signifier of limited evidence in the Atlas: a more consistent graphical language that bridges both static and interactive illustrations should be explored.

Leaving the grey hexagons blank, as we illustrate in *Figure 8*, would also be more internally consistent with blank circles representing limited evidence in attribution studies, as Figure's explanatory text describes:

The confidence level for the human influence on these observed changes is based on assessing trend detection and attribution and event attribution literature, and it is indicated by the number of dots: three dots for high confidence, two dots for medium confidence and one dot for low confidence (filled: limited agreement; empty: limited evidence)
(AR6 WGI 2021)

Overall, the graphic looks clean and appealing, but it is open to debate whether the information on uncertainty is being represented well, so that people can read and understand the information off the chart correctly and efficiently.

CLIMATIC IMPACT DRIVERS (CIDS) IN SPM

Climatic impact drivers (CID) refers to many different physical climate system conditions such as heatwaves and cold spells, snowstorms and avalanches, cyclones and dust storms, floods and droughts, and other means, events, extremes, that can affect ecosystems and societies. *Figure SPM.9* presents a synthesis of AR6 WGI reference regions where CIDs are projected to change. High and medium confidence are differentiated with dark and light shades within a stacked bar chart, where the bars sit against a background of an even lighter 'envelope' that represents the number of regions where the analysis is relevant.

There are several sensible design choices made here. Lighter shades have been chosen to represent less confidence, and the lighter ink is more distant from the axis. See *Visualising Uncertainty: A Shport Introduction* (Levontin et al. 2020) for more on hue, saturation and colour value, as well as modifications such as blurring and pixelation, to convey uncertainty. The phrases "number of land & coastal regions" and "number of open ocean regions" both appear twice, relatively prominently, to help preclude the misinterpretation that the chart is something to do with the magnitude of projected changes, rather than the number of areas in which changes are projected. The relatively prominent separation of the Open Ocean is also appropriate; however, on the other hand (as discussed below) it is perhaps still not prominent *enough*, perhaps inviting illegitimate comparisons across the two columns. Furthermore, the 'Assessed Future Changes' legend is formatted in a way that opens it to misinterpretation: does it refer to the whole chart, or only column B?

A summary of discussion on this figure (SPM.9) at the intergovernmental negotiations offers further insights into the politics of visualisations. Representations are never 'objective' or 'neutral' but reflect subtly cultural, political and social values — a fact that is rarely acknowledged, but that might be explored by close textual analysis of deliberations, or notes based thereon.

The US suggested specifying that all regions are "projected to" experience changes in at least five CIDs, instead of "will," and specifying this is the case "at 2°C warming." LUXEMBOURG requested adjusting the visualization so that the upper end of scales on the number of regions aligns with the maximum number of land and ocean regions considered. CANADA called for specifying the number of regions for which each CID is applicable, noting that for instance, only some regions have snow glaciers. The REPUBLIC OF KOREA and the US requested clarifying whether changes relate to increases in frequency, intensity, or duration, noting this is not evident for all CIDs. The NETHERLANDS, SPAIN, and MEXICO called for presenting information in a more region-specific manner to increase policy relevance. Other comments related to: reinstating a map showing the regions that are considered in the figure; including meteorological droughts; and referring to coastal and "open ocean" CIDs, instead of "oceanic." The US asked what type of assessment was conducted for agricultural and ecological droughts, noting some indices are highly dependent on temperature. The authors noted they did not use any metric based on temperature, primarily relying on soil moisture. The figure was approved, with revisions including the addition of an "envelope" representing the maximum number of regions for which a CID is relevant.
(Bansard and Akanle Eni-ibukun, n.d.)

Poor visualisations is one of the costs of the institutional arrangement for agreeing on visualisation that precludes a possibility of testing the proposed amendments to graphics with audiences. One risk is that multiple amendments will be considered separately and approved as good ideas, but interact in adverse ways. A potential benefit of the deliberative process is the generation of relatively ample explanatory notes, although there may also be a tendency to over-rely on them throughout AR6 WGI. With any iterative design process, there is

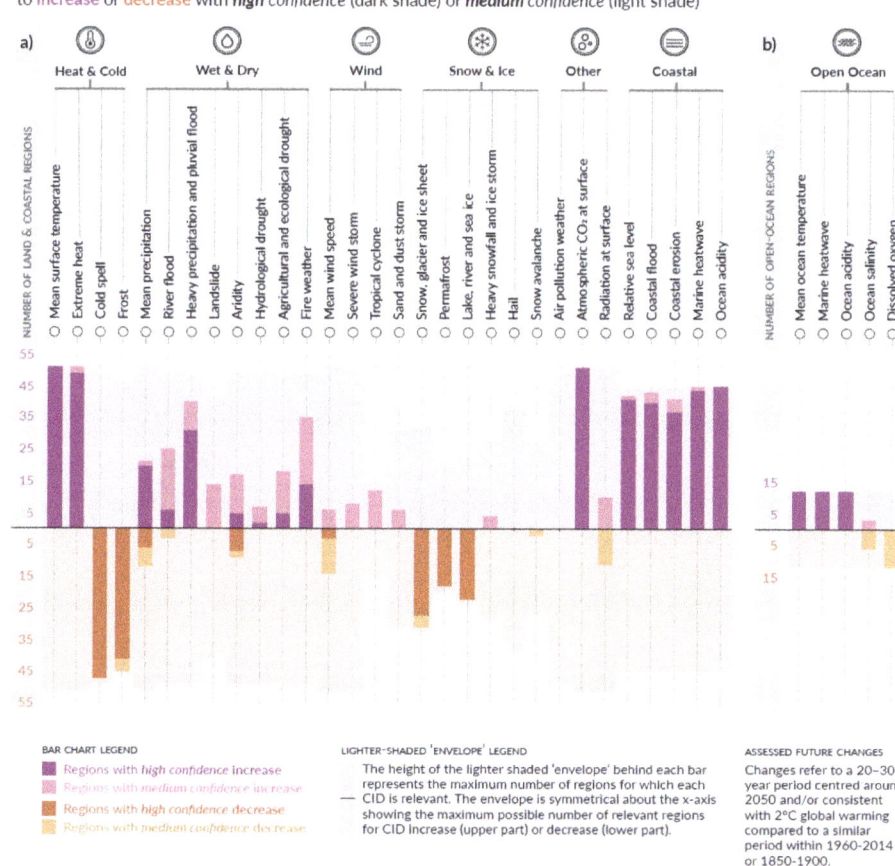

Figure 9. Partial reproduction of SPM. 9 (IPCC WGI et al. 2021).

always the risk that the final stage of amendments prior to a release will introduce entirely new problems. This can partly be addressed by insisting on further review where amendments are other than very minor; in the context of visualisation, however, even an apparently very minor amendment can sometimes have a large impact on how the visualisation works.

In the case of the SPM.9, the added 'envelope' (the pale, symmetrically ragged background to the bars) is a relatively poor visualisation element which is open to being misinterpreted or ignored. For example, the number of regions for which a CID was found to be significant might easily be confused with the magnitude of an impact, despite the text telling us otherwise. It is also misleading in the way that extreme events over oceans appear 'less likely' (the smaller envelope on the right). However this is only due to the fact that there are much fewer regions. Increases in hazards, such as heat waves and acidity, are in fact expected to occur over 100% of the area (ocean), yet they look less likely than heat waves on land that are also projected to occur over 100% of the area (landmass), only because the area (landmass) was subdivided into more parts, making the envelopes larger and the heights of the bars in the figure higher. Further, it is left unclear what the baseline is (is it starting in 1890 or 1960?).

Other approaches could be explored and tested. There could be an argument for transposing the chart sideways. On the downside, the distinction between increase and decrease would be less marked on such a rotated version, and would require careful and prominent labelling. On the other hand, the labels of each CID might be more easily read. There also might be a slightly easier on-ramp for the audience, likely to start at the top of the list with some relatively obvious CIDs (mean surface temperature, extreme heat, cold spell). On the actual visualisation, the eye is drawn to spend more time at the centre of the diagram.

Why is the figure whose main point is the geographical extent of specific changes not plotted on a map, perhaps with fewer CIDs represented or more aggregation? Another option to explore would be a set of mini-maps (perhaps one for 'Heat & Cold,' one for 'Wet & Dry,' and so on). In Figure 9, the wide range of different CIDs considered and the ambitious compression of information has led to the ambiguities noted by the delegates from the Republic of Korea and the USA ('increase' or 'decrease' in what sense?), which could perhaps be resolved by differentiating into separate mini-maps.

Overall, the figure is once more clean and elegant, with several sensible choices, but there may be room for further experimentation and improvement.

Poor visualisations is one of the costs of the institutional arrangement for agreeing on visualisation that precludes a possibility of testing the proposed amendments to graphics with audiences.

THE AR6 WGI INTERACTIVE ATLAS

The interactive Atlas represents a major step forward in communicating climate risk by the IPCC. In particular, there is much more consistency to representing uncertainty in maps. Further, researchers tested proposed visualisations with the audiences. It is always recommended to do so. The research found:

> *[...] wide-ranging interpretations and varied understandings of climate information amongst respondents due to the choice of visuals. In addition, Taylor et al. (2015) found that preferences for a particular visualization approach do not always align with approaches that achieve greatest accuracy in interpretation. Choosing appropriate visuals for a particular purpose and audience can be informed by testing and evaluation with target groups.*
> (AR6 WGI 2021)

Who is the Atlas for? The intended audience includes everyone, including policymakers, but not necessarily in all situations:

> *Communication aimed at informing the general public about assessed scientific findings on climate change have a different purpose and format than if intended to inform a specific target audience to support adaptation or mitigation policies (Whetton et al., 2016). The growing societal engagement with climate change means IPCC reports are increasingly used directly by businesses, the financial sector, health practitioners, civil society, the media, and educators at all levels. The IPCC reports could effectively be considered a tiered set of products with information relevant to a range of audiences.*

> *The Interactive Atlas does provide access to a collection of observational and modelling datasets, presented in a form that supports the distillation of information on observed and projected climate trends at the regional scale. Access to the repository of underlying datasets enables further processing for particular purposes. As noted above, it is not the intention nor the ambition of this IPCC assessment and the Interactive Atlas component to provide a climate service for supporting targeted policies. For this an increasing number of dedicated climate change assessment programs have been carried out, aiming at mapping climate change information relevant for adaptation and mitigation decision support.*
> (AR6 WGI 2021)

Representing uncertainty as clearly and eloquently as the Atlas endeavours is not without risks. Communicating about uncertainty and reliability is seen by many scientists as the basis of maintaining trust in science within a larger society (cf. e.g. O'Neill, 2012; Stocker et al., 2013; Van Der Bles et al., 2020; Padilla et al. 2021). During the COP26 Universities Network's Climate Risk Summit, we asked participating scientists whether they believed that uncertainty should be communicated even when uncertainty is small — 100% replied 'yes'.

Nevertheless, uncertainty in climate science has been derided, politicised, and weaponised across the political spectrum (Silver 2013). Uncertainty has served both to sow doubt about the urgency of addressing climate emergency and to heighten a sense of emergency. The obstacles to reasonable climate action often are not clarity and credibility, but rather economics and politics, and so it is often certitude that is demanded by decision-makers, environmental activists, and concerned citizens. And it is certitude that is sometimes provided (often with good cause) by the scientists.

Hopefully the Atlas will serve to increase popular understanding of both models' usefulness and their limitations. Nevertheless, it is clearly only a first step, and one which poses many questions. Which users have appropriate knowledge to correctly interpret the displays? Can the Atlas come with more resources aimed at developing the knowledge and graphicacy needed to interpret it? What VR, AR and other immersive storytelling implementations may spin off from the Atlas? Does the Atlas presage more interactive decision support tools which are more explicitly designed to integrate modelling and stakeholder deliberation, and what dangers might this pose for unaccountable "black boxes" in participatory decision-making processes? The Interactive Atlas is interactive, but is it playful? Does it encourage learning, creativity, collaboration, exploration and the sharing of knowledge? How do the Atlas's maps compare to the many other alluring interactive maps available online (such as Google Maps)? The IPCC's texts and visuals have been created with the tacit assumption that others will translate them into many different appropriate contexts; does the Atlas supply appropriate resources for interactive designers?

SEVEN RECOMMENDATIONS FOR THE IPCC AND THE MODELLING COMMUNITY
Recommended areas for action and further research

1) Communicate key assumptions around model uncertainty: "Global model includes all relevant regional forcings and realistically simulates all relevant regional scale processes and feedbacks and their dependence on large-scale climate. Parameterisations are valid in future climate" (IPCC WGI et al. 2021). For example, all future projections depend on the assumptions that existing knowledge of the processes that shape the climate system is accurate and applicable in the future. Under what conditions would this assumption be invalid? Can the processes change, e.g. if the climate crosses a tipping point? Can our knowledge about them change so as to lead to entirely different forecasts? Only qualitative answers to these questions are often possible, and measuring consensus (see below) becomes especially important for communication.

2) Explore how to better foster interdisciplinarity. When developing visualisation formats, or other means of communicating model uncertainty, favour interdisciplinary teams across the sciences, social sciences, arts and humanities, as well as non-academic participants, especially core end users. The case to do so is even stronger in respect of interactive formats such as the Atlas and any successors, and might include for example social scientists and arts and humanities with expertise in AI and automation and critical data studies, as well as more obvious fields such as the environmental humanities.

3) Encourage scientists to adopt a common vocabulary for discussing models' predictive skill, methods to assess whether a model is fit for purpose, and procedure for weighing or rejecting models. Conduct workshops dedicated to finding common approaches to communicating the results of these evaluations.

4) Improve representation in the modelling community. There is a need for a wider discourse on model validation, the subjectivities it involves—this is one reason to include in the research (e.g. workshops mentioned above) a greater diversity of participants. Similarly, collect and report data on representation (especially race and gender) among the climate modelling teams, and take strong measures to improve representation. Modelling is a quantitative way to create narratives about our futures, and narratives empower us to intervene in these futures via shared cultural imaginaries. African futures, for example, should not be forecast by teams that exclude Africans.

5) Develop more best practice for communicating the reliability of forecasts. Find ways to disengage if necessary. One of the hardest things for a modeller to say is, "I don't think my model is good enough for the question you are asking." Where there is high uncertainty but no feasible opportunity to communicate it to the relevant decision-maker given the available time and resources, there is the danger that modelling can no longer serve transparency or robust decision-making. Visualisations, such as *Figure 11*, can help scientists communicate how a model's skill varies across temporal and spatial scales—it is generally easier to predict changes for large areas in the near future, than on a finer scale and far into the future.

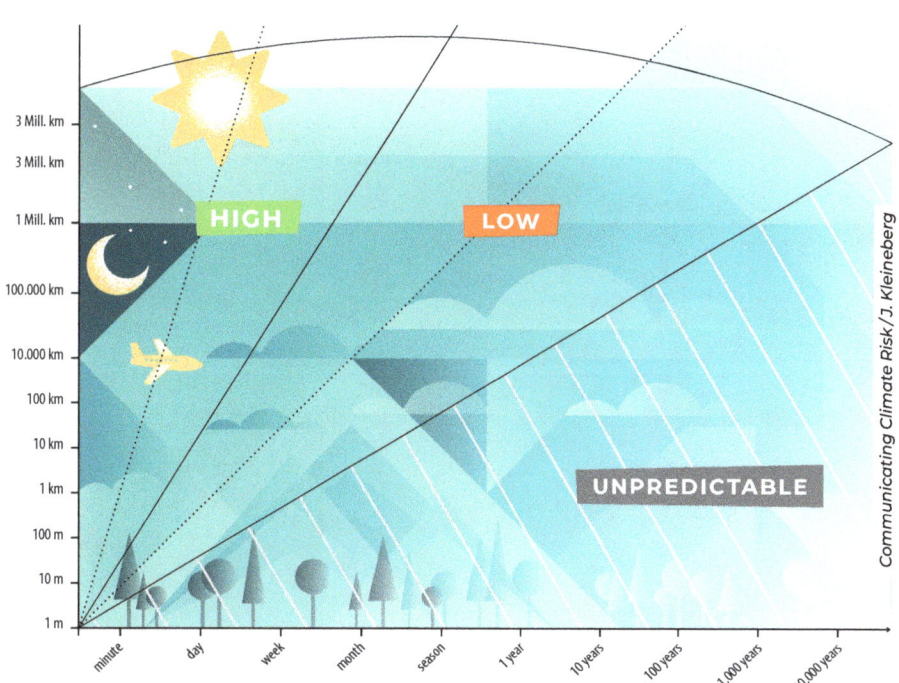

Figure 10. Illustrating how model prediction skill depends on spatial and temporal scales.

First, conduct expert elicitations and/or literature review to scope a list of relevant uncertainties, and group them in pertinent ways (e.g. data and processes). Use a formal process to investigate perceptions of uncertainties identified in the scoping stage among the scientists collaborating on a specific modelling project.

Figure 11. Prioritising uncertainties based on a formal expert elicitation process that also accesses consensus (Leach et al. 2014).

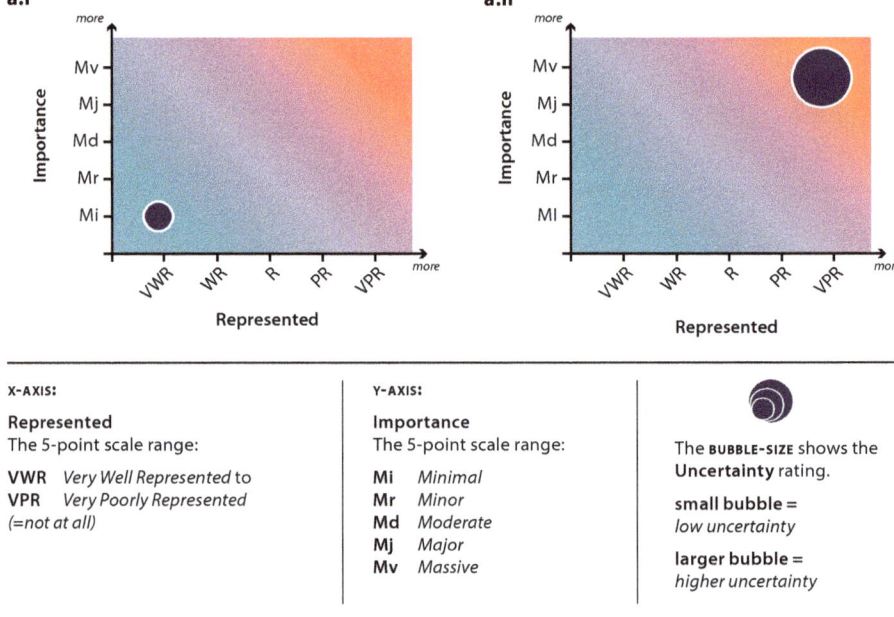

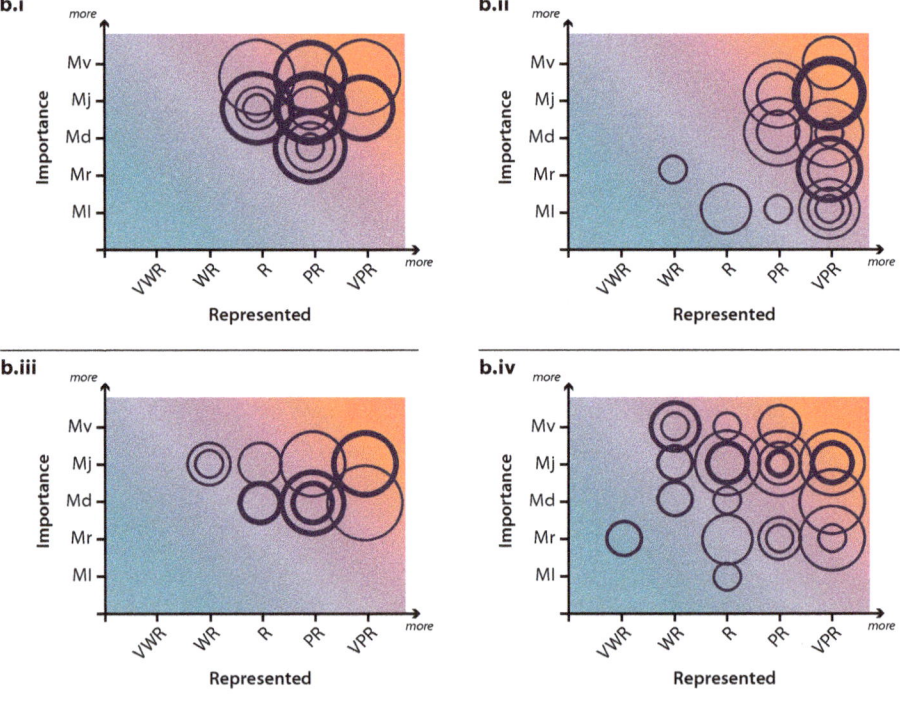

Visualisation approach suggested by Leach et al. 2014.

6) Address a mismatch between the expectations of decision-makers and perceived ability of models to make predictions meaningful to policy on regional scales:

While the ability of global models to simulate large-scale indicators of climate change has improved since AR5 (Chapter 3), the simulation of regional climate and climate change poses an additional challenge. Users demand regional climate projections for decision making and have high expectations regarding accuracy and resolution (Rössler et al., 2019a), but some scientists consider such projections still a matter of basic research (Hewitson et al., 2014a).

Policymakers often want forecasts on specific temporal and spatial scales. Currently, models are rarely fit for purpose to make such predictions. Even models that appear reliable when it comes to predicting averages might not be so when it comes to predicting rare events that live in the hard to estimate tails of probability distributions. It is not only harder to make predictions about the tails, having less data to estimate rare events means also having less data to evaluate the quality of predictions. The IPCC AR6 are open about such difficulties but not necessarily transparent because of the language used to communicate this:

In particular extreme events are often caused by specific, in some cases persistent, circulation patterns (Sections 11.3–11.7). It is therefore important for climate models to reasonably represent not only continental, but also regional climate and its variability for such extremes. As explained in Section 3.3.3, standard resolution GCMs can suffer biases in the location, occurrence frequency or intensity of large-scale phenomena, such that statements about a specific regional climate and its change can be highly uncertain (Hall, 2014).

7) Measure and visualise consensus (or its lack) on uncertainties. First, conduct expert elications and/or literature review to scope a list of relevant uncertainties, and group them in pertinent ways (e.g. data and processes). Use a formal process to investigate perceptions of uncertainties identified in the scoping stage among the scientists collaborating on a specific modelling project.

A visualisation approach suggested below (Leach et al. 2014) can be a useful tool to prioritise uncertainties that need to be communicated. It is also a useful exercise for helping researchers reflect on their current research in new and fruitful ways, and perhaps shape future priorities.

Three aspects of each source of uncertainty should be investigated (Figure 11a):

- **Importance:** believed potential to affect modelling results (e.g. how sensitive are model results to small changes in the source of uncertainty). Shown on y-axis.
- **Level of uncertainty:** ranging from "low" where a variable is believed to be well understood to "high" where there is little information about the variable or it is known to be highly uncertain. Shown on x-axis.
- **Representation:** to what extent analysis already accounts for this source of uncertainty. Shown by bubble size.

The background of *Figure 11* intends to provide an additional visual cue as to which uncertainties should be prioritised but the standard 'traffic light' red-green spectrum has been replaced to make the figure colour-blind-friendly (Katsnelson 2021). Sources of uncertainty that end up in the upper-right "red" corner *(Figure 11 aii)* are high priority: they are those that respondents believed to be important, are associated with high levels of (epistemological) uncertainty, and are not yet to be properly accounted for in modelling or risk assessment. Those in the bottom-left "green" corner *(Figure 11 ai)* can probably be left out of wider conversations with stakeholders, as they are believed not to impact results, and are well understood and accounted for.

There is often an assumption that scientists share views on uncertainty. But formal elicitations can reveal surprising differences. *Figure 11b* demonstrates how results might look based on actual surveys we conducted (Leach et al. 2014). Each ring is a response from a scientist. Since the answers are on discrete 5-point scales some answers will overlap and this is represented by ring thickness. Scientists might agree on everything: the importance of a particular source of uncertainty, on how uncertain they are about it, and on how well it is already accounted for or 'represented' in the model *(Figure 11 b.i)*. Or elications might show a total lack of consensus *(Figure 11 b.iv)*.

Once perceptions of uncertainty are clarified and priorities are identified, we can plan how to communicate them. Caveat: Scientists can be wrong at predicting how important a source of uncertainty is.

AUTHOR CONTRIBUTIONS:
Conceptualization: PL and JLW; Research: PL; Writing: JLW and PL; Figures: JK and PL.

REFERENCES

Abramowitz, Gab, Nadja Herger, Ethan Gutmann, Dorit Hammerling, Reto Knutti, Martin Leduc, Ruth Lorenz, Robert Pincus, and Gavin A. Schmidt. 2019. 'ESD Reviews: Model Dependence in Multi-Model Climate Ensembles: Weighting, Sub-Selection and out-of-Sample Testing'. *Earth System Dynamics* 10 (1): 91–105. doi.org/10.5194/esd-10-91-2019

Bansard, Jennifer, and Tomilola Akanle Eni-ibukun. n.d. 'Summary of the 54th Session of the Intergovernmental Panel on Climate Change and the 14th Session of Working Group I: 26 July - 6 August 2021'. *Earth Negotiations Bulletin*. enb.iisd.org/climate/IPCC/IPCC-54-WGI-14/summary

Bassil, Noah R. 2011. 'The Roots of Afropessimism: The British Invention of the "Dark Continent"'. *Critical Arts* 25 (3): 377–96. doi.org/10.1080/02560046.2011.615141

Bles, Anne Marthe van der, Sander van der Linden, Alexandra L. J. Freeman, James Mitchell, Ana B. Galvao, Lisa Zaval, and David J. Spiegelhalter. 2019. 'Communicating Uncertainty about Facts, Numbers and Science'. *Royal Society Open Science* 6 (5): 181870. doi.org/10.1098/rsos.181870

Bock, L., A. Lauer, M. Schlund, M. Barreiro, N. Bellouin, C. Jones, G. A. Meehl, V. Predoi, M. J. Roberts, and V. Eyring. 2020. 'Quantifying Progress Across Different CMIP Phases With the ESMValTool'. *Journal of Geophysical Research: Atmospheres* 125 (21). doi.org/10.1029/2019JD032321

Budescu, David V, Han-Hui Por, and Stephen B Broomell. 2012. 'Effective Communication of Uncertainty in the IPCC Reports'. *Climatic Change* 113 (2): 181–200.

Dieckmann, Nathan F, Robin Gregory, Ellen Peters, and Robert Hartman. 2017. 'Seeing What You Want to See: How Imprecise Uncertainty Ranges Enhance Motivated Reasoning'. *Risk Analysis* 37 (3): 471–86.

INED. 2019. 'Projections by Continent'. Ined - Institut National d'études Démographiques. 2019. ined.fr/en/everything_about_population/data/world-projections/projections-by-continent/

IPCC WGI, P. Zhai, A. Pirani, S. L. Connors, and WGI. 2021. 'IPCC, 2021: Summary for Policymakers'. In *Climate Change 2021: The Physical Science Basis. Contribution of Working Group I to the Sixth Assessment Report of the Intergovernmental Panel on Climate Change*. Cambridge University Press.

Iturbide, Maialen, Fernández, Jesús, Gutiérrez, José Manuel, Bedia, Joaquín, Cimadevilla, Ezequiel, Díez-Sierra, Javier, Manzanas, Rodrigo, et al. 2021. *Repository Supporting the Implementation of FAIR Principles in the IPCC-WGI Atlas* (version v2.0-final). Zenodo. doi.org/10.5281/ZENODO.3691645

Janzwood, Scott. 2020. 'Confident, Likely, or Both? The Implementation of the Uncertainty Language Framework in IPCC Special Reports'. *Climatic Change* 162 (3): 1655–75. https://doi.org/10.1007/s10584-020-02746-x.

Jarosz, Lucy. 1992. 'Constructing the Dark Continent: Metaphor as Geographic Representation of Africa'. *Geografiska Annaler: Series B, Human Geography* 74 (2): 105–15. doi.org/10.1080/04353684.1992.11879634

Katsnelson, Alla. 2021. 'Colour Me Better: Fixing Figures for Colour Blindness'. *Nature* 598 (7879): 224–25. doi.org/10.1038/d41586-021-02696-z

Kisembe, Jesse, Alice Favre, Alessandro Dosio, Christopher Lennard, Geoffrey Sabiiti, and Alex Nimusiima. 2019. 'Evaluation of Rainfall Simulations over Uganda in CORDEX Regional Climate Models'. *Theoretical and Applied Climatology* 137 (1–2): 1117–34. doi.org/10.1007/s00704-018-2643-x

Leach, Adrian W., Polina Levontin, Johnson Holt, Laurence T. Kell, and John D. Mumford. 2014. 'Identification and Prioritization of Uncertainties for Management of Eastern Atlantic Bluefin Tuna (Thunnus Thynnus)'. *Marine Policy* 48 (September): 84–92. doi.org/10.1016/j.marpol.2014.03.010

Masson-Delmotte, V., P. Zhai, A. Pirani, and S. L. Connors. 2021. 'Climate Change 2021: The Physical Science Basis. Contribution of Working Group I to the Sixth Assessment Report of the Intergovernmental Panel on Climate Change'. Cambridge University Press.

Meehl, Gerald A., Catherine A. Senior, Veronika Eyring, Gregory Flato, Jean-Francois Lamarque, Ronald J. Stouffer, Karl E. Taylor, and Manuel Schlund. 2020. 'Context for Interpreting Equilibrium Climate Sensitivity and Transient Climate Response from the CMIP6 Earth System Models'. *Science Advances* 6 (26): eaba1981. doi.org/10.1126/sciadv.aba1981

Padilla, Lace, Sarah Dryhurst, Helia Hosseinpour, and Andrew Kruczkiewicz. 2021. 'Multiple Hazard Uncertainty Visualization Challenges and Paths Forward'. *Frontiers in Psychology* 12: 1993. doi.org/10.3389/fpsyg.2021.579207

Schmidt, Gavin. 2021. 'RealClimate: #NotAllModels'. 9 August 2021. realclimate.org/index.php/archives/2021/08/notallmodels/

Silver, Nate. 2013. *The Signal and the Noise: The Art and Science of Prediction*. Penguin Economics. London: Penguin Books.

Chapter 5: CLIMATE FINANCE AND CLIMATE RISK

INTRODUCTION
Climate finance affects us all, yet for many, the world of finance appears opaque and confusing

▶▶▶ *"In truth, sustainable investing boils down to little more than marketing hype, PR spin and disingenuous promises from the investment community."*
—**Tariq Fancy**, *Former CIO for Sustainable Investing at BlackRock*

▶▶▶ *"Private finance is judging which companies are part of the solution, but private finance, too, is increasingly being judged. Banks, pension funds and asset managers have to show where they are in the transition to net zero. And people are voting with their money."*
—**Mark Carney**, *UN Special Envoy for Climate Action and Finance*

▶▶▶ *"Money talks."*
—*Proverb*

This is a chapter about **finance**. Where is the money for mitigation and adaptation actually coming from? Is it being invested in the right ways? How will climate transition impact the financial sector more broadly?

It is also about **communication**. Like climate science, **climate finance can be an intimidating topic for non-experts.** However, in the case of climate science, there are endless projects devoted to communicating findings with wider publics. The same is hardly true of climate finance.

Despite its relative opacity, **the financial sector is creating its own narrative about climate transition**. The framings and ideas put forward by central banks, investor coalitions, and financial institutions, can carry a lot of weight. They can also migrate outside the financial sector, and shape the views of policymakers, publics, and other actors.

Furthermore, **financial markets themselves also tell stories**. They communicate information about the climate risk strategies of various actors. The stories told by the price of an asset, the rate of return on an investment, and so on, may contradict what companies explicitly say in their reports.

If climate transition is to benefit from broad participatory expertise, as described in Chapter 3, then more resources must be devoted to demystifying finance. That doesn't just mean introductory primers like this chapter. It also means widening participation in the design and governance of financial systems. It means making financial activity much more legible to, and auditable by, a much wider range of actors. For now, let us begin with the big picture, painted in broad strokes.

Even by optimistic estimates, we are not investing nearly enough in climate transition. The fossil fuel industry still gets more investment than climate transition. **Nor are we investing in the right places.** More that 80% of climate finance is invested in the same nations where it originates, rather than where mitigation is cheapest and adaptation needs are most pressing. Sub-Saharan Africa, for example, currently receives less than 5% of global climate finance.

Currently the vast majority of climate finance is **public sector finance**. It comes from governments. However, beguiling promises are emerging from some corners of **private finance**, claiming to be on the verge not only of reconfiguring the economy to be ecologically sustainable—Net

Subsections

Introduction	Scenario analysis and stress testing
The climate finance gap	Challenges for scenario analysis
Challenges to reallocating capital	Emerging trends in scenario modelling
The major players in global finance	Climate risk at the enterprise scale
Sidebar: Key terms	Climate risk into financial risk
An anatomy of climate risk	Stranded assets and impairment
Unlocking private sector climate finance	Double materiality
Sidebar: Who benefits from framing climate change in terms of financial risk?	Dynamic materiality
	Scoping the policy space
Improving climate-related reporting	Acknowledgements
Climate-related reporting in context	References
Sidebar: Who is on the frontline of climate risk?	

Zero is "nothing less than shorthand for retooling global capital markets to work toward an economy and society that can be sustainable"—but doing so in ways that serve global justice—"As the captains of private finance begin to steer global capital toward achieving Net Zero, many are realizing that efforts to stem climate risk are unlikely to succeed on the systemic level if we leave behind the most vulnerable populations, communities and countries" (Lee 2021). Over the course of this chapter, we will furnish this big picture with further details.

THE CLIMATE FINANCE GAP
Everybody knows that climate change means big social changes, but few yet appreciate how drastic these really are

▶▶▶ *"The future is already here. It's just very unevenly distributed."*
— **William Gibson**

We need to close the climate finance gap, the gap between what *is* being invested, and what *should* be invested. However, a "finance gap" may feel a bit abstract, so we let's start by picturing the physical work of climate transition.

There are vast tracts of forests and wetlands to be restored. There are billions of buildings to be insulated for warmth. We will need hardened rail tracks that won't buckle during heatwaves. Wind farms sprouting from land and sea. Fleets of electric buses, trams, bikes, rolling through elegant new urban infrastructure. Flood barriers should be appearing everywhere. So should scaffolding—more frequent storms meaning repair work becomes a regular part of the rhythm of everyday life. Obsolete fossil fuel infrastructure must be retrofitted for new uses, or dismantled and reused. The meat industry must rapidly downscale, while also improving food security, and protecting the freedom and well-being of farmers and other workers. Many other industries must downscale too. Meanwhile, brand new sectors are burgeoning—precision fermentation, bioenergy, carbon neutral cement and steel, technologies for capturing carbon at source, or sucking it from the sky, still to be refined and rolled out at scale. The very molecular composition of the places where we live and work must be transformed.

Each of us may picture climate transition differently, and climate transition will look different in different places. These visions are not utopian: even at best, our world will still be beset by war, disease, natural disasters, and by shocks that today are barely on our radar. Yet in the midst of everything, the work of climate transition can still continue, and in ways that express the intelligence, the imagination, and the values of those who carry it out. The short version is: **everything must change**.

Such changes are starting to happen, but they are still very limited. The stories told by our governments contradict the stories told by our markets. All over the planet, humans are as busy as ever, creating and transforming things. Yet such activity does not yet encompass our collective wisdom about what needs to be done. Instead, we continue to build a future of hurricanes, famines, floods, the collapse of social and political structures, the spread of uninhabitable deserts. The 2020s are the decade of delivery, yet we are in the grip of an ominous inertia. So how can we do better?

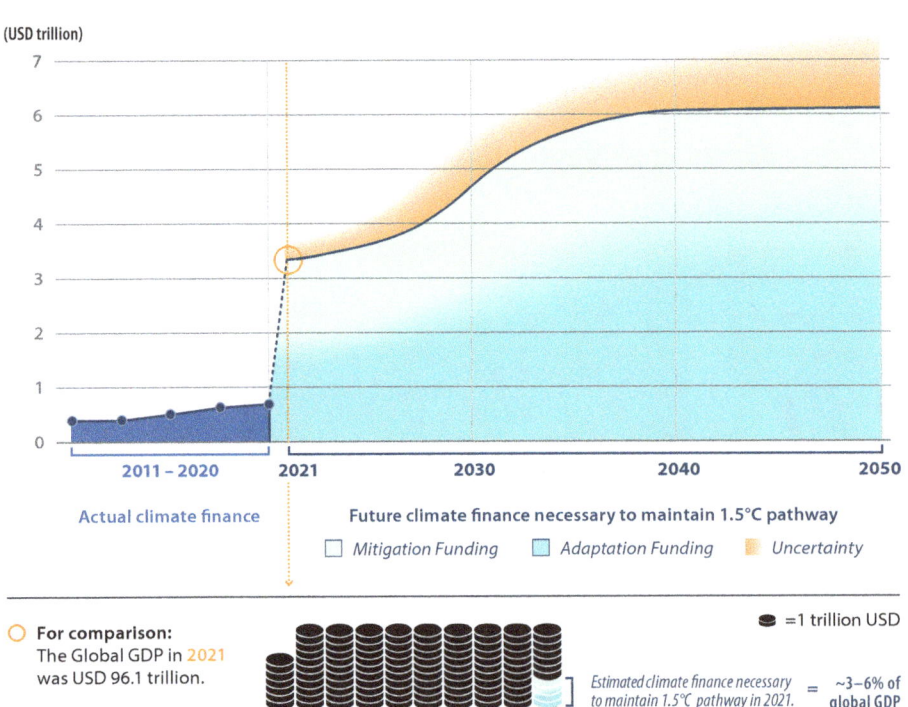

The IPCC estimates that 3-6% of the global GDP need to be invested by 2030, which means increasing investment three- to six-fold from recent levels. Delays in climate action push up future costs; uncertainty over the level of climate finance increases with time.
Sources: the Global Landscape of Climate Finance (2021), IPCC AR6 WG3 (2022) report, Worldbank.org.

Figure 1. Future climate finance necessary to maintain 1.5°C pathway.

More finance needs to be allocated to climate transition, and to be allocated very differently.

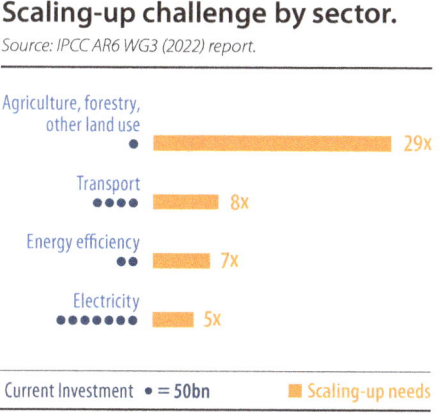

Scaling-up challenge by sector.
Source: IPCC AR6 WG3 (2022) report.

Figure 2. Investment in agriculture and forestry needs to increase 29-fold by 2030, while investment in the electricity sector needs to increase five-fold.

Spending more money will be a good start. The IPCC estimates that we need to invest 3-6% of global GDP[1] by 2030, which means increasing investment three- to six-fold from recent levels. Figure 1 gives an estimate of how much finance is needed to meet internationally agreed climate targets.[2]

As well as investing more, we need to **invest *differently*** (see Figures 2 and 3). For example, the IPCC highlight the lack of priority given to adaptation investment, despite explicit demands from Least Developed Countries. A study of sixteen African LDCs revealed that the desired ratio is on average 2:1 for adaptation to mitigation finance, with countries such as Eritrea and Uganda requesting in their intended Nationally Determined Contributions (NDCs) that approximately 80% of climate finance be used for adaptation (IPCC AR6 WGII). Such requests have gone unheeded, with the majority of funds getting earmarked for mitigation.

Investment also needs to better address its own negative side-effects (cf. McCauley et al. 2019; Sovacool et al. 2019). Some climate policies could **damage biodiversity** (e.g. bioenergy crops or mining for green transition), for example. Furthermore, **some climate policies could have devastating effects on the economies of developing countries**. As the world decarbonises, developing countries may struggle with higher energy prices, with agricultural and pastoral land lost to offsetting schemes, and with falling export revenue under environmentally sustainable regulatory regimes. Loans to deliver climate transition may burden debtor countries with hefty repayments, or come with technical assistance or other conditions that erode these countries' policy autonomy. Some scholars call the current climate finance policies **"green structural adjustment"** for the Global South – an extractive system designed to benefit foreign investors and companies who stand to make money from green transition (Bigger and Webber 2021). While these and other exposures may be concentrated within developing countries, they are also **problems for the entire world**. As the IPCC states, "Flows of commodities and goods, as well as people, finance and innovation, can be driven or disrupted by distant climate change impacts on rural populations, transport networks and commodity speculation" (IPCC AR6 WGII).

The potential for risks to cascade globally through social, political, economic and ecological channels is intrinsically difficult to model. Nonetheless, significant transfers of finance from richer countries — for example, through a robust international carbon market designed and governed for this purpose — can go a long way toward addressing it. However, such flows are currently very limited. Indeed, net flows are reversed from what they need to be: currently finance is still leaving some developing countries in greater quantities than it is entering (cf. UN ECA 2015, UNCTAD 2020, Ndikumana and Boyce 2022). The reasons for this are complex, and include loopholes in tax systems, perceptions of better investment opportunities in the Global North (because of infrastructure, legal systems, labour markets), legacies of colonialism, and unequal distribution of power in the global economic system.

---

1 This amount is comparable to the largely hidden economic support for fossil fuels, estimated to be around 7% of the global GDP by the IMF, accounting for subsidies and externalities.

2 Clearly, estimating the costs of climate transition is no simple task. A recent net zero pathway from the International Energy Agency (IEA) estimated that finance would have to rise to about $5 trillion by 2030, and remain at that level until at least 2050. McKinsey has recently produced a very high estimate: "Capital spending on physical assets for energy and land-use systems in the net-zero transition between 2021 and 2050 would amount to about $275 trillion, or $9.2 trillion per year on average, an annual increase of as much as $3.5 trillion from today" (Krishnan et al. 2022). The McKinsey methodology has however come under criticism for its assumption of a very slow roll-out of renewables and a heavy reliance on negative emissions technologies (NETs) to accomplish alignment with Paris goals. Of course, speaking of the 'cost' of climate transition can also be misleading in some contexts, since the cost of not transitioning is much higher: some analysts prefer to frame climate transition as a net windfall.

CHALLENGES TO REALLOCATING CAPITAL
We need to allocate more money overall to climate transition, and we need to allocate it more efficiently and justly. What are some of the current obstacles?

> ▶▶▶ *"Given the urgency and the challenges of the climate crisis and the just transition, sustainable and ESG investing alone will not deliver us a 1.5 degree C and a just transition. We believe that all industries will need to be transformed, and will need to innovate, and that certainly includes the finance industry."*
> — **David Blood**, Just Climate

Finance is a human invention, yet it is currently failing to serve vital human interests, let alone the interests of the wider natural world. More finance needs to be allocated to climate transition, and to be allocated very differently. There are a number of stories being told about how this transformation of priorities could happen. Within the financial sector, the prevalent story tends to involve **improved assessment and communication of climate risk**.

Companies and financial institutions already have legal obligations to disclose the risks they are facing. Until recently, such disclosures have tended to ignore climate. However, **mandatory climate risk disclosures**, often based on the TCFD framework, are now gradually coming into play. Informed by such disclosures, financial institutions should be able to deploy their extensive expertise in analysing risk, and modelling potential future scenarios, to reallocate investment. Investor coalitions such as GFANZ can make good on their climate promises.

Crucially, such disclosures may also provide more policy levers for **governments, regulatory bodies, and central banks**. By gaining a clearer view of the landscape of climate risk, they can formulate more effective policy to alter that landscape. Furthermore, when policy is enacted to make climate-aligned activities more appealing, mandatory disclosures should help its signals to propagate quickly and effectively to a range of actors.

Let us say that we accept this story. What would be the biggest challenges? Even if we assume widespread political will to make the necessary changes, the **global nature** of climate transition creates complex challenges, with the potential for policy in one jurisdiction to undermine policy in another. Another challenge is that practically everyone involved will be developing new capabilities. Few companies have robust climate risk management. Key tools and standards (e.g. from the ISSB) are works-in-progress. Likewise, central banks face challenges integrating climate into their existing policy remits.

Relying on companies to report on their own climate risks can also give rise to **conflicts of interest**. This means that **audit and accountability** mechanisms should also rapidly evolve to address potential for negligence or fraud. Similarly, **independent data collection, analysis and communication** of climate risk need to improve. The three major ratings agencies, and the four major professional services networks, are among those leading the charge here: however, favoring these incumbents means trade-offs with more participatory and potentially more just approaches (cf. Newell, Geels, and Sovacool 2022).

More broadly, support is needed to strengthen public sphere institutions (including media, social movements, education and research sectors, and civil society organisations) capable of robust independent investigations and research, to reduce the reliance on self-reporting. **Greenwashing** is currently rife within finance. This means that investors may already think they are helping to fund climate transition, when really they are not. Greenwashing refers to when something is labelled as environmentally sustainable in ways that are false, misleading, or exaggerated. There are many types of greenwashing, from mildly misleading upbeat messaging to concerted attempts to spread disinformation. For our purposes here, a key point is that the current regime of Environmental, Social, Governance (ESG) metrics is nowhere near fit-for-purpose. One recent study found that the vast majority of equity funds labelled ESG-friendly were not aligned with the Paris climate targets. Strikingly, more than half of climate-focused ESG funds were also not aligned (InfluenceMap 2021). In the EU context, the EU's Corporate Sustainability Reporting Directive (CSRD) which came into force on January 1st 2024, the EU Taxonomy, and a recently proposed EU regulatory framework on the transparency and integrity of ESG rating activities are all expected to bring more rigour into ESG reporting and result in greater influence of ESG and climate considerations in investment decisions.

Climate finance also faces many other **"supply side" challenges**, especially in the developing world. What this means is that even when finance is available in principle, would-be funders and investors often find themselves frustrated by a lack of appropriate projects. For example, markets for green investments such as low-carbon steel, or electric car infrastructures, remain relatively small and fragmented. In the case of public sector sources (the majority of finance available), much more is theoretically allocated than is actually disbursed. Reasons for this include the high proportion of loans (rather than grants), and unfeasible co-financing requirements (Savvidou et al. 2021; IPCC AR6 WGII).

What could happen if the supply of climate transition projects doesn't keep pace with investor demand? Even the extremely modest recent increase in climate finance has led to **fears of a green bubble**. If this happened, it would imply money pouring into low-quality projects which don't deliver the carbon reductions the world is counting on (*The Economist* 2021).

It is also crucial to recognise that **many things that need to happen are simply not profit-making opportunities**. Investor coalitions like the Glasgow Financial Alliance for Net Zero (GFANZ) place great store in blended finance solutions, where private finance can team up with philanthropy or the public sector to fund such projects. Blended finance comes with its own host of practical and ethical complexities. For example, critics of blended finance point to a shortfall in transparency and accountability, with trade-offs that should be debated by stakeholders getting transformed into mere technical problems to be "solved," sometimes behind closed doors (Tan 2022).

Finance doesn't only need to flow where it is needed — **finance also needs to move out of investments that are not climate-aligned**. There is little likelihood of this happening while these investments are reliable and profitable. And (complicating matters further) there are also cases where it would be better to *increase* finance to such activities temporarily, for the purposes of decarbonising them.

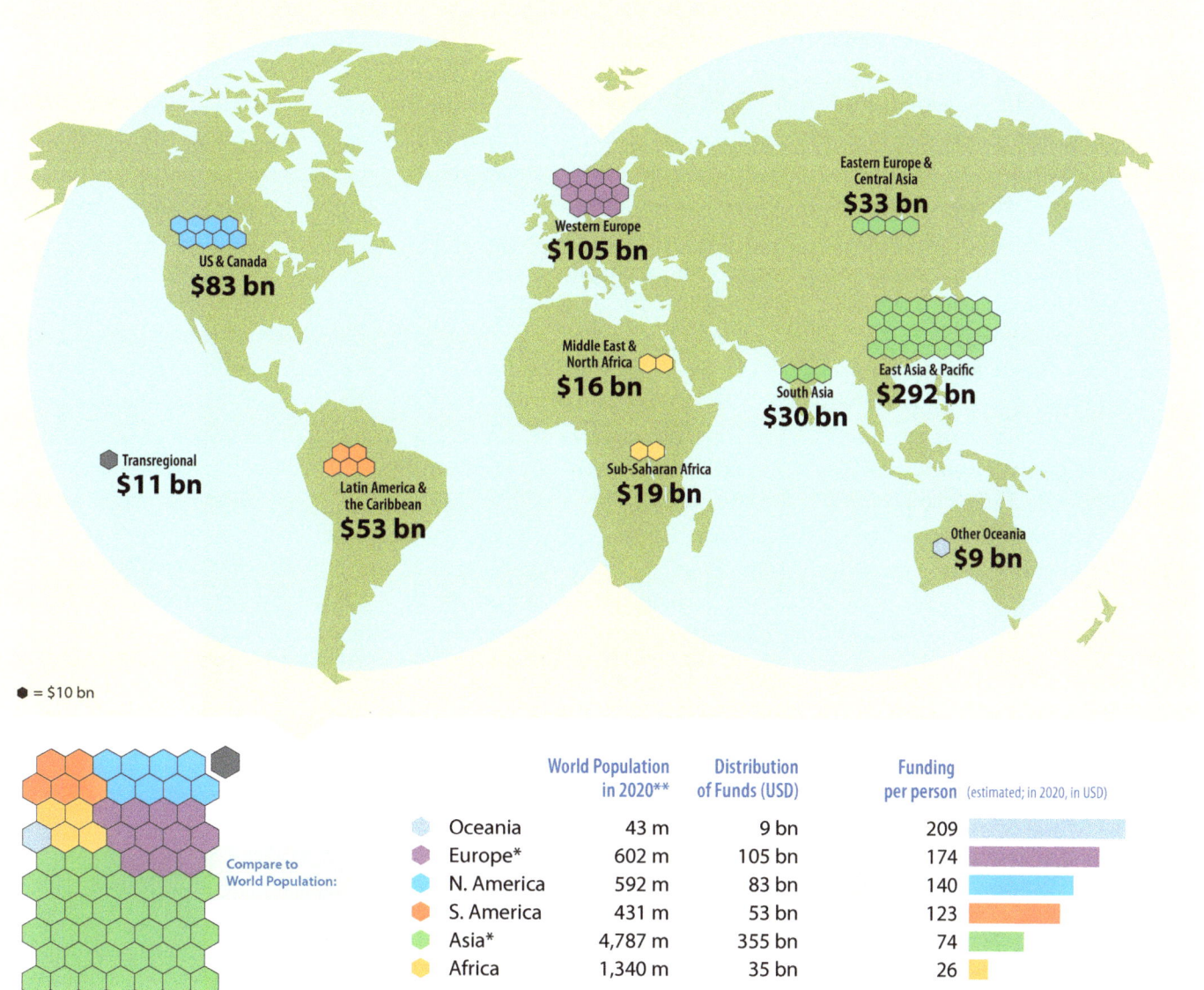

Figure 3. Destination regions of climate finance.

THE MAJOR PLAYERS IN GLOBAL FINANCE
Who's who in the world of finance

If you are new to the topic of finance, by now you may have many questions about the different players involved. In this section we offer a quick introduction. It may feel quite dense: but you can always refer back to it later. As you read this section, you could ponder:

- Where are the levers of change? In other words, how might each type of actor influence reallocation of finance for climate transition (positively and/or negatively)?
- Who does each type of actor primarily communicate with?

On the sell-side, **companies** sometimes need to raise finance to do what they do. To raise this finance, they sell financial products, including shares and bonds, to investors. They often collaborate with **financial institutions**, such as **investment banks**, in order to do this. 'Financial institution' is a fairly broad term, which typically covers investment banks, as well as commercial banks, insurance companies, and other types of businesses that deal with financial products. **Governments** and **municipalities** also issue bonds. Financial products can also sometimes be issued directly, without extensive involvement by financial institutions.

On the buy-side, these financial products (also called securities, assets, or instruments) are bought and sold by **investors**. Types of investors include pension funds, sovereign wealth funds, endowments and foundations, insurance firms, mutual funds, hedge funds, private equity, government-affiliated authorities, development banks, and high net-worth individuals or families. Many of these are **institutional investors** (also often known as **asset owners**), organisations that invest on somebody else's behalf. They have a legal obligation to act in their clients' best interests (**fiduciary duty**), which in principle goes beyond narrow short-term financial interests (there are efforts in many national jurisdictions to explicitly redefine 'fiduciary duty' in the context of ESG). Such institutional investors may manage their own assets, outsource management to specialist **asset managers**, or do a mix of both.[3]

A **stock exchange** is an institution which matches buyers and sellers of financial products. When a private company "goes public" by listing its shares on a stock exchange for the first time, this is called an Initial Public Offering (IPO). There are around twenty major stock exchanges in the world. Some of the larger ones include the New York Stock Exchange, Nasdaq, the Shanghai Stock Exchange, and Euronext. Stock exchanges have listing requirements, which form another potential point of intervention for climate alignment: e.g. more rigorous disclosure criteria for IPOs, or banning certain types of listing.

Investment decisions are partially guided by **rating agencies** (Moody's, S&P and Fitch) who evaluate the risk of financial products and assign them ratings. They can give investors guidance over and above what companies disclose about themselves, or other information that is publically available. In addition to ratings agencies, there is a burgeoning ecosystem of firms providing data and analytics related to climate, sustainability, and even social justice, supporting some financial actors to do their own ESG-style analyses or to drill into specific details of interest. As one recent study put it: "Disclosure could be terrible, yet markets could still price risks appropriately if large traders, credit rating agencies, and others found alternative ways to incorporate climate-related information" (Bolstad et al. 2020). However, the same study found that rating agencies had yet to adequately reflect climate risk in their ratings. Furthermore, when ratings do reflect climate risk, this isn't necessarily transmitted into actual market prices.

Investment decisions are also guided by **certification schemes** like the Climate Bonds Initiative. Approved verifiers are hired by the

Where are the levers of change?
Who does each type of actor primarily communicate with?

---

[3] There are one or two simplifications there. For example, sometimes assets are managed and owned by the same entity, and there can be various other layers that make the "actual" owner of a financial asset difficult to identify or define. Some of the biggest and best-known financial institutions also work both on the sell-side and the buy-side (for instance JPMorgan Chase and Goldman Sachs). Sometimes 'asset owners' has a narrower definition, e.g. pension funds, SWFs, endowments and foundations. In this chapter, we use a fairly broad definition. An even broader definition might include the other ways that governments own assets (e.g. state-owned enterprises; Development Finance Institutions; cf. OECD 2021; CFI 2021). Likewise, sometimes 'investors' means specifically shareholders, as distinguished from creditors and/or lenders. Again, in this chapter we use the words 'investment' and 'investor' in a broad and inclusive sense.

companies and financial institutions that issue financial products, to check those products against the certification standard. Certified green bonds currently represent only a small fraction of the total global bond market.[4]

Approved verifiers include the Big Four **professional services networks** (Deloitte, Ernst & Young, KPMG and PwC). These same actors also shape the landscape by selling audit, tax and legal advisory services, and by conducting market and future trends research. Together with smaller **consulting firms**, they also support companies to undertake climate-related disclosure, and to interpret the relevance of climate science to their business.

Then there are **investor coalitions** (e.g. Glasgow Financial Alliance for Net Zero, Climate Action 100+, PRI, and many others), networks of asset managers and asset owners. These coalitions are formed to influence the companies they invest in. The coalitions engage investee companies to improve their sustainability, set expectations, and divest if they are not met.[5] As shareholders, they also generally have the power to choose which auditors to appoint.

Every currency zone also has a **central bank**. Central banks have special discretion over the creation and production of money. They also perform some regulatory functions. In most cases, a central bank is associated with one county: for example the Federal Reserve is the central bank of the USA, the Bank of Uganda is the central bank of Uganda, and the Bank of England is the central bank of the UK. In a few cases, there are central banks overseeing monetary policy for multiple countries, including the European Central Bank (member states of the EU) and the Bank of Central African States (member states of the CEMAC). At one time, most central banks were more closely integrated into governments. Today most central banks have become more independent, on the basis that their main function is to stabilise prices, and regulate the money supply to prevent economies from either having not enough capital or more capital than can be productively deployed. The influence of elected officials is seen as potentially detrimental to these purposes. However, different central banks have different degrees of independence, and all are ultimately answerable to legislatures in the long term.

Central banks exist at the interface between the public sector and the private sector. Central banks such as the Bank of England and the European Central Bank have been particularly active in promoting the inclusion of climate factors in stress testing (see later in this chapter). The expectations of central banks also tend to be closely monitored by the providers of risk assessment tools and data, and other consultancy services, so the signals sent by central banks can have wide ripples throughout the finan-

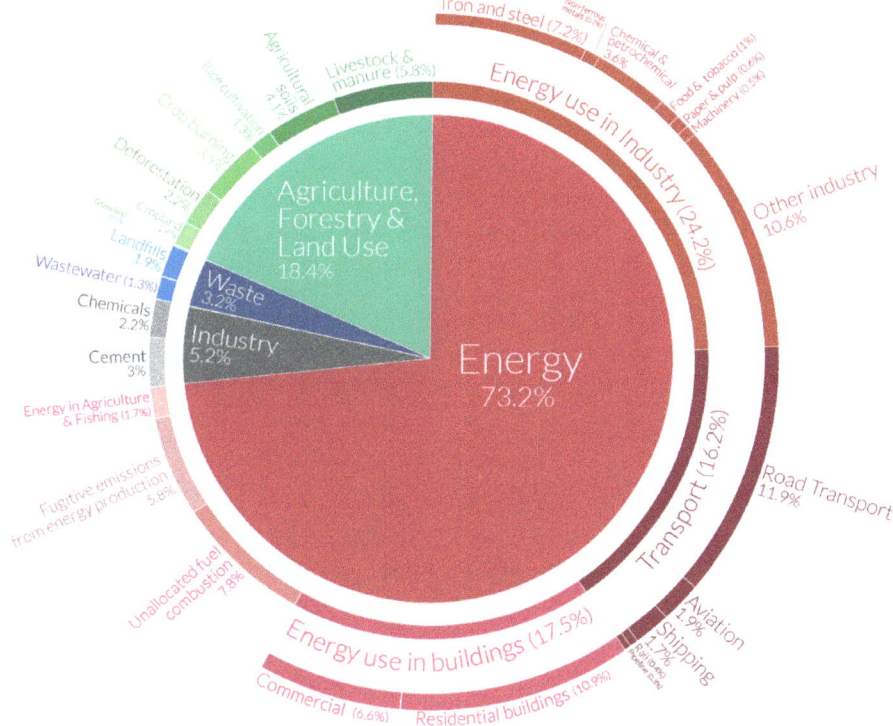

Figure 4. Global greenhouse gas emissions by sector.

---

[4] An even smaller fraction of these finance projects in Africa, where the climate finance gap is most stark. "The dynamics of developing a green bond market are complex and require sound technical expertise. There is a general lack of capacity in Africa, especially within the regulatory agencies and stock exchanges" (Marbuah 2020).

[5] Divestment is often treated as a last resort, and there is an argument that it is not effective in a liquid market (i.e. if there are plenty of less scrupulous investors happy to buy up the divested shares). But there are also good arguments in favour of divestment. While the impact of divestment can be difficult to isolate from other factors, in at least some cases it seems to have led to higher borrowing costs for the companies in question. Partial divestment can also create dialogue with companies that have been resistant to engagement. Furthermore, ruling out divestment, or perpetually deferring divestment, can damage the credibility of the engagement.

cial system. Currently, the majority of climate finance comes from **the public sector**. One sometimes hears that governments cannot afford climate transition, or that technology will make it cheaper to address in the future. This is misleading, insofar as it ignores predictions that the costs of delaying transition are exponentially increasing. Some governments might unwisely ignore the wider space of policy options available to them. Governments can tax and spend. They can borrow and spend. They can redirect subsidies, or create incentives through tax breaks. They can invest in research, ensuring that new technologies are developed and implemented in the public interest. They can build infrastructure necessary for climate transition investments to be profitable, or legislate that it should be built. They can socialize risk through blended finance, thereby de-risking projects from the investor perspective. They can lead by transitioning public sector operations, in some cases lowering costs for all by tapping into economies of scale. They can reallocate vast state-owned pension funds.

They are ultimately in charge of how the money supply itself grows, and for what purposes.

What *is* true, however, is that decisions about exactly how to finance climate transition can have complex consequences. These consequences involve **controversial topics**, including inflation, exchange rates, different methods of measuring carbon footprints (territorial vs. consumption), the balance of power between different countries, and the relationship between states and markets. Furthermore, policy levers are much more available to some governments than to others. Many developed countries have optimistic but not implausible net zero targets, relatively established national carbon accounting practices, intermediate milestones, and carbon markets and institutions that can allocate finance in line with their goals. There is still much work to be done, but at least within the borders of countries like the UK, emissions have been falling, and will account for the smaller and smaller share of future global emissions.

For effective climate transition, however, finance must be urgently channelled to developing countries, most of which are in a very different situation. These are the countries that will account for the majority of future emissions, and have large populations vulnerable to climate impacts (see Figure 5 for comparison between geography of populations affected by climate change in the future vs. research to study these impacts). Developing countries have huge current infrastructure deficits, while urbanising at unprecedented rates: the cities will need added housing stocks, food, water, energy, heating and cooling, transport and wastewater treatment, flood control and other types of resilience engineering. Their current access to finance is woefully inadequate for global climate transition goals. Little materialises from corporate bond markets, and not enough from private markets in general. What does come through usually passes via **development banks** primarily set up by the richer countries. Development banks can be wholly public, or can have a mix of public and private ownership. They invest in private sector projects in low and middle-income countries. A **bilateral development bank** is set up by one country, e.g. the Netherlands Development Finance Company FMO or the UK's CDC Group. A **multilateral development** bank is set up by several countries, e.g. the World Bank or the African Development Bank. With some exceptions (e.g. EBRD, IFC), development banks make their loans at the sovereign government level.

When the public sector and private sector collaborate on investments, it's called **blended finance**. This may also refer to collaborations between philanthropic funding and the private sector. A related term is **concessional finance**, which is effectively when worthwhile projects in developing countries get cheaper access to capital.

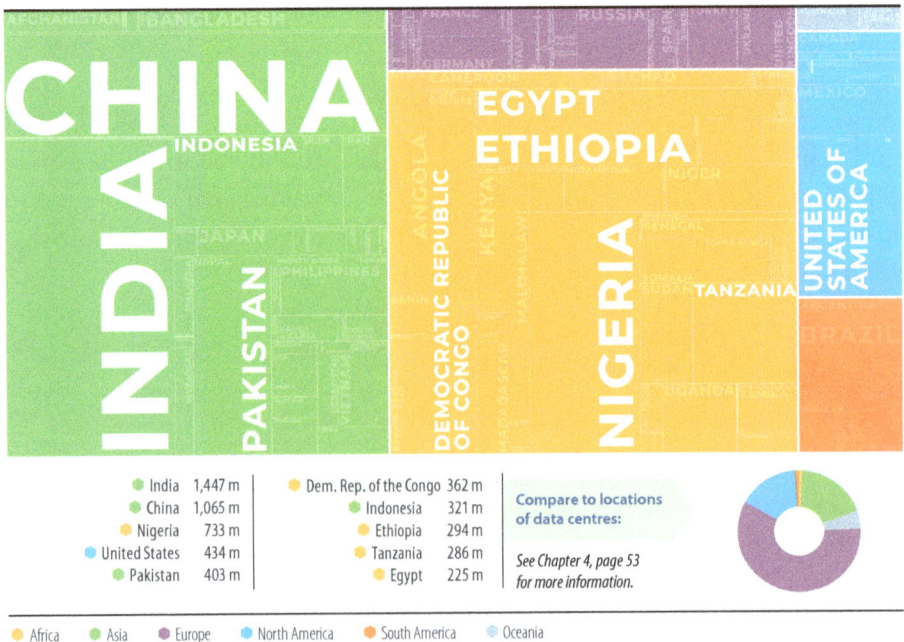

Population projection: **Top 10 countries with the largest population in 2100.**
(Source: Our World in Data)

- India 1,447 m
- China 1,065 m
- Nigeria 733 m
- United States 434 m
- Pakistan 403 m
- Dem. Rep. of the Congo 362 m
- Indonesia 321 m
- Ethiopia 294 m
- Tanzania 286 m
- Egypt 225 m

Compare to locations of data centres:
See Chapter 4, page 53 for more information.

- Africa
- Asia
- Europe
- North America
- South America
- Oceania

Figure 5. Geographies of affected populations vs. climate risk research.

There are other relevant actors (brokerage firms; alternative trading systems; cryptocurrency exchanges; market makers; specialists; unions; insurers; the Bank for International Settlements; taskforces like the TCFD, TNFD and TSVCM; regulators and agencies like the Securities and Exchange Commission; and others), but that should be enough to give you a flavour. There is one thing they practically all have in common: **they are all interested in risk**. Like it or not, these actors have tremendous influence on shaping wider understandings of climate risk.[6]

---

6   To further help you find your way around the world of finance, the Laudes Foundation offers a useful online map: maps.laudesfoundation.org.

CLIMATE FINANCE KEY TERMS
SEE ALSO "INTRODUCTION" IN THIS CHAPTER.

ALTERNATIVE INSTRUMENT
An investment that doesn't fall into any 'conventional' class of investments such as shares, bonds, or cash. Examples of alternative instruments include hedge funds, commodities, private equity funds, land, intellectual property, and real estate.

ASSET
Something owned by somebody. In finance, assets usually refers to investments such as bonds, shares, or funds.

AUDITOR
Usually this means the independent firm appointed to verify a company's mandatory reporting (which traditionally has consisted of financial accounts). There is significant confusion around the actual legal obligations of auditors, often referred to as the "audit expectation gap." Loosely speaking, auditors have a narrower remit and less accountability than is often assumed. A lot of big companies are audited by one of the Big Four professional services networks (Deloitte, E&Y, KPMG, PwC). The Big Four have come under some criticism for "still quietly signing off unmodified accounts for businesses that have no clear future in a net-zero world" (Landell-Mills 2021).

BOND
Buying a bond is a very common way of making an investment. In some ways, this is similar to a loan. Loans are already widely understood — somebody borrows money from you, then pays it back with interest. The main difference with a bond is that it is *tradeable*. In other words, if you buy a bond directly from the bond issuer, then you have essentially lent them money. You can then hold the bond until it matures, and in the meanwhile, collect interest payments (called coupons). What if you don't want to hold the bond? Then you are free to sell it to someone else, without needing the borrower's permission. Whoever you sell it to becomes the new bondholder. Bonds can be issued by companies, municipalities, or governments. To get a bit more technical, bonds have the following characteristics: maturity, face value, coupon rate, bond price, and yield. The yield of the bond normally reflects the returns of the bond (includes both the coupon payments and the bond price change). Since bonds are essentially contracts, they can get as complicated as imagination and law allow, e.g. involving factors like conditional clauses that get triggered only if environmental targets are met. Bonds and loans are both called debt instruments, distinguished from equity instruments.

CARBON PRICE
Carbon pricing seeks to capture the actual costs of GHG emissions and ensure that the responsible party pays for them. To do this it needs to value both damage being done to the climate right now, as well as the cost for future generations. This is sometimes called the social cost of carbon. A carbon price can be established by means of a carbon tax, and/or other mechanisms like carbon trading. A carbon price is almost certainly a necessary instrument of climate transition, however, the extent to which a carbon price alone can drive change is a subject of controversy. Furthermore, there is no universal agreement on how to estimate a carbon price. One reason is that most (although not all) economists think that harms or benefits in the future should be weighed less heavily than harms or benefits right now, but disagree by how much (what 'discount

rate' should be applied). Further, historical emissions that account for the vast majority of the carbon budget have not been subject to a carbon price. The wealth, technology and infrastructure effectively acquired at 'subsidised' prices are concentrated in the Global North, and translate directly into lower economic costs of future decarbonisation of respective economies. And, as IPCC AR6 WGIII notes: "For a globally uniform carbon price, carbon intensive and energy exporting countries bear the highest economic costs because of a deeper transformation of their economies and of trade losses in the fossil markets."

CARBON MARKETS

Carbon markets are mechanisms where certain actors can pay for the right to emit carbon. Carbon emissions allowances can be acquired via auctions, free allocation, or other-the-counter (OTC) transactions. Carbon markets commonly use a cap-and-trade mechanism, where polluters are given an emissions allowance over a predetermined period. The idea is that regulators cap the overall level of emissions low enough to drive climate transition, while the trading aspect creates flexibility in how we get there. If a market participant has a surplus allowance at the end of the period, they can sell it to another polluter to allow them to emit carbon. There are Compliance Carbon Markets (CCMs), where national, regional, or international regimes regulate carbon allowances (e.g. European Union Emissions Trading System), as well as Voluntary Carbon Markets (VCMs).

CLEAN DEVELOPMENT MECHANISM

A mostly lacklustre attempt to support green investment in developing countries, set up in 2006. The CDM was intended to give developing countries flexibility in how they met their Kyoto Protocol targets. By meeting CDM requirements, countries were able to earn Certified Emission Reduction credits (CERs), with one credit being equivalent to one tonne of CO_2. These credits can then be sold to wealthier countries, who claim the saved emissions as part of their own efforts to meet international emissions targets. The CDM is still active, although its mandate technically expired in 2020, along with the Kyoto Protocol.

CLIMATE TRANSITION

The changes we need to make to mitigate climate change and to adapt to its effects.

CSR

Corporate Social Responsibility. CSR doesn't really have a strict definition, but generally refers to all practices undertaken by companies to have a positive influence on society and the environment. Within finance, the term ESG (Environmental, Social, and Governance) now tends to be a more common term than CSR, since it provides ways of measuring CSR performance.

DEGROWTH

Degrowth (also known as post-growth) represents a diverse set of political, social and economic theories united by their criticism of increasing Gross Domestic Product (GDP) as an overriding policy goal. GDP currently measures government spending, household spending, investments and exports; it leaves out a lot of the things that everyone agrees they want, such as care for the elderly or a healthy environment. An economy re-organised on degrowth principles will not necessarily imply negative GDP growth (although in some cases it might, especially in the Global North). Degrowth proposes using metrics that more accurately reflect the wellbeing of people and planet.

DISCLOSURE

A disclosure is when a company communicates something about itself, or what it knows about its situation. Often used in the context of a company's legally mandated reporting.

ESG

Environmental, Social and Governance. ESG is about companies looking beyond profits and growth, and seeking to identify and quantify the benefits and harms they create for all stakeholders. ESG and sustainability are very similar terms, and the two are sometimes used interchangeably. The terms do have distinct histories, and ESG is more relevant within finance. ESG information is disclosed by companies, and also compiled by independent analysts (e.g. Refinitiv). ESG scores can be used in the decision-making of financial market participants. For instance, ESG scores are used to screen companies for inclusion in ESG funds, or factored into investment decisions and supported by shareholder engagement. At the time of writing, there are deep and well-documented concerns that ESG information flows are incapacitated by systematic greenwashing and a lack of true climate additionality. Investments in ESG-friendly portfolios are not doing the necessary work of climate transition, and there is a risk that they create a false sense of progress.

EXPOSURE

Exposure is a key concept in risk analysis, e.g. the IPCC currently divides climate risk into hazard, vulnerability, exposure. In the financial world, exposure tends to mean the amount of money that an investor has invested in a particular financial product. So it is the amount of money the investor stands to lose. But exposure does not necessarily have negative connotations: you might hear someone talking about wanting to increase their exposure to something, meaning they want to own more of a financial product which they think will go up in value. Within finance, exposure is sometimes essentially a synonym for risk. Furthermore, higher exposure (risk) implies higher returns (positive or negative). There are therefore some subtle tensions and discrepancies between the way many climate scientists and finance professionals tend to think about exposure.

EXTERNALITY

Carbon emissions are the most important example of externalities we are considering here. Whenever an actor (e.g. a company) values something differently from how society as a whole values it, economists refer to the difference as an externality. It is external to the decisions that the company will make, and therefore those decisions will be suboptimal, considered from the standpoint of society as a whole. Externalities can actually be positive, as in the case of some education or research and development (R&D), or they can be negative as in the case of GHG pollution. Economists and policymakers are understandably interested in how externalities can be removed, and factored into a company's decision-making. Carbon taxes exist in various jurisdictions as a way of doing this: if set at the right level, they can potentially make the company pay a cost that reflects the cost to society. Of course, the question of how valuable something is to "society as a whole" is always philosophically and ethically complicated.

FINANCE

There is no easy way to define this term, but it is generally to do with ways to raise money to carry out various kinds of projects. The word capital is sometimes (not always) used in similar ways.

FINANCIAL INSTITUTIONS

Investment banks, retail banks, insurance companies, etc. See "The Major Players in Global Finance."

FINANCIAL PRODUCTS

Shares, bonds, (index) funds, derivatives, etc., that can be bought and sold. Just think of a financial product as an investment contract seen from the investor's perspective. For example, a company wants to borrow some money so it can undertake a project — so it issues bonds for investors to buy. These bonds are one kind of financial product. The investor can hold onto them and receive interest on the loan, or they can sell them on. Terms very similar to *financial product* (but not identical) include *instrument* or *security* or *financial asset.*

FUND

A fund is a type of financial product. It is a portfolio of investments (e.g. shares, bonds, cash, other funds) owned by a pool of investors. Three important kinds are mutual funds, hedge funds, and exchange-traded funds (EFTs). Additionally, these types of funds can be created as an **index fund**, which means that the fund's composition is based on an index: a kind of weighted model built out of the changing values of financial assets selected according to some criteria (e.g. the major companies in a particular region or sector). ESG index funds are funds that have been assessed based on sustainability criteria.

INDEX

A mathematical construct that captures the performance of a set of financial products. These products will have been selected according to some criteria and weighted according to some methodology. This allows the creation of index-tracking funds, which (roughly speaking) allow investors to invest in a market as a whole, or in a particular 'themed' subsection (e.g. tech funds).

ISSB

International Sustainability Standards Board.

LABEL

A financial product may have one or more labels to attract investors. Some labels involve third-party certification. Unfortunately, the current labelling regime is far from being fit-for-purpose. Financial products that are labelled sustainable are not necessarily sustainable; climate finance products are not necessarily aligned with Paris Agreement commitments, etc. At best, labels enable comparisons between similar products.

MAINSTREAM REPORTING

The information that certain organisations are required to produce by law. Historically, financial reports have been the main component. Efforts are underway to integrate climate transition (and other sustainability issues) into mainstream reporting.

MATERIALITY

Roughly speaking, something is material if it is important enough to mention (especially important enough to mention to investors and other stakeholders). Financial reporting and sustainability reporting have traditionally had distinct concepts of materiality. Roughly speaking, financial reporting treats an issue as material if it could reasonably affect the decision-making of a stakeholder, especially the financial decision-making of an investor. Sustainability reporting tends to treat issues as material to the extent that they impact stakeholders or the environment. There is currently a lot of new thinking happening around materiality. It remains to be seen whether a concept of materiality can be operationalised that will force material climate risks and opportunities to effectively coincide with the necessary action for climate transition.

NET ZERO

A situation in which carbon emissions are reduced, and any remainder are offset by additional carbon removals elsewhere in the system. Net Zero targets are mandated in some national legislations but remain voluntary in others. Many large companies have similarly set themselves Net Zero targets with specific deadlines. Achieving global Net Zero by 2050 is projected to give about 50% chance of limiting warming to below 1.5 degrees this century, provided the total emissions before 2050 are also within the carbon budget.

PATHWAY

We often hear talk about pathways to Net Zero. The crucial point here is that, in order to stay within the remaining carbon budget, an entity can't just achieve Net Zero by a particular date, but also has to consider what it cumulatively will emit along the way. A later Net Zero date does not necessarily imply higher than an earlier one: it all depends on the speed with which emissions fall. More broadly, the word *pathway* can also be used as a rough synonym for *strategy* ("our pathway to deliver net zero by 2025 in collaboration with our stakeholders") or for *scenario* ("these three sets of assumptions can be used to build potential three pathways").

SHARE

A share is a type of financial product. It is an ownership stake in a company. Shareholders have certain voting rights, and from time to time receive dividends (a portion of the company's profits), but are not personally liable for the company's debts. Most shares can be easily bought and sold. Also known as stocks. There are many different kinds (e.g. common and preferred stock), but we won't get into the detail here.

SUSTAINABILITY

Sustainability encompasses all kinds of social and environmental awareness. It is closely related to ESG, and sometimes used as synonyms. But sustainability is the broader of the two terms, and has wider recognition across society.

SUSTAINABLE FINANCE

A financial product (e.g. a bond) that takes ESG factors into account. Green finance takes environmental issues specifically into consideration. Climate finance seeks to support climate change mitigation and/or adaptation projects.

TCFD

Taskforce on Climate-related Financial Disclosures.

VOLUNTARY REPORTING

Information that companies publish about themselves which is not legally required. In the past there has been a strong "two tier" effect, with investors paying far less attention to voluntary reporting than to mandated mainstream reporting. This remains mostly the case, although efforts are underway to include climate-related information (and other sustainability information) in mainstream reporting.

VULNERABILITY

Is a degree to which a system is able to cope with an adverse event, slow negative trend, or an increase in variability. Vulnerability is determined by financial resources available to cope with the unexpected and adaptation finance more generally. Allocating resources to reduce vulnerability can significantly lower climate risk.

AN ANATOMY OF CLIMATE RISK
A few broad categories

For climate finance, a key issue is the extent to which market prices do or don't reflect climate risks. This is relevant for investment focused on mitigation and adaptation, of course, but also for *any* investment, since any investment is likely to impact and be impacted by the future of the climate.

Furthermore, as we have already highlighted (see 'Challenges to Reallocating Finance'), some climate risks and opportunities are deliberately engineered by policymakers. A new law or regulation will show up in an enterprise's risk management practices: the risk of being non-compliant, the risk of reputational damage or fines and penalties, the risk of adapting less effectively than one's rivals to the new rules, and so on. In this sense, **climate risks can be instruments of governance**.

Let's remind ourselves of some of the big categories of climate risk. First, physical risk and transition risk are generally differentiated. **Physical risk** refers to direct exposure to hazards created by the changing climate: losses from damage inflicted by wildfires, floods, hurricanes; working days lost from heatwaves; supply chains disrupted by storms, and so on. These impacts are already happening, and economic losses are predicted to continue to increase exponentially with warming. Physical risks are also considered in terms of the persistence or frequency of their hazards. An **acute hazard** refers to something short term, such as an extreme weather event. A **chronic hazard** is a longer-term trend, such as rising sea levels, or rising average temperatures.

Transition risk refers to changes in the socio-economic sphere. For example, carbon prices or other policies aimed at steering capital towards a sustainable economy can change the financial position of a company, the value of its assets, its operating costs, or expected rewards on investment. Transition risks may be driven by policy changes, changing investment priorities, consumer behaviour, or technological innovation. Like physical risks, transition risks are already creating impacts. By and large, companies have been paying far more attention to transition risks than to physical risks, partly because transition risks are more tractable and operate on shorter time scales. Sometimes transition risks within the legal system are considered separately as **liability risks**. Currently it seems that exposure to climate litigation is both underestimated by companies historically responsible for emissions, and very poorly priced in by the markets.

Many risks may involve feedback loops or cascade effects. **Stranded asset risk** is the risk that an asset will lose its value, with unburnable fossil fuel reserves being the classic example. The scope of potential stranded assets also extends towards other sectors — e.g. Internal Combustion Engine Vehicle Fleets in the transportation sector.

The risk of stranding and the timeframes involved depends multiple factors including the nature of the asset and the legislative environment governing it. This currently leads to the primary interest being fossil fuel

---

RISK as a function of **hazard** *(events and their likelihood and severity; e.g. how hot, or how much rain)*, **exposure** *(who is affected)*, and **vulnerability** *(how sensitive people are when exposed)*.

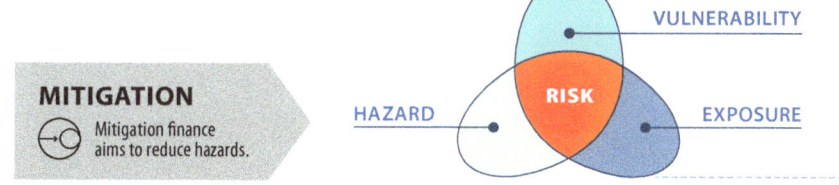

An **acute hazard** refers to something short term, such as an extreme weather event. A **chronic hazard** is a longer-term trend, such as rising sea levels, or rising average temperatures.

Vulnerability is a degree to which a system is able to cope with an adverse event, slow negative trend, or an increase in variability. It is determined by financial and other resources available to cope with the unexpected. Allocating resources to reduce vulnerability can significantly lower climate risk.

Exposure refers to who and/or what is at risk — e.g. financial investments, or humans and other living creatures, ecosystems, infrastructure, buildings, belongings, activities, institutions, cultures, etc. Financial actors do not always see exposure as a negative, insofar as increased exposure can sometimes mean increased returns.

Figure 6. Adaptation and mitigation finance and climate risk.

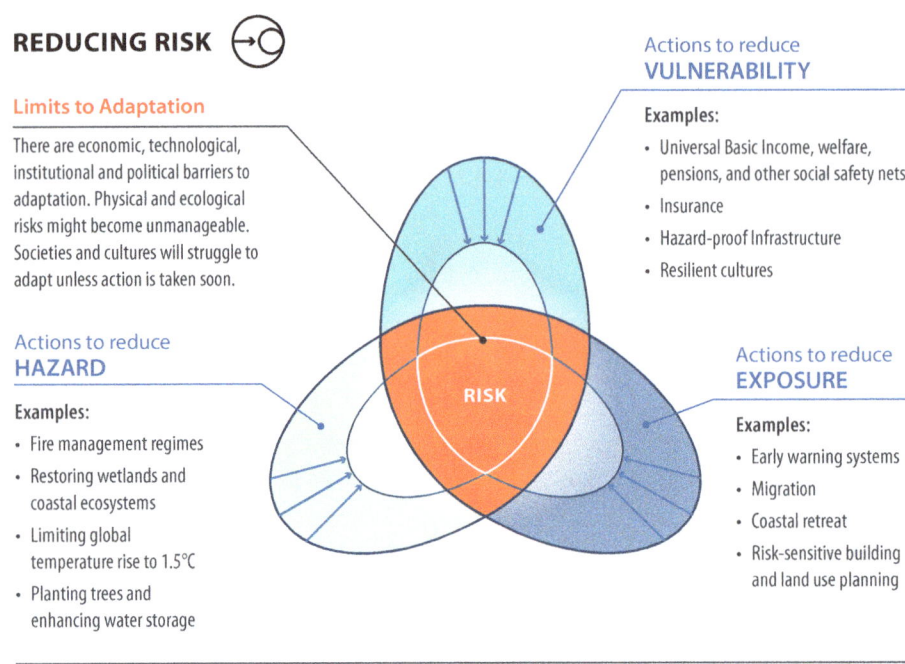

Figure 7. Reducing risks.

reserves, transportation and distribution infrastructure, and power infrastructure. But the scope of assets that could become stranded may grow over time. Such stranded assets might then have knock-on effects on the wider global economy, creating transition risks even for companies without any direct exposure to those assets (see "Stranded Assets"). Picture the global financial crisis of 2007-2008, or the Great Depression of the 1930s — or more optimistically, picture an era of intensified **creative destruction**, in which resilience means not only absorbing or adapting to shocks, but also using shocks as opportunities for transformation (see "Scoping the Policy Space"). One way to attempt to address the complex interconnections among risks is with **scenario analysis** that integrates physical and transition risks (see "Scenario Analysis and Stress Testing").

A climate risk is typically conceptualised as an interaction between a **hazard** (or sometimes **driver**), **exposure**, and **vulnerability** (Figure 6). So far we have mostly been talking about hazards. Exposure refers to who and/or what is at risk — for example humans and other living creatures, ecosystems, infrastructure, buildings, belongings, activities, institutions, cultures, etc. Vulnerability refers to the conditions which make these exposed elements susceptible (and/or resilient) to harm. The terms are defined so that it is possible to be exposed to a hazard yet *not* vulnerable: for example, living in a floodplain with excellent flood defence systems, or if you are a farmer, having a perfect insurance policy against crop failure.

A frequent failure of climate risk communication is to focus on hazards, without addressing exposures and vulnerabilities. Vulnerabilities can often be reduced significantly by investing in adaptation, including technological and infrastructural adaptation, insurance, disaster warning systems, and poverty reduction (Figure 7). These risk concepts can operate at many different scales — a region or country, a city, a sector, a portfolio, a company, an asset. Of course, they do operate in different ways in different contexts. But to generalise just a little, the complexity of climate risk is pushing past the limits of traditional methods of horizon scanning and risk management, and the associated decision support tools.

UNLOCKING PRIVATE SECTOR CLIMATE FINANCE
One or two promising signs suggest how private climate finance might start to flow

So far this chapter has been quite gloomy. But there are many brighter notes too. Let's not forget that the world has more than enough money for climate transition. First, there is **public sector finance** (see "Scoping the Policy Space," near the end of this chapter, for more detail).

There is also **private sector finance**. Driven by the IPCC, civil society actors, environmental social movements, and other factors, private sector finance is showing signs of cultural shift. New technologies are also transforming the financial landscape, with promising possibilities of large returns on investment that is aligned with climate transition.

Investors have formed large coalitions to drive climate transition. "Climate alignment" has emerged as an overarching concept. The new **Glasgow Financial Alliance for Net Zero** (GFANZ) has over $130 trillion in assets under management.

Its membership consists mostly of asset managers and asset owners, all of whom are committed (at least on paper) to science-based net zero targets.[6]

---

6 "Under management" meaning that the signatories in many cases don't own the investments themselves, but rather are investment banks and the like who are investing money on their clients' behalf. Moreover, some of their assets are locked up in ways that would make them difficult or impossible to reallocate (e.g. in mortgages). See "The Major Players in Global Finance" for more.

Other signs of a shift include:

- Financial institutions integrating climate risks and opportunities into their mainstream risk management, e.g. via stress testing.
- Developments in portfolio alignment tools, used to gain more holistic understandings of climate performance.
- Growing recognition of the scale of greenwashed financial products, and the need for better labelling.
- Growing recognition of science-based targets.
- Better understanding of how sustainability and climate fit within financial institutions' fiduciary duty to clients.

However, we need to be clear who we are talking about here. These are investors, not philanthropists. They have shown no dramatic shifts in the levels of risk and return they deem acceptable. Their interest in climate transition is at least partly motivated by the enormous earning potential it represents.

So how do investors intend to accomplish climate transition? Investors want **climate transition to be priced into the financial markets, reflecting risks and opportunities**. Ideally, the financial system should be reformed so that the risk-return profile of every investment is consistent with a just, resilient, and 1.5 degree future. Assets that are incompatible with such a future should be phased out altogether, at an appropriately rapid pace. In the ideal version of events, it would be foolhardy or impossible to invest in non-aligned ways, even if you tried. However, pricing in climate transition is extremely challenging, especially in the narrow sliver of time available.

One big step would be a **global tax on carbon**, set at an ambitious level, subject to appropriate mechanisms of review and revision. There are already carbon taxes in some jurisdictions. By itself, such a tax will be highly regressive in many parts of the world (developing countries whose economies are much more dependent on fossil fuels), so it needs to be accompanied by large international financial transfers, and policies to protect vulnerable groups from side-effects (such as higher prices or job losses). **Cap-and-trade schemes** are also being tried by many countries in order to impose a price on carbon. But even in the absence of a global carbon tax, there are areas where useful progress can be made.

Investor coalitions like GFANZ have several tools to help price in climate transition. They can talk to companies to set expectations and timeframes; as shareholders of companies, they can exercise voting rights, and propose resolutions (**engagement**). If companies keep falling short, investor coalitions can sell their investments (**divestment**). Partial divestment can also be used to catalyse more meaningful engagement.

Transparency is another key area. The way companies report climate risks, opportunities, and impacts is set to change, becoming more mandatory, more standardised, and more subject to independent assurance. This is true for both financial and non-financial companies. The new International Sustainability Standards Board (ISSB) and EU Taxonomy on sustainable activities are intended to help improve transparency.

However, **the promised revolution in climate and sustainability reporting deserves a cautious welcome**. To really happen, it will need to be properly resourced and governed across society. Initiatives to improve data quality and transparency always sound like a good idea, but sometimes the reality can be a proliferation of bureaucracy which does not really serve these goals. Independent audit and assurance is currently rare, and conflicts of interest are rife. The applicability of traditional financial audit methodology and expertise to climate disclosures has not yet been carefully explored. In particular, it is far from clear how "materiality" — which has always been key to how financial disclosures work — can be made fit-for-purpose for climate disclosures. Crucial aspects of climate risk are difficult to consistently quantify. Forcing companies to think in great detail about climate risk, and to disclose their findings, may also help to drive them to more sustainable business practices. It may even help, to some extent, to reallocate finance. But there is a danger that we **expect too much of improved reporting**. The main importance of improved reporting is not what it can accomplish by itself, but that it can support **other kinds of regulation and policymaking**.

Meanwhile, emerging climate data analytics may mobilise more sophisticated modelling and larger, richer data-sets, to produce better intelligence about climate risks and opportunities (see "Emerging Trends in Scenario Analysis"). Yet insofar as this occurs, it also gives rise to challenges around the ownership, interpretation, and accountability of this intelligence (see "Challenges for Scenario Analysis" and "Dynamic Materiality"). Where technical experts and decision-makers have substantially different understandings of the key models being used, this fits the definition of deep uncertainty. Lacking unequivocal recommendations, decision-makers must be guided by open dialogue with stakeholders and communities, as well as the ethos captured in vision, mission, and core value statements. In short, across business, finance, and policy, effective climate decision-making means *both* evolving existing risk management practices, and being prepared to step outside of risk management frameworks altogether.

Here, it is also worth noting that not all elements of climate transition — in the sense of a just and resilient transition to net zero — can be articulated as climate risks and opportunities. Climate risks and opportunities are signals about what climate transition requires. But they are not perfect signals that we can simply follow to arrive at a 1.5 degree future. Ben Caldecott makes a similar point when he describes the difference between Climate Risk Management (CRM) and Alignment with Climate Outcomes (ACO):

> *"While there is some overlap between CRM and ACO they have different objectives and often different results. [...] CRM can make little or no contribution to ACO [...] These synergies between ACO and CRM are clearly important, and it makes sense to maximise them at every opportunity. But that is different from saying there is always a positive relationship between them both, or that CRM automatically and inevitably leads to ACO. It does not."*
>
> (Caldecott 2020).

Finally (and this is the really interesting part), to the extent that pricing climate risk and opportunities into global markets *can* be achieved, it implies tremendous disruption. But it would be a disruption that in principle could be controlled — rather than a disorderly climate transition, or the devastating chaos of a failed transition[7]. In fact, let's give that disruption an even more optimistic spin, and call it an era of intensive **creative destruction**. That means it is not only the 'creative' but also the 'destruction' side of things that demands of us new concepts, new approaches, innovative policy design, and more effective and democratic decision-making. Business and finance are human inventions, and can be transformed to support a flourishing human and more-than-human world. New industrial policies such as Biden's Inflation Reduction Act, and new regulations such as the EU taxonomy, seek to turbocharge innovation in the business and financial spheres, which are also anticipating flourishing – green transition is also an economic opportunity that global financial centres and industrial powerhouses are keen to capitalise on. See "Scoping the Policy Space" below for a little more on creative disruption.

---

7   At COP28, the world reached an agreement to transition away from fossil fuels, making 'transition chaos' less likely.

WHO BENEFITS FROM FRAMING CLIMATE CHANGE IN TERMS OF FINANCIAL RISK?

BY ITS NATURE, climate transition expertise draws on many different kinds of knowledge and skills. There are implications to emphasising the financial risk management aspects of climate transition. The overarching narrative which does so is not politically and ethically neutral. Rather, it embeds assumptions about how decision support and decision-making for climate transition will be distributed across different geographies, and across different sociological groups within those geographies. To take one simple example, the UK has a well-developed financial services sector, and therefore (on this prevailing paradigm) is well-positioned to provide the world with cutting-edge climate risk intelligence. To take another example, any company's appointment of a Climate Transition Lead may be relatively more likely to prioritise experience of financial risk management, against other relevant forms of expertise such as environmental science or stakeholder engagement (which are nevertheless taken into account). In fact, such a role is probably not really called Climate Transition Lead — but rather Climate Risk Lead. These affinities can feed into, overall, a decision-making system that reinforces systemic racism by relying on expert credentials correlated with social, political, educational, and cultural backgrounds that are unrepresentative for likewise systemic reasons.

IMPROVING CLIMATE-RELATED REPORTING

Companies are increasingly being required to change the way they communicate climate-related information. It's an evolution that deserves a cautious welcome

▶▶▶ *"Companies need to do more. Corporate reporting should address the company's impact on the environment, the resilience of its business model and the impact of climate change on its financial statements"* (FRC 2020).

There is a diverse ecosystem of approaches to pricing or qualitatively assessing climate risks, and little is settled about terminology, scope or methods for such analyses. A few important worth mentioning include ISSB standards, TCFD recommendations, SASB standards, GRI standards, EU Taxonomy and other taxonomies, SBTi standards, CBI standards, GHG Protocol, and the Oxford Principles.

The snappy version is: **efforts are underway to make climate risk part of companies' mainstream reporting**. Mainstream reporting refers to the information that companies are required by law to communicate about themselves, mostly on an annual basis. These reports are aimed at investors (and to some extent regulators). In the past, financial statements have always been the core of mainstream reporting.

Climate-related information, when provided, has been part of **voluntary reporting**. This means it has been more closely connected with marketing, branding, and stakeholder relationship management. Voluntary reporting can also be part of how companies push themselves to change. Further, collecting and analysing ESG-related data does not only serve public-facing transparency—many internal company findings might stay hidden so as not to risk releasing proprietary information that might harm competitiveness, but still be useful to the company's internal efforts to reform. Some companies have used voluntary reporting to become more competitive in a future characterised by tighter climate regulation and more detrimental climate impacts.

As many companies have anticipated, voluntary standards are being replaced by mandatory ones, partly via the guidelines and standards created by the **Taskforce on Climate-related Financial Disclosures** (TCFD) and the **International Sustainability Standards Board** (ISSB). The ISSB is very new, and its approach is firmly rooted in financial accounting. The ISSB is governed by the IFRS Foundation, who also oversee the International Financial Reporting Standards (IFRS), accounting standards used across most of the world, with various local flavours. The USA is the big exception to IFRS—US public companies use GAAP, which does not specifically refer to climate risk, but is commonly interpreted to include such risks if they are material.

What if the company in question is an investment bank or other financial institution? When a company's decisions involve the activities of thousands of other companies, each at a different point in its climate transition journey, disclosure becomes complicated. That's where **climate analytics** such as **portfolio temperature assessment** come in. Available data on the companies can be combined with climate models to assess consistency with different global net zero pathways (discussed further under "Scenario Analysis and Stress Testing").

The TCFD and ISSB work should also hopefully dovetail with, at a minimum, new regulations on the horizon in the United States from the Securities and Exchange Commission (SEC), and in the European Union through the Corporate Sustainability Reporting Directive (CSRD) and Sustainable Finance Disclosure Regulation (SFDR). A promising outcome would be for the ISSB to become the global standard that integrates the best aspects of its many forerunners, and introduces a few bold new ones.

There are certainly challenges to shifting climate risk into mainstream reporting. As we'll see, mainstream reporting and voluntary reporting have fairly distinct concepts of **materiality** (meaning, roughly speaking, what is important enough to mention). The attempts to combine them, such as double materiality and/or dynamic materiality, are very much works-in-progress (see "Double Materiality" and "Dynamic Materiality").

Mainstream reporting and voluntary reporting have distinct concepts of materiality...

CLIMATE-RELATED REPORTING IN CONTEXT
Even if climate reporting does improve, its role in climate transition is not completely straightforward

▶▶▶ *"In deciding whether to provide resources to an entity, users need to understand how sustainability-related risks and opportunities are likely to affect the value, timing and certainty of the entity's future cash flows and therefore users' assessment of enterprise value"*

— *ISSB Prototype* 2021

So will disclosure that is more standardised, more mandatory, and more science-based help to reallocate private finance, in ways that are consistent with a decent chance of keeping warming below 1.5 degrees? Or could disclosure "improvements" end up redirecting capital in maladaptive ways, for example, away from developing countries struggling with the bureaucratic costs of reporting? Similarly, the burden of disclosure regulations might put innovative smaller enterprises, SMEs and start-ups at a disadvantage when they try to secure funding. Another way in which these new regulations can prove maladaptive is by stymying investment in carbon-intensive activities such as mining which have a complex but significant role to play in the green transition.

The evidence that reporting is feeding valuable information to the markets so far is discouraging. In 2020 Carbon Tracker surveyed 107 companies and found that a total of zero followed good practice on climate risk reporting, and that 70% of reports were disconcerting in quality.[8] Whether the expected mandatory reporting based on best practice (e.g. fostered by the Climate Financial Risk Forum (CFRF)) turns out to be transformative remains to be seen.

Let's remember that **reporting is only one of the potential levers** for reallocating capital. Tax incentives, regulatory policies, institutional capacity, labour markets, resource prices, litigation risk, and technological developments have arguably far more influence. Active stakeholder engagement and grassroots pressure could play important roles, and hence are indispensable as tools to promote a climate transition that is not only quick but also just.

Reporting is certainly linked to these many other areas. Anything that makes a company's activities more legible is likely to be empowering for stakeholders and enabling for policymakers. But such linkages are stronger in some geographies than in others.[9] In the Global South, where there tends to be greater emphasis on development and adaptation, improved reporting may have relatively weak impact on decarbonisation specifically.

More broadly, wherever public concern for climate change is weak, improved transparency may be met with indifference from investors, consumers, and policymakers alike. Furthermore, in countries whose public sectors are heavily invested in fossil fuels, it may not be credible that better data on its own will drive divestment. If the importance of such investments is their role in funding vital public services or development projects, or if there are overriding geopolitical considerations, decision-makers may not see any relevance in the improved data.

SCENARIO ANALYSIS AND STRESS TESTING
To deal with the giddying complexity of climate risk management, companies are making greater use of climate scenario analysis and stress testing

In a recent survey of financial firms, nearly 80% of respondents said regulators now require reporting of climate-related risks. Two-thirds reported significant increases in staff working on climate risk. The availability of data and reliable models were cited as key short-term concerns, with regulatory uncertainty also significant (GARP 2022). **Climate scenario analysis** is used by many corporations and (increasingly) financial firms, to manage risks and opportunities. Simply put, scenario analysis means imagining the future in order to plan for it. Scenarios are snapshots of future states of the world, or pathways that describe how events may unfold over time.

Some scenarios, such as the IPCC's Shared Socioeconomic Path-

---

8   https://carbontracker.org/reports/flying-blind-the-glaring-absence-of-climate-risks-in-financial-reporting/

9   However, these variations are by no means fixed. The EU's proposed Carbon Border Adjustment Mechanism (CBAM), which would impose tariffs on imports according to their carbon intensity, is an example of the EU's efforts to exert its economic power and project the influence of its emerging reporting regime onto other geographies, particularly in the Global South.

ways (SSPs), are described as **global reference scenarios**. They can aid in communication and collaboration among multiple actors, by making analyses more comparable. Scenario analysis often involves large amounts of quantitative data, modelling, and assumptions. However, more free-form approaches can also be useful: storytelling about the future that asks, "What if?"

Scenarios inform critical thinking—they are not necessarily "predictions," and it is not always the case that the most likely scenario is the most useful. Often an interesting scenario will reveal how entities or assets which appear quite similar in the present may diverge in the future. Just like participatory processes, good scenario analysis is often iterative rather than static. That is, scenario analysis can be conducted regularly, and the learnings from each analysis can be fed into the way the next one is run. At the same time, scenario analyses can be continually refreshed in line with the latest expectations and projections. The environmental, economic, and social data that underpins scenario analysis is continually evolving. Scenarios need to reflect these changes.

One way that financial institutions use scenario analysis is to investigate how a portfolio will respond to different hypothetical impacts. This is known as **stress testing**, and involves modelling the response of the portfolio and the wider financial system in which it is embedded. **Climate stress testing** is usually underpinned by historical observation data and climate modelling, as well as potential transformations of the policy environment. Stress testing can also encompass, for example, natural capital and biodiversity risk. Central banks, especially via Network for Greening the Financial System, have been key in encouraging the use of stress testing.

Similar techniques can be used to extrapolate a future scenario from what is being done in the present. **Portfolio temperature assessment** is a modelling approach that combines data on companies' emissions with science-based scenarios, in order to calculate the degree of global warming implied by a particular portfolio of investments (Smith 2021). For example, an assessment can conclude that a portfolio is consistent with 2.7 degree warming rather than the

WHO IS ON THE FRONTLINE OF CLIMATE RISK?

OVER 40% OF THE WORLD'S POPULATION ARE "HIGHLY VULNERABLE" TO CLIMATE CHANGE, according to the IPPC. A recent HSBC report suggests that the ten most vulnerable countries are India, Pakistan, Bangladesh, Philippines, Sri Lanka, Columbia and Mexico, Oman, Kenya and SA (Paun, Acton, and Chan 2018). Distinguishing physical risk and transition risk, however, paints a richer picture (see table).

Of course, other methodologies could produce different lists. It is surely significant that none of the world's very poorest nations (by GDP per capita) appear on these lists, whereas some of the wealthier ones such as Australia, Qatar, Kuwait, and Saudi Arabia, are deemed especially vulnerable to climate transition risk, because their economies are so entangled with the fossil fuel industry. That's not to say that these wealthier countries are not confronting significant physical risks too. For instance, the Gulf region faces extreme risks around increased temperatures, potential for vector-borne diseases, and stress on water and agriculture. Nonetheless, it may be worth taking such lists with a pinch of salt. Might the relative limitations of climatic and economic data from Africa, and related lower reliability of climate risk projections, have unduly lessened the perception of risk to the continent, in monetary terms?

HSBC RANKING	PHYSICAL RISK	TRANSITION RISK
1	Philippines	Bahrain
2	Thailand	Kuwait
3	Pakistan	Qatar
4	Sri Lanka	Oman
5	Bangladesh	S. Arabia
6	Vietnam	Kazakhstan
7	India	Malaysia
8	China	Columbia
9	Oman	Australia
10	Columbia	UAE

goal of 1.5. Leading methods include Arabesque, CDPWWF Temperature Rating Methodology, Lombard Odier, MSCI, Paris Agreement Capital Transition Assessment (PACTA), Transition Pathway Initiative (TPI), and S&P Trucost, and there is significant variation in the approaches taken. Portfolio temperature assessment does not provide an answer to (and according to some critics, could even incentivise) practices of **brownspinning**, in which carbon intensive assets are sold to new owners, without actual reductions in global carbon emissions.

Portfolio temperature assessment is one methodology to improve alignment to **science-based targets** — a set of formal guidelines developed by SBTi to help align portfolios with reductions needed to stay below 1.5 degree Celsius warming (Yan et al. 2021). So far adherence has been lacking: one review of the Climate Action 100+ initiative, with $35 trillion assets under management, found that only 9% are committed to science-based targets, and even fewer have concrete plans to meet them.

The increasing recognition of science-based targets within business and finance is worth celebrating. For now the term "science-based" is closely associated with the work of a specific body, the SBTi. However, it is also worth noting that scientists can hold different views, and therefore there can in principle be different targets claiming to be science-based (sometimes with different degrees of legitimacy). Scientific expertise's self-regulatory mechanisms may well come under new pressure as the influence of science-based targets grows.

CHALLENGES FOR SCENARIO ANALYSIS
The models and data which underlie scenario analysis have many limitations, and it can be challenging for technical experts to communicate these to decision-makers

Interestingly, there are historical links between scenario analysis and fossil fuels: Royal Dutch Shell was an early developer of the methodology with its 'Shell Scenarios.' In recent years, the TCFD has played a key role in the spread of climate scenario analysis, recommending the use of scenarios that are plausible, distinctive, consistent, relevant, and challenging. Not only is scenario analysis being more widely used, its methodologies are also evolving. However, there are still many serious challenges and limitations to be addressed.

Modelling climate risk requires detailed and highly resolved climate models, macroeconomic models, and assumptions about future technology and society and how quickly these can change. Like any complex models, these models embed political and ethical values, which need to be made explicit for scrutiny and debate. Similarly, **models used in scenario analysis give rise to challenges around interpretation and communication** (Gambhir et al. 2021). Decision-makers who are not technical experts may acquire a false sense of precision and confidence. On the other hand, decision-makers may dismiss the most inconvenient results as mere technical glitches.

Different methodologies currently in use rely on different scenarios ranging in their assumptions and scope. Although a narrower range of scenarios would not be desirable, this does create obstacles for comparing risk assessments that differ greatly in terms of depth (Bingler and Colesanti Senni 2020). One of the key issues in matching scenarios to investor interests is timing—climate scenarios are generally long-term, extending to 2050 or 2100. For many investors, 'long term' may mean anything beyond the next five years. Reputational risks do generally have longer time horizons (Fulton and Weber 2015), though of course we should be cautious of relying too heavily on reputation as a driver for good decision-making.

The common providers of climate scenarios include IPCC, NGFS, OECM, PRI Inevitable Policy Response (IPR), as well as various

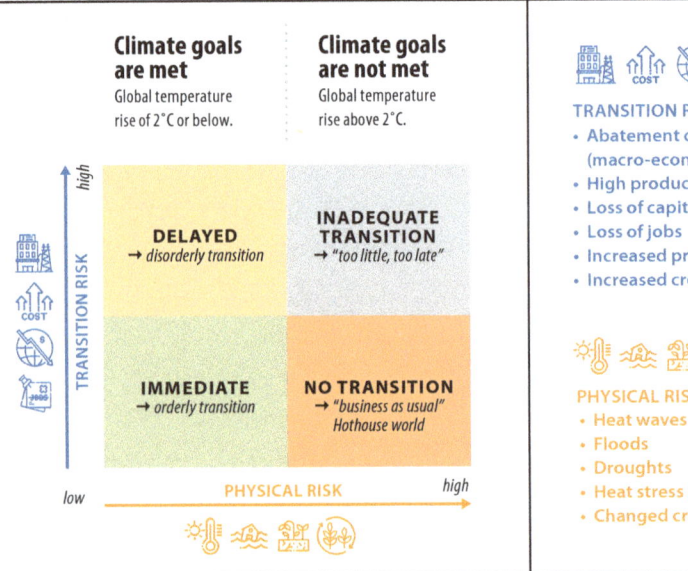

Figure 8. Mapping scenarios onto a grid of transition and physical risks.

commercial providers of risk assessments (2DII, MCSI, South Pole, Oliver Wyman, Moody's ESG Solutions, and others), who may develop bespoke scenarios (Figure 8 illustrates broad scenarios and risks).

In a recent survey of the scenarios used by UNEPFI, all scenario sets now include at least one future path that is compatible with 1.5 degree warming (Smith 2021). However, these 1.5 degree pathways often build in questionable assumptions, especially in the **overshoot scenarios** where 1.5 degree warming is temporarily exceeded before coming down to the target range (well below 2 degrees) by the end of the century.

In particular, most of them (including the influential EIA energy transition scenario) involve negative emissions technologies (NETs) being scaled up later in the century to remove large amounts of carbon (Smith 2021). For the large and long-lasting overshoot scenarios, the heavy reliance on NETs, extending into next century, may appear irresponsibly optimistic.

When we turn to the "**worst case scenarios**," we also find issues. Of the methodologies surveyed, all have been sticking with the out-of-date RCP 8.5 scenario to measure maximum physical risk (Smith 2021). This scenario, from the AR5 reporting cycle, was based on a lack of policy response together with high growth and fossil fuel use. This somewhat misleadingly became labelled the "business as usual" scenario, but more recent work has clarified that RPC 8.5 was always intended as only one potential future associated with a lack of policy response, higher than expected population and economic growth rates or high climate sensitivity — arguably, a pessimistic one. On the other hand, the IPCC AR6 scenarios do not reflect risk cascades and tipping points (see Chapter 3, Communicating around Tipping Points). In this respect, the widely used worst case scenarios may be overly optimistic.

EMERGING TRENDS IN SCENARIO MODELLING
Scenario modellers are wrestling with the complex interdependencies of climactic and socio-economic factors, while also seeking to represent more granular scales while accounting for uncertainty, and balancing interpretability, plausibility and salience

Practices around scenario modelling are evolving. Assessing exposure across global supply chains, markets and investments requires highly resolved models, sometimes on a scale as small as a meter. **Insurance companies** have the most experience with using such **downscaled models** in making detailed assessments of physical risk. They are now in the process of leveraging their experience to supply the rapidly growing market for future scenarios to price in climate risk at the level of products and services.

Scenario modelling is attracting public investment, often in collaboration with the private sector. The integration of climate data (physical risks) and socio-economic data (transition risks) continues to be a lively area of research.

Some scenario analysis focuses on either physical risk or transition risk. However, scenario analysis also often now compares multiple scenarios that **integrate physical and transition risks**, modelling their non-linear interdependencies (Gambhir et al. 2021). It is important for risk assessments to include not just primary impacts of climate change (heat waves, droughts, floods, rising sea levels, etc.) but secondary consequences that involve social or ecological changes (biodiversity risks, migration, conflicts, public health impacts, consumer behaviour, economic shocks, inequality, gendered impacts), as these are clearly pertinent albeit very difficult to model, especially while accounting for uncertainty (Harrington, Schleussner, and Otto 2021). These cascading effects can manifest on bigger scales (country by country) as well as local scales. For example, there might be useful quantitative predictions on sea-level rise, but the same scenarios probably do not account for the impacts of greater salinity on adjacent agricultural land or real estate, even in cases where it would be especially pertinent (Smith 2021).

These integrated approaches also seek to consider scenarios in terms of both costs and benefits, counting not only avoided physical impacts but also positive growth in innovation and net investments. However, in a world zooming past the parameter space that has been observed, justifying assumptions about the future for predictive macroeconomic modelling is even more difficult than deciding which assumptions about the physical world are likely to hold long-term (Gambhir et al. 2021).

Another area of development is the use of **digital twins** (detailed simulation-based versions of companies, cities, etc.), combining Machine Learning (a form of AI) with the accumulating wealth of data from sources such as satellites and other sensors. Although this is an exciting field, there are also good reasons to be cautious around these novel forms of analysis and decision support (see "Dynamic Materiality"). We've seen a growth in companies (RMS, Verisk, XDI) providing nearly real-time data on physical risks at a granular spatial scale as well as predictive modelling for scenario use in risk assessments. There is also momentum towards greater sharing of data and scenarios, as well as the development and adoption of **open source tools**, often as a result of collaborations between private companies and public research, for example, ClimInvest and EU EU's Copernicus Climate Change Service (E3CS).

There is great scope for improving the complexity, depth, consistency, and scope of various scenarios. However, all these developments are likely to make already opaque models less transparent and their assumptions, especially with regards to accounting for uncertainty, more difficult to communicate. Few scenarios in use have ever been peer-reviewed, and even more worryingly the providers of risk products themselves are not always able to identify key assumptions or understand their implications (Smith 2021). Many assessments are using the same publicly available climate data, but models differ greatly. The question of what the result might be were a different model used is rarely asked. The few experiments that were conducted suggest that model uncertainty is very high, and that it is rarely taken into account or communicated. There is a risk that investors who are aware of these issues will simply conclude that all assessments are uninformative, inconsistent, and offer little value for decision-making.

The general drive towards standardisation includes an evolution in best practices for specifying scenarios in terms of common assumptions, parameter ranges, and how uncertainty is taken into account. Standardisation will hopefully improve the **interpretability** of risk assessments in finance that is currently low, as a thorough recent review of the existing methodology notes (Bingler and Colesanti Senni 2020):

> *"Interpretability of the tool output is an important criterion for usability. Since the tool output is usually a figure, assumptions and drivers are easily hidden in a single number. However, these could have a significant impact on the final output. The output interpretability criterion thus assesses whether the model structure, key drivers, and assumptions are well reported by tool providers, and whether the tool output itself is communicated in direct relation to key assumptions and model limitations. This is important for tool users and other users of the tool output (like investors or supervisory authorities) to better understand what is actually measured by the tool, and what the output really tells."*

CLIMATE RISK AT THE ENTERPRISE SCALE
What's a day in the life of a risk professional?

▶▶▶ *"Risk managers are focused on protecting their investment portfolios from potential damages done by a worsening climate rather than helping prevent that damage from occurring in the first place."*
— **Tariq Fancy**, *former BlackRock chief investment officer for sustainable investing*

▶▶▶ *"Now the crux of complex systems, those with interacting parts, is that they convey information to these component parts through stressors …"*
— **Nassim Nicholas Taleb**, *Antifragile: Things that Gain from Disorder*

The scenario analysis described in the past few sections is just one part of **risk management**. Risk management involves actively identifying and assessing risks, dealing with them, and communicating about them (while protecting sensitive information). It is a form of decision-making under uncertainty. Managing a company's risks is also about managing its opportunities.

Many kinds of organisations — financial institutions, corporations, public bodies, and others — practice some form of risk management. On one level, risk management can reveal opportunities that help a company to better meet its objectives. On a deeper level, risk management might even help a company to recognise when it needs to reassess its objectives, and conduct deeper transformation. The bigger companies are, increasingly, being asked to share publicly how they manage risk. The Taskforce for Climate-Related Financial Disclosures (TCFD) asks companies to describe processes for identifying, assessing, and managing climate risks. The emerging standards of the International Sustainability Standards Board (ISSB) are following suit.

Financial institutions often have a variety of large teams specialising in many kinds of risk, and many niche roles within each team. A broad distinction can be drawn between **risk analysts**, who work with models and other tools to provide actionable information, versus **risk managers**, who focus more on controls, compliance, and decision-making.

In a **non-financial company**, risk management tends to be a different affair. Some companies choose to have no formal risk management framework at all. That doesn't mean they act with reckless abandon! — they may nevertheless follow processes which allow them to manage risk, even without using the concepts and terminology of risk management. However, many companies do use formal risk management frameworks. When a company uses Enterprise Risk Management (ERM), it seeks to embed risk management in all its decision-making. The aim here is for risk management not to feel like an extra set of hoops to jump through. Sometimes it works, sometimes it doesn't.

Depending on the industry, risk management may also be regulated to a greater or lesser degree, and may require the company to open its operations to various kinds of assessment or multilateral stakeholder agreement. So a day in the life of a **risk professional** really depends on the type of organisation they work for, where it is located, and their own specific responsibilities and experience.

Despite all this diversity, we can pull out two broad insights about putting climate risk into risk management. First, climate risk analysis is often conducted by technical specialists, or outsourced to consultancies, yet it informs decisions which senior leadership take on a broader basis. So effective communication between technical experts who provide the risk analyses, and the decision-makers who rely on them, is always a key challenge (see the chapter "AR6 and Modelling Uncertainty"). Given the complexity of the existing models and data sets, and their trajectory toward increasing complexity, this challenge is set to grow.

Second, climate risk introduces complex connections among more "traditional" risk categories, however these are taxonomised. Risk professionals of all kinds are probably interested in how climate risks transmits into the risk types they are familiar with (see "Climate Risk into Financial Risk"). But at the same time, they're interested in what may get lost in translation: those novel features of climate risk that require new tools, concepts, methods, or attitudes (see "Double Materiality" and "Dynamic Materiality").[10] For both these reasons, climate risk management needs both to evolve, and to be clear about what it is and is not doing to contribute to a rapid and just climate transition.

CLIMATE RISK INTO FINANCIAL RISK
How does climate risk translate into financial risk? And how doesn't it translate?

▶▶▶ *"[...] as climate-related events are uncertain and likely to grow over time, their evolution will arguably involve non-linearities and tipping points. As a consequence, the largely backward-looking traditional approach based on historical loss experience will probably fail to capture the forward-looking elements of these risks [...]"*
— *Financial Stability Institute*

Climate risk is challenging for risk managers, because it cuts across so many other risk types. Those in charge of managing a company's risk are ultimately interested in prioritising limited resources to mitigate risks and capitalise on opportunities. Should limited budget be spent on a new insurance policy? On flood fortifications? On procuring a new software system? Risk mitigation measures take money, so naturally risk managers are asking themselves, **"How do climate risks transmit into financial risks?"**

A similar question is being asked within financial institutions, by risk professionals using scenario analysis, sensitivity analysis, and stress testing. And a similar question animates the work of interdisciplinary teams of consultants building tools and models to assess exposure to climate risks for a range of clients and contexts.

How do climate risks transmit into financial risks? This is an important question, but also a dangerous one. Climate risk has many characteristics that are not adequately analysed in terms of financial risk, or any of the categories of risk covered by traditional tools. Climate change is a global problem, in a complex interconnected world. It can be challenging for any entity to see beyond the horizons of its immediate risks and opportunities. It's tempting to imagine that if each and every entity manages these, the world will be doing enough to align with the Paris Agreement. This is not the case.

But all is not lost. In simple terms, we need to do two things: expand risk management to encompass climate, while also being clear about risk management can and cannot solve. **Risk management can evolve.** Rapid and just climate transition requires companies to be realistic about their outward impacts, open-minded in picturing the future, and prepared

---

10 In a previous section, we explained that a risk can be broken down into hazard, vulnerability, and exposure. Is this the only way of thinking about climate risks? No it isn't—in fact, previous IPCC reports used a different framework, in which "vulnerability" and "exposure" were combined into one concept. Certain ISO standards break risk elaborate on vulnerability with other subcomponents: sensitivity, potential impact without adaptation, risk given adaptation. The three subcomponents risk we use here are useful abstractions, even if reality can seldom be so neatly subdivided. In practice, a risk professional would consider any risk holistically, and wouldn't talk about one subcomponent without talking about the others.

to make big changes to their business models. Double materiality and dynamic materiality are promising signs. More work is now needed for risk management to become a space where the most progressive insights of all stakeholders are identified, tested, and integrated. Second, it is important that companies (and the individuals who work in them) always think more widely, beyond risk management, to understand the realities of climate change and climate action. Starting points include: (a) each company's mission, values and vision; (b) deepening understanding of what climate analytics can and cannot provide to decision-makers; (c) participatory multi-stakeholder planning; (d) broader considerations of transformative climate justice.

STRANDED ASSETS AND IMPAIRMENT
What's the worst that could happen?

▶▶▶ *"The threat of climate-related risks stranding assets has spurred work by financial supervisors and central banks, who have announced new supervisory expectations and climate stress tests to help improve the solvency of individual financial institutions, as well as the resilience of the financial system as a whole."*
— **Ben Caldecott**

▶▶▶ *"It is difficult to get a man to understand something, when his salary depends upon his not understanding it."*
— **Upton Sinclair**

An **asset** is some resource that some entity, such as an investor or company, owns and/or controls. **Stranded assets** are assets that have lost their value, or have even been converted into liabilities. The topic of stranded assets first appeared within regulatory economics in the 1990s. In this period the topic was quite closely linked to the question of compensation. Stranded assets had something of a reboot in the 2010s, and are now closely associated with climate transition risk. One vivid example of asset stranding is when new regulation renders reserves of fossil fuels unburnable. However, asset stranding is also a much broader phenomenon. How will more sustainable agriculture impact the market for fertilizers? What might traditional pastoralists have to fear as it grows more profitable to reforest pastures to sink carbon? Or a shrimp boat owner from integrated mangrove-shrimp aquacultures? Ben Caldecott writes: "Assets become stranded all the time and this is often the result of the relentless process of 'creative destruction' in dynamic economic systems. New technologies replace old ones, new companies outcompete incumbents, and this constant process changes societies" (Caldecott 2015).

Stranded assets are important from a number of perspectives, including who decides which assets get stranded; who absorbs the loss and who compensates whom; how best to meet the energy requirements of development; how best to integrate stranded asset risk into corporate strategy and governance; how to ensure companies are transparent about risks of assets becoming stranded; and how stranded asset risk can become involved in risk cascades involving e.g. unemployment, lost profits, reduced tax income, credit liquidity, and overall financial stability of the global economy.

From a policy perspective, stranded assets again raise the question of how the costs and benefits of climate transition ought to be distributed. Kefford et al. (2018) suggest $541 billion worth of fossil fuel power plants could be stranded by 2060, with China and India the most exposed. Under what conditions should support be available to the owners or other stakeholders of stranded assets? What form should this support take? Any such policy requires very careful design. It has the potential to help align climate transition with the broader concerns of transformative climate justice. In the context of stranded assets accumulating in developing countries, REDD+ is the only existing international mechanism for compensation, its singularity highlighting the policy gap on climate justice. Perverse incentives should be minimised, so that no one is unduly rewarded for failing to foresee what they should reasonably foresee, and have the means to avoid.

[…] partial compensation or grandfathering—a way of gradually phasing out and supporting (potential) losers of the transition—can be employed to smoothen the transition […] But slow phasing-out policies—exempting carbon intensive industries from new rules—may at the same time sustain lock-in problems as the market becomes distorted and investments are not pushed towards low carbon technologies […](Bos and Gupta 2019)

When an asset gets stranded, what does this actually look like? How is it assessed and communicated in practice? Often it means the old value gets crossed out, and a new value written in — what accountants call **impairment**. The practice of testing for impairment is based on a body of quite technical laws, regulations, and formulae. Some assets have to be tested on a regular basis, and whenever there is an indicator of potential impairment; other assets, only when there is an indicator. At the moment, none of the rules about impairment testing are particularly climate-centric. A 2018 review of UK-listed companies noted that even though investors were "becoming increasingly interested in disclosure around climate change in impairment testing," the authors could only find "one company making overt references to the implications of adapting to climate change and other environment-related constraints or opportunities, such as shortages of key resources, foreseeable regulatory change or shifts in demand for the company's goods or services" (FRC 2019). IFRS IAS 36, which deals with impairment, does not mention climate factors triggering an impairment test. The Climate Disclosure Standards Board have published some high-level guidance for impairment assessment that is aligned with IAS 36 (CDSB 2022).

Impairments may sound a bit like confessions. The owners are admitting to themselves, and to everyone, that something is not worth what they expected. Confession can be hard. It may be easier to delay, to tell yourself you'll do it later, when the time is right. One study explored whether companies reduced their impairments during the 2008 financial crisis; as you might guess, they did: "companies recognized less impairments during the crisis, including companies in countries that have used external financial aid, suggesting that managers may use impairment recognition as a way of practicing earnings management" (Gaio, Gonçalves, and Pereira 2021).

With respect to asset stranding, we also want to reflect again on how a metaphor can insinuate certain moods and attitudes: "the way we think influences the way we speak, but the influence also goes the other way" (Boroditsky 2011). So forget, for the moment, all about finance, and just imagine that something or someone has been stranded. Your friend missed their connection and is now stranded at the airport. Or perhaps the tide has come in, and now you and the other picnickers are stranded on a tidal island. In everyday speech, *stranding* has a negative connotation, and implies unfinished business. Sure, something might be stranded forever. But so long as it is stranded, you're probably wondering about how to rescue it. Are these associations really appropriate for reserves of coal, oil or gas left untouched in the ground? From some perspectives, yes. Are they appropriate if we re-create their energy in cleaner ways, and provide for the livelihoods that once depended on their extraction? From the broader perspective of the global economy, this could be a stranding worth celebrating. Maybe another word is in order? Relinquished assets, superseded assets, composted assets. Maybe you have an idea about what to call them?

DOUBLE MATERIALITY
Sometimes it feels like everyone is threatened, but nobody's responsible for creating hazards. Double materiality seeks to change that — but there are challenges in formulating and applying the concept…

Materiality is about what matters.[11] If something is material, it means you should care about it, and include it in your decision-making. It may mean you should disclose it too, so that other decision-makers can include it in their decisions. Materiality has specific legal definitions for accountants and auditors, and is also well-embedded in best practice in both sustainability and risk management. See Figures 9 and 10, which focus on reporting of emissions. However, climate change is changing what matters, how it matters, and to whom. Traditional approaches to materiality are looking increasingly creaky and outdated.

Double materiality is one ongoing attempt to evolve the concept.

Double materiality refers to an emerging approach, where companies' mainstream reporting includes the climate risks they are driving, not only the climate risks they are facing. So double materiality seeks to synthesise two existing ways of approaching materiality. Within mainstream financial reporting, issues have traditionally been treated as material if they might impact the company's financial position, e.g. bottom line or access to capital. This is often understood as meaning that issues are material only if they could reasonably influence the decision-making of investors or lenders. By contrast, within voluntary sustainability reporting, issues are described as material if they significantly impact the world in some way, whether or not such impacts have financial consequences

---

11 Within philosophy, and the arts and humanities broadly, "material" can mean something else altogether. Furthermore, there are close connections between new materialism and climate-related fields of inquiry such as the environmental humanities, the energy humanities, ecocriticism, ecopoetics, animal studies, etc. We won't get into the details here, but some good entry points include the work of Anna Tsing, Jane Bennett, Timothy Morton, and Stacy Alaimo.

Accurate reporting of emissions can help direct investment to achieve CO2 reductions across the value chain.
Illustration for a generic fashion brand or retailer.

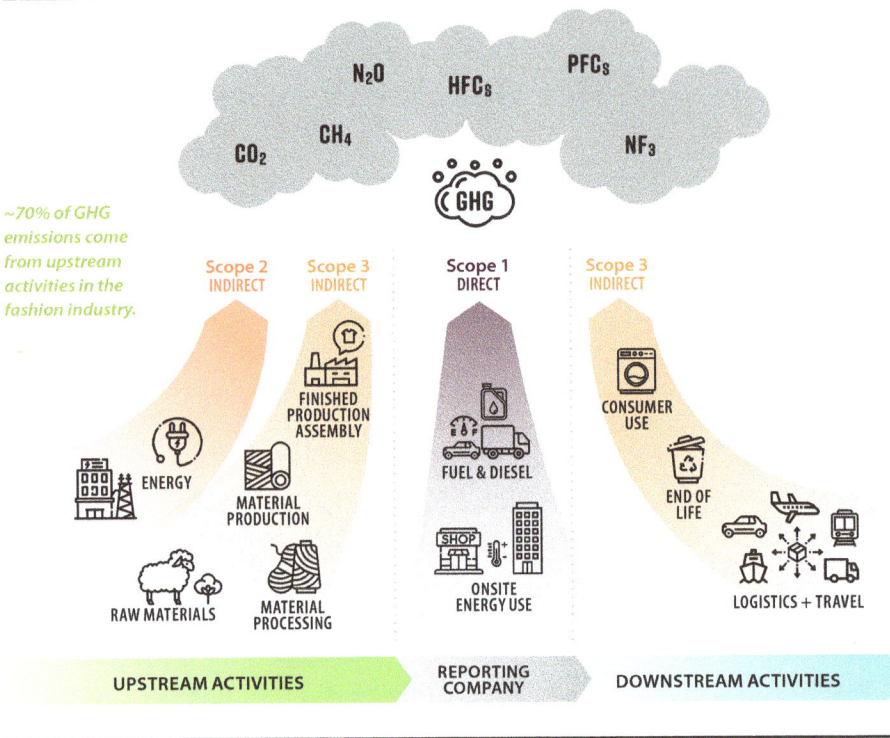

Figure 9. Illustrating reporting of corporate emissions.

for the company.[12] How do companies determine these impacts? Mostly just by asking. That is, on the sustainability side, stakeholder mapping and engagement have traditionally been key to determining materiality.

Arguably, a big problem for mainstream financial reporting is that a company's negative impacts are "somebody else's problem" by default. They only really concern the company if they might have financial consequences for the company.[13]

It's true that there are many channels through which this could happen, so companies are seldom blasé about it. For example, a bad reputation could spook customers or other investors; or employees might object to company policies or activities; or a new regulation might be imposed, favouring rivals who were better prepared; or there could be legal challenges; or the degradation of the local environment could harm employees, customers, and other key stakeholders; or activists might take direct action against the company. In all these ways and more, negative externalities can become re-internalised.

From the evidence of its prototype frameworks, the International Sustainability Standards Boards will remain focused on single materiality: its standards will require companies to disclose climate-related risks that could affect the decision-making of investors and lenders. They won't ask companies to try to quantify all impacts on all stakeholders as part of their mainstream reporting.[14] As the Global Reporting Initiative suggest, not only is sustainability reporting "highly relevant in its own right as a public interest activity," but also "most, if not all, of the impacts that have been identified through this process [of sustainability reporting] will eventually become financially material" (GRI 2021).

However, some take the view that this doesn't go far enough. If it is only "most" and not "all" of its negative impacts that a company eventually addresses, then this may not be compatible with global climate goals. Furthermore, the timeframe implied by "eventually" may signal incompatibility. Then there is the fact that processes for re-internalising these negative externalities are not cost-neutral for society, but draw on resources that could be allocated more usefully. In other words, if companies don't disclose their

---

12 Occasionally 'double materiality' is used in a slightly different way, to essentially mean non-financial disclosures only.

13 A textbook illustration of externality would tend to focus, in the first instance, on an unsympathetic agent passing off costs to innocent victims. For example, an unscrupulous company pollutes heavily, raking in the profits, while the local community endures environmental degradation, or pays for its clean up with their taxes. This is what we normally think of when we think of negative externalities. However, the relationship between externalities and climate justice is not quite so straightforward. Situations may arise where an externality happens to be borne by those who reasonably should be paying for it, even if they are not responsible for generating it. To bring this into focus, consider the carbon emissions of poorer developing countries, who may have very little cumulative emissions (and therefore very little responsibility for climate change), and whose emissions are relatively weighted toward providing basic necessities. Pricing in an externality is not always and everywhere automatically the best policy. This topic sometimes comes up in debates around "polluter pays" vs. "beneficiary pays" vs. other approaches to climate justice.

14 In fact, according to the current draft wording, they won't even ask companies to disclose risks that are not "significant" (meaning there is a danger of circularity, whereby a company claims an undisclosed risk must not have been significant, otherwise they would have disclosed it).

impacts, it becomes somebody else's job — perhaps regulators and policymakers, or do-gooding customers, or NGOs and civil society actors, or roving newshounds, or ratings agencies, or perhaps nobody at all — to identify them and make them financially material for the company.

Double materiality has already been embedded in the EU's recent CSRD disclosure regime. It is also part of a broader shift, from financial reporting aimed at investors, to reporting of material information to all stakeholders — including investors, regulators, customers, suppliers, employees, unions, local communities, and others. Double materiality was first proposed by the European Commission in 2019. As described in a 2021 report from the European Financial Reporting Advisory Group:

> ***Double materiality.*** *The operationalisation of the concept of double materiality is key to sustainability reporting standard-setting in the EU. The standard-setter should therefore adopt conceptual guidelines addressing the definition and implementation of the concept of materiality in each of its two dimensions. Double materiality requires that both impact materiality and financial materiality perspectives be applied in their own right without ignoring their interactions:*
>
> ***a) Impact materiality:*** *Identifying sustainability matters that are material in terms of the impacts of the reporting entity's own operations and its value chain (impact materiality), based on:*
>
> *(i) the severity (scale, scope and remediability) and, when appropriate, likelihood of actual and potential negative impacts on people and the environment;*
>
> *(ii) the scale, scope and likelihood of actual positive impacts on people and the environment connected with companies' operations and value chains;*
>
> *(iii) the urgency derived from social or environmental public policy goals and planetary boundaries.*
>
> ***b) Financial materiality:*** *Identifying sustainability matters that are financially material for the reporting entity based on evidence that such matters are reasonably likely to affect its value beyond what is already recognised in financial reporting. The determination of financially material effects on the reporting entity can rely on non-monetary quantitative, monetary quantitative, or qualitative data, while recognising the dynamic relationship between them. Many impacts on people and the environment may be considered 'pre-financial' in the sense that they may become material for financial reporting purposes over time (so-called 'dynamic materiality'). Financial materiality for sustainability reporting cannot be extrapolated from financial materiality for financial reporting.*

However, the work of uniting these two traditions is far from simple. A recent GRI report identifies some of the challenges in applying double materiality, including:

> *[...] poor disclosure of the process of determining material sustainability issues; variation in the approach used by organisations to apply the GRI concept of materiality; stakeholder engagement is used to increase transparency and accountability but also to manage risks by reducing materiality attached to reporting information; organisations often lack skills to apply materiality to sustainability issues; assessment of materiality favours short-term financial interests; and, the materiality assessment process often falls outside the scope of sustainability assurance engagements.*
>
> *(Adams et al. 2021)*

Double materiality appears to be a work-in-progress, partly because of the distinctiveness of the two materiality traditions. For example, the use of a risk framing appears to be somewhat sporadic in the discussions around outward impacts. Companies are not being invited to risk scan on

Scopes explained
Illustration for a generic fashion brand or retailer.

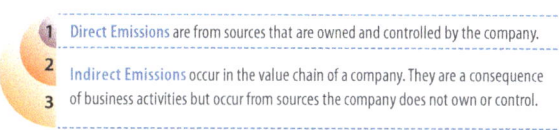

Scopes help to systematically define different emission areas, and are a widely utilised tool in reporting.

1. Direct Emissions are from sources that are owned and controlled by the company.
2. Indirect Emissions occur in the value chain of a company. They are a consequence of business activities but occur from sources the company does not own or control.

Scope 1 emissions
are direct emissions from owned or controlled sources, generated while performing business activities.
- Fossil fuels or biomass burned on-site (e.g. for heating plants, offices, retail spaces)
- Fuel used in vehicles owned or controlled by the company
- Fuel for back-up power generators

Scope 3 emissions
are all other indirect emissions that occur in the value chain of a company. They are a consequence of business activities but occur from sources the company does not own or control.
- Emissions generated in the company's supply chain (upstream and downstream: extraction, production, transportation of purchased materials; fuels, services)
- Travel (business travel, employee commuting)
- Emissions generated from waste disposal (including waste generated in operations and production of purchased materials and fuels, as well as disposal of sold products at the end of their life)
- Leased assets
- Investments

Scope 2 emissions
are indirect emissions generated by the production of purchased energy.
- Purchased electricity, steam, heating, cooling

Figure 10. Scopes explained.

Double materiality appears to be a work-in-progress, partly because of the distinctiveness of the two materiality traditions.

behalf of every key stakeholder (let alone every stakeholder) with the same degree of thoroughness and detail that they might do for themselves, but the limits of their responsibilities under double materiality are not yet clear. More subtly, the two traditions may be challenging to unite elegantly because they already blur and overlap in various ways. For example:

- As already mentioned, a company reporting on a single materiality basis may still include climate-related information in its main report, if there is some plausible mechanism (such as investor sentiment) to hold the company accountable.
- A company reporting on a single materiality basis may still include climate-related information in its secondary reports, subject to voluntary frameworks (e.g. TCFD and GRI or SASB) and perhaps also legal requirements (e.g. the UK's Companies Act 2006 and more recent legislation mandating TCFD for many companies). These may include impacts that investors and lenders factor into their decision-making. Furthermore, the voluntary or less-tightly-regulated reporting processes such as TCFD, GRI and/or SASB may end up internally informing the mainstream reporting.
- Contrariwise, the inclusion of climate-related information within a company's main reporting does not give a strong guarantee that it will be used by investors and lenders.
- The distinction between reporting aimed at investors and lenders, vs. reporting aimed at all stakeholders, is rather stylised. Investors and lenders are reasonable to be concerned about climate-related information for its sake.
- Initiatives such as TCFD and the ISSB can encourage the markets to see climate-related information as a self-fulfilling indicator of financial performance (what the sociology of finance sometimes calls "performativity").[15]
- Audit and assurance is stronger in connection with mainstream reporting than with voluntary reporting, but it is still much weaker and limited in scope than is commonly assumed (sometimes called the "audit expectation gap.")
- As the next section explores, the concept of "dynamic materiality" can further blur the line between single materiality and double materiality, by emphasising that issues that are not material for investors and lenders today could rapidly become so in the future.

In short, with or without an explicit double materiality framing, there are significant challenges to incentivising market participants to make decisions on the basis of climate-related disclosures.

DYNAMIC MATERIALITY
Dynamic materiality seeks to reflect the urgent timescales of climate transition, and the need to reflect stakeholder diversity—but it is as yet ill-defined and associated with some dubious hype

Another term currently getting a lot of attention is **dynamic materiality**. The term does not have a strict and widely recognised definition. However, like double materiality, it emerges from attempts to transform the traditional concept of materiality (rooted in accounting and finance) to work better for sustainability and climate transition.

Dynamic materiality reflects the recognition that whether or not something is material may **change over time**. For example, it could change because of the disruptive power of physical climate risks, or because of swiftly shifting consumer sentiment, or because risk cascades rapidly transform the environment in which an entity operates. In this way, dynamic materiality blurs the distinction between single materiality and double materiality—climate risk issues (and other sustainability

---

15 This concept is perhaps most familiar from financial bubbles: the price of something rises, more investors buy it, driving up the price, and so on. However, the presence of such reinforcing feedback loops is not necessarily associated with bubbles.

So can materiality be evolved to support robust disclosures consistent with rapid and just climate transition? Are double materiality and dynamic materiality complementary concepts, or competitors? Or neither, or both? What do you think?

issues) that investors don't care about today may be all they think about tomorrow. Dynamic materiality is linked with efforts to make companies even more forward-looking and responsive to new data in their management of risks and opportunities. Moreover, dynamic materiality reflects the recognition that **materiality is multi-dimensional**, and the same issue can be more material to some stakeholders and less material to others. Although it has potential to do so in ways that centre inclusivity, equity, and climate justice, it does not necessarily embed these values.

Currently, dynamic materiality has both **stakeholder capitalism** and **techno-solutionist** aspects. On the one hand, it imagines more regular micro-assessments, and more regular streams of information connecting companies and their various stakeholders. This means there could potentially be more involvement of stakeholders in the governance and day-to-day activities of a company. One theme we have already extensively explored is how climate transition demands improvements and innovations in democratic governance throughout society. In this respect, dynamic materiality holds some promise.

However, dynamic materiality is also often associated with novel applications of **AI and big data** to determine materiality. Although AI and big data do have important roles to play in climate risk decision support, strong caution is advised. In recent years there have been well-attested problems associated with novel applications of AI including explainability, algorithmic bias, algorithmic opacity ("black boxes" resistant to inspection), inappropriate levels of trust or mistrust in automated analyses, ethical and political value judgments made to seem "neutral," and a history of cutting key stakeholders out of the loop of analysis, deliberation and decision-making. These and other unintended consequences are set out in the overlapping fields of critical algorithm studies, critical data studies, and critical internet studies.

These problems may be compounded when the climate analytics in question are proprietary, and sealed off from scrutiny. Even within peer-reviewed literature, there are many instances of AI "solutions" being mobilised within problem spaces to which they are categorically ill-suited. Given that a lack of decision-useful data is a common complaint in climate risk management, and there is a danger that AI will become an excuse to shoehorn "non-traditional data sources" (e.g. ESG corpora, social media data) into filling gaps they cannot fill. These difficulties are compounded by frequent mismatches between the types of information demanded within financial risk management and the types of information climate modelling can reliably supple: "The challenge of deploying intelligence from climate science to manage climate-related financial risks across the economy is profound" (Fiedler et al. 2021).

We therefore recommend separating the concept of dynamic materiality from particular proposed technological implementations, and instead defining dynamic materiality more formally. Dynamic materiality can be defined as an approach to materiality which (a) represents the materiality of an issue as a multi-dimensional construct, containing qualitative and/or quantitative data, and reflecting differences between different stakeholder groups, and which (b) embeds such a representation within data monitoring and/or participatory processes to enable it to be refreshed on a timescale appropriate to its use by key stakeholders.

In June 2023, the ISSB published its first two disclosure standards, defining risks that need to be disclosed as material ('if omitting, obscuring or misstating it could be reasonably expected to influence investor decisions'). The ISSB has yet to provide clarity on how these definitions are to be applied in practice. Without clear answers, there is every possibility that the standards will fail to support the informational requirements of climate transition.

So can materiality be evolved to support robust disclosures consistent with rapid and just climate transition? Are double materiality and dynamic materiality complementary concepts, or competitors? Or neither, or both? What do you think?

SCOPING THE POLICY SPACE
What are some of the policy tools available to steer us safely through a time of intensified 'creative destruction'?

▶▶▶ *"Finance will not drive the net-zero transition on its own. Finance is an enabler, a catalyst that will speed what governments and companies initiate. If there is commitment to move to a sustainable, resilient and fair energy system, and the right policies are made, finance will be there."*
— **Mark Carney**

▶▶▶ *"[…] we have seen that in the spurts and vicissitudes of the process of creative destruction […] perfect and instantaneous flexibility may even produce functionless catastrophes […]"*
— **Joseph Schumpeter**

This chapter has emphasised the prevailing narrative within the financial sector. This narrative relates how **reforms are underway to improve the flow of climate-related information** through business, finance, policy, science, technology and society as a whole. The informational framework that is emerging is mostly a mixture of concepts from financial reporting and audit, sustainability reporting, and risk management. It is far from perfect, but it is evolving rapidly. Targeted public investment in key forms of data collection, such as scaling up data for measurement, reporting and verification (MRV) on soil carbon sequestration projects, can help to catalyse improvements in information flows. So too can novel digital technologies, innovations in areas such as AI and data analytics, data visualisation, decision support systems, participation and engagement tools, blockchain-based finance and governance, as well as research to address issues around bias and explainability.

All these measures are seen as stepping stones toward a Net Zero world. As they are achieved, consumers can be expected to more clearly comprehend what they are paying for, workers what they are working for, and investors what they are investing in. Company executives can gain a stronger sense of who their suppliers and partners are. Yet these are still only stepping stones. Where they are leading to is improved policy. Their larger significance lies in how they might make the climate implications of diverse activities, by diverse entities, legible to policymakers.

Governments, central banks, local authorities, and intergovernmental organizations, are all seeking to see the policy space more clearly, including what markets can feasibly deliver and on what timeframes, where market participants require different incentives, where markets require deeper redesign, and where non-market options ought to be pursued.

When it comes to the content of such policies, however, the prevailing story tends to turn a little vague. So to conclude this chapter, we briefly sketch a few of the policy options that are available, or that may become available, in the near future. We do not intend anything in this section as a recommendation (nor as a caution). Rather, we want to give a sense of the wider context within which climate finance and climate risk communication exist. We want to emphasise that improving climate risk management, and making climate-related investments more profitable and less risky, is only one aspect of climate transition governance.

Of course, this is also not a comprehensive account, not even of policy that is being pursued, let alone proposed. We can start with **fiscal policy**. Tax is a powerful instrument, not only to raise funds, but also to influence prices. **Carbon taxes** can put a price on carbon emissions and encourage switching to low-carbon alternatives. **Cap-and-trade** and other mechanisms can also impose a price on carbon. Government spending can include **supply-side interventions**, with governments acting as the "investor of first resort" (Macfarlane 2019) through innovation agencies and development banks. Low disbursement rates are currently an issue, when climate finance is compared with development finance as a whole. Options to address this include making available more **concessional finance**—funding provided as grants, or as loans on more favourable terms—as well as softening co-financing requirements, and greatly expanding the range of projects and activities funded. Climate finance can also be reallocated by creating more equitable access to **Special Drawing Rights**, supplementary foreign exchange reserves within the IMF.

Government spending can also include **demand-side interventions**, using procurement policy to encourage and reward innovation in support of climate transition. What governments *don't* spend can be as important as what they do. Subsidies in agriculture and energy, as well as other sectors, can be redistributed to support climate transition outcomes. As the IPCC states, "Demand-side mitigation and new ways of providing services can help avoid, shift, and improve final service demand. Rapid and deep changes in demand make it easier for every sector to reduce GHG emissions in the short and medium term" (IPCC AR6 WGII).

Where carbon intensive activities prove unresponsive to these incentives, tougher **environmental standards** and **direct bans** can be used. Governments can also **nationalise key resources** for climate transition purposes, through compulsory purchase (also known as eminent domain). Where resources come into public ownership, there are opportunities to improve **participatory governance** (see more below).

Broad-based taxes on net wealth (**wealth taxes**) do not target carbon directly, but can raise capital for climate transition, and if appropriately deployed can improve resilience by reducing inequality. Initiatives to strengthen **global tax transparency and governance**, such as the OECD/G20 Inclusive Framework on Base Erosion and Profit Shifting, can improve tax effectiveness by reducing avoidance and evasion. Cryptocurrency presents some relatively new challenges for multi-jurisdictional tax governance.

One especially complex and challenging form of taxation is the **carbon tariff**, such as the EU's proposed Carbon Border Adjustment Mechanism. The primary function of a carbon tariff is to prevent **carbon leakage**, where reducing carbon emissions in one jurisdiction would increase emissions in another (e.g. because production moves to the jurisdiction where carbon is uncosted or cheaper). The concept of carbon leakage has controversially been used to justify giving large emission allowances to hard-to-abate sectors.

Carbon tariffs can have serious implications for the exports of developing countries, exacerbating inequality and jeopardising orderly climate transition. **Debt restructuring**, including debt cancellation, debt-for-nature swaps, and debt-for-efficiency swaps, are among the many options for mitigating such issues. **Loss and damage mechanisms**, or **Carbon Debt** linked payments in the future, can also use attribution science and legal processes to appropriately manage financial flows from developed to developing countries.

Whatever fiscal policies are taken, they can be designed to be recession-ready, so that climate targets are not gambled on the ups and downs of national, regional, and global economy, but will be met in all reasonably foreseeable scenarios.

Monetary policy includes managing the money supply and interest rates, and related governmental and central bank activities. Over a hundred central banks have joined the Network for Greening the Financial System, and are coordinating various policy responses aimed at reallocating capital in more climate-aligned ways. Central banks are also promoting and coordinating stress testing exercises, analysing how the financial system may respond, for example, to a rapid shift in climate policy, and/or in investor sentiment, and working to prepare accordingly.

A key tool of any central bank is the bank rate, the rate at which it charges domestic banks to borrow money, and through which it influences interest rates. Central banks also purchase assets, especially in **Open Market Operations** (OMO) and sometimes **Quantitative Easing** (QE). They can put downward pressure on interest rates by creating new money and buying bonds, or upward pres-

EXAMPLE CENTRAL BANK REMITS		
South African Reserve Bank	**The European System of Central Banks**	**The United States Federal Reserve**
"The primary objective of the Bank shall be to protect the value of the currency of the Republic in the interest of balanced and sustainable economic growth in the Republic."	"Without prejudice to the objective of price stability, the ESCB shall support the general economic policies in the Union with a view to contributing to the achievement of the objectives of the Union as laid down in Article 3 of the Treaty on European Union." The first statement of Article 3 reads: "The Union's aim is to promote peace, its values and the well-being of its peoples."	The objective of the Fed is to "maintain long run growth of the monetary and credit aggregates commensurate with the economy's long run potential to increase production, so as to promote effectively the goals of maximum employment, stable prices, and moderate long-term interest rates." The Fed is belatedly looking at scenario analyses of how climate might pose risks to this "long run potential to increase production."

sure by selling them. Crucially, this means that there are policy options around *which* assets they purchase. Central banks can favour green bonds and (especially since the green bonds market is currently relatively small) apply other criteria to support climate transition. **Collateral frameworks** determine which assets will be acceptable as collateral, and which will be unacceptable or only acceptable subject to a discount ('haircut'); this is another area where central banks can favour greener assets.

Critics argue that favouring green or ecologically benign bonds could damage perceptions of central bank independence and neutrality, especially in the US context (*The Economist* 2022). Truly "neutral" operations have always been illusory: "[a]ll along the monetary policy implementation process, central banks make choices which favour some assets more than others and thus shape relative prices, as well as relative funding conditions for firms" (Senni and Monnin, 2020). In fact, because of which sectors issue the greatest volume of bonds, central banks have historically been skewed toward carbon intensive bonds.

How much legal leeway do central banks currently have to support climate transition? Most central banks do not yet have explicit sustainability mandates (less than 15%). Many do have mandates which incorporate sustainability more indirectly (around 40%), since they are tasked with supporting national economic policy, so long as it is consistent with their core objectives (usually price stability). Furthermore, even those pursuing a narrow mandate of price stability can legitimately consider climate risk, price stability is impacted by climate (Dikau and Volz 2021).

When sustainability is mentioned, it is sometimes in the context of sustainable growth. Indeed, many central bank mandates mention growth, although this could be open to reinterpretation as non-GDP measures of growth. As the IPCC notes, "GDP is a poor metric of human well-being, and climate policy evaluation requires better grounding in relation to decent living standards" (IPCC AR6 WGII). **Beyond GDP** approaches have in principle attracted widespread sympathy within European policy and beyond; some countries have well-developed mechanisms for collecting alternative progress metrics. Levers to drive more effective use of non-GDP metrics are one aspect of the complex and varied field of **degrowth and post-growth theory**.

Central banks have unequal powers: decisions on interest rates by central banks in large economies often have implications for currencies in other countries, namely by affecting the cost of debt and trade balances, thus limiting options for central banks in developing countries. Central banks in emerging economies might also have limited data and analytical capacity to assess and prepare for climate risks, as a working paper from the South African Reserve Bank notes: "emerging market central banks currently have limited capacity to assess climate risks and their effects on financial stability, growth, and inflation" (Arndt, Loewald, and Makrelov 2020).

Just like central banks, **regulatory agencies** have unequal powers, and in some cases exert significant influence beyond their borders. In the USA the **Securities and Exchange Commission** (SEC), founded at the height of the Great Depression, has a mission to protect investors, maintain fair markets and facilitate formation and flow of capital. It has significant scope to influence the manner of climate transition, e.g. through rules on climate risk disclosures.

Stock exchanges have listing requirements, which are another potential point of intervention for climate alignment, e.g. more rigorous disclosure criteria for IPOs, or banning certain types of listing. Laws and regulations on **insolvency** and **limited liability** can also be reengineered in support of an orderly climate transition.

The unprecedented coordination challenges of climate transition suggest opportunities for innovative forms of governance. **Blockchain technology** currently attracts interest in this respect. This comes with the caveat that distributed ledger technologies contain intrinsic energy inefficiencies, and especially so when they take a proof-of-work approach (as is the case with Bitcoin). However, there is interest in the potential of blockchain technology to financialize natural assets; to create digital co-operatives and other participatory platforms; to downscale investments to the level of communities (or even individuals); to lower the costs of reporting requirements in developing world contexts; and to track and verify climate-related claims (e.g. around additionality of carbon removals). None of these use cases is hardwired into the technology itself, and blockchain is capable of operationalising centralised, hierarchical governance structures as well as decentralised, participatory ones.

More broadly, policy can support scaling existing forms of **community ownership and governance**, and innovative approaches to democratically empowering stakeholders, and recognising and cultivating stakeholder expertise. This can include, for example, **citizen assemblies** and other forms of sortition, as well as devolving more significant powers to **local partnerships** with mixed memberships drawn from education, health and care, charities and voluntary sectors, unions, and SMEs. **Workplace democracy** is another key area. Reform of corporate governance and employment law can be tied to climate and sustainable development objectives, drawing on cooperativism, codetermination, and participatory economics,[16] and innovations such as Inclusive Ownership Funds, in order to address challenges around the proper assessment, audit and disclosure of climate risks and opportunities, and shortcomings in existing risk management frameworks. More broadly still, reduced working weeks, Universal Basic Income and Universal Basic Services, and diverse proposals and pilots associated with post-work, also have potential to alter the dynamics of information flow throughout society, by transforming the availability and quality of "free time" and widening the scope for effective people-led policymaking. Some of the deeper engagements with democratic reform in recent history have taken place in several South American countries, and the rest of the world can learn from the successes and failures.

This is just a brief glimpse into the available options. To gain a better sense of the breadth of the possible, we might reflect that there is no reason in principle why *any* of the organisations, institutions, frameworks, or other entities mentioned in this chapter should remain permanent, or should have roles in the future that resemble their roles today. All can be reformed, repurposed, or dismantled.

To understand how swiftly the line between the feasible and the unfeasible can shift, it is helpful not only to look to the century ahead, but also to the century behind us. The terms **Green Deal and Green New Deal** are often used in relation to climate transition policy. Of course, these terms mean different things in different contexts. We don't want to get into the details here. The point is that, by invoking the US New Deal of the 1930s, these terms invite a more historical perspective on today's climate challenges. Back in the 1930s, the context from which the New Deal emerged was characterised by fiery debates, including many proposals going much further than what the New Deal finally delivered. Some of these ideas represent paths-not-taken, others were incorporated into policies in adapted forms. For example, the Technocracy movement sought to make scientific and technical analysis much more central to economic decision-making, proposed a currency backed by energy, and had a deep interest in automation (and a disdain for democracy). The chemurgy movement, active at roughly same tim,e was interested in the use of agricultural byproducts for energy and manufacturing, in ways which foreshadowed today's interest Negative Emission Technologies, bioeconomy, and nature-based solutions.

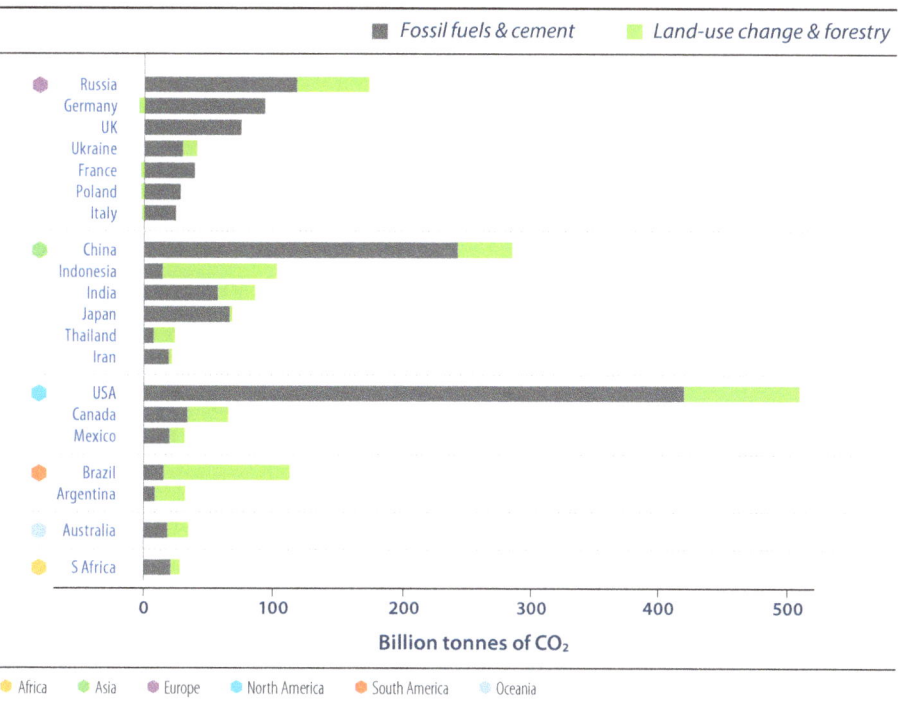

Figure 11. *Historical responsibility for emissions; top 20 countries arranged by continent.*

Climate change necessitates **adaptation and innovation**. A great many companies, so the prevailing story goes, will adjust themselves to new regulatory regimes and re-engineered risk landscapes. They will combine incoming information about their operating environment with their own local knowledge and experience. They may adopt new business models. They may innovate in ways that ultimately support (though in some cases will undermine) climate transition. Many will not passively accept the changes in the risk environment, but

---

16   **Participatory economics** ("Parecon") proposes that strong workplace democracy can take over most or all the allocative functions of finance, while also acknowledging challenges around (a) scoping the appropriate constituency for each individual deliberation and decision, and (b) knowledge asymmetries within workplaces and their potential to undermine democratic process. Albert (2003) recommends operationalising two principles: (a) that parties to a decision should have input into that decision in proportion to its impact on them, and (b) that roles within an enterprise should be designed as "balanced job complexes," with due regard for how they concentrate or disperse decision-making power.

will seek to actively participate in shaping the risk landscape (and this too will have mixed consequences for climate transition).

But there is another side to this story which is every bit as crucial. **Some companies will ultimately fail to adapt**. They will suffer from stranded assets or other negative impacts; they will go out of business; their carbon intensive activities will cease; new sustainable enterprises will take their place; their employees eventually will find work elsewhere. Recent technological advances have contributed to a more optimistic vision for investors, and there is a tendency to dwell more on the 'creative' side of **creative destruction** than on the 'destruction' side. Nonetheless, the prevailing narrative acknowledges the destruction too, disguised by euphemism and upbeat messaging. The assumption is that stranded assets, impairments, insolvencies, debt restructurings, companies going into administration, underemployment, job losses (however temporary), will be part even of an 'orderly' transition scenario. In other words, these are not only seen as hazards to be avoided on the road to Net Zero. These destructive impacts are also seen as part of the mechanism of change.

In this sense, the transition narratives which prevail within the financial sector imply **profound upheaval and deep uncertainty**. Although this is not widely acknowledged, this is something they share with more overtly radical narratives of system change and climate transition, those rooted in environmental social movements, campaign organisations, and activism and protest.

When it is frankly confronted, it raises a number of questions. Can any country, company or financial institution really be relied upon to promote the information which could spell its own timely demise? How will society absorb the costs of these rapid reallocations, both through public services and more informal networks of support and care? Will unemployment be coupled to poverty and suffering, or might it mean the support of social welfare, rich opportunities for education and retraining, and greater freedom to shape new livelihoods through participatory governance? When vulnerabilities to transition risk are concentrated in certain regions or countries, how will this be reflected in the realm of geopolitics? Enthusiasts of creative destruction may find it easy to proclaim that some companies should perish so that others may arise—but who would say the same about entire countries?

All these questions and more are implicit in the term **just transition**. The future is deeply uncertain, and we can say with confidence that it will not feature steady, controllable, incremental progress. Communicating climate risk may contribute to a financial system more capable of coping with rapid, global and unpredictable changes. But it is still only a small part of a story that is still being written.

ACKNOWLEDGEMENTS

We would like to thank Arie Krampf, Simon Dikau, Kasim Buckley, Panagiotis Tzouvanas, Saeed Sanei, and Courtnae Bailey for reviewing, discussing and suggesting additional content for this chapter.

AUTHOR CONTRIBUTIONS

Conceptualization: JLW and PL; **Research:** JLW and PL ; **Writing:** JLW; **Figures:** JK and PL

REFERENCES

Adams, Carol A., Abdullah Alhamood, Xinwu He, Jie Tian, Le Wang, and Yi Wang. 2021. 'The Double-Materiality Concept: Applications and Issues'. *Global Reporting Initiative.* globalreporting.org/media/jrbntbyv/griwhitepaper-publications.pdf

Arndt, Channing, Chris Loewald, and Konstantin Makrelov. 2020. 'Climate Change and Its Implications for Central Banks in Emerging and Developing Economies'. Publications > Working Papers, June. resbank.co.za/en/home/publications/publication-detail-pages/working-papers/2020/10001

Bigger, Patrick and Sophie Webber. 2021. 'Green Structural Adjustment in the World Bank's Resilient City'. *Annals of the American Association of Geographers,* 111:1, 36-51, doi: 10.1080/24694452.2020.1749023

Bingler, Julia Anna, and Chiara Colesanti Senni. 2020. 'Taming the Green Swan: How to Improve Climate-Related Financial Risk Assessments'. *SSRN Electronic Journal*. doi.org/10.2139/ssrn.3795360

Bloomberg, Michael. 2016. 'Phase 1 Report of the Task Force on Climate-Related Financial Disclosures'. TCFD. assets.bbhub.io/company/sites/60/2020/10/Phase_I_Report_v15.pdf

Boroditsky, Lera. 2011. 'How Language Shapes Thought'. *Scientific American* 304 (2): 62–65.

Bos, Kyra, and Joyeeta Gupta. 2019. 'Stranded Assets and Stranded Resources: Implications for Climate Change Mitigation and Global Sustainable Development'. *Energy Research & Social Science* 56 (October): 101215. doi.org/10.1016/j.erss.2019.05.025

Caldecott, Ben. 2015. 'Why Stranded Assets Matter and Should Not Be Dismissed'. *The Conversation*. theconversation.com/why-stranded-assets-matter-and-should-not-be-dismissed-51939

CDSB. 2022. 'Accounting for Climate: Climate-Related Checklist for IFRS Financial Statements'. CDSB. cdsb.net/sites/default/files/cdsb_accounting_for_climate_checklist_2022_v4.pdf

Dasgupta, P. 2021. 'The Economics of Biodiversity: The Dasgupta Review'. *HM Treasury*.

Dikau, Simon, and Ulrich Volz. 2021. 'Central Bank Mandates, Sustainability Objectives and the Promotion of Green Finance'. *Ecological Economics* 184 (June): 107022. doi.org/10.1016/j.ecolecon.2021.107022

Fiedler, Tanya, Andy J. Pitman, Kate Mackenzie, Nick Wood, Christian Jakob, and Sarah E. Perkins-Kirkpatrick. 2021. 'Business Risk and the Emergence of Climate Analytics'. *Nature Climate Change 11* (2): 87–94. doi.org/10.1038/s41558-020-00984-6

FRC. 2019. 'Thematic Review: Impairment of Non-Financial Assets'. Financial Reporting Council. frc.org.uk/getattachment/4daee650-59fe-43b0-904c-ba9abfb12245/CRR-Thematic-Review-Impairment-of-Non-financial-Assets-final.pdf

Fulton, Mark, and Christopher Weber. 2015. 'Carbon Asset Risk:- Discussion Framework'. *World Resources Institute.* wri.org/research/carbon-asset-risk-discussion-framework

Fulton, Mark, and Sue Reid, eds. 2018. 'In Sight of the Clean Trillion: Update on an Expanding Landscape of Investor Opportunities.' *Ceres.* edx-files.s3.amazonaws.com/climate/Ceres_In_Sight_Clean_Trillion_May10_2018.pdf

Gaio, Cristina, Tiago Gonçalves, and Anabela Pereira. 2021. 'Financial Crisis and Impairment Recognition in Non-Financial Assets'. *Revista Brasileira de Gestão de Negócios 23* (July): 370–87. doi.org/10.7819/rbgn.v23i2.4108

Gambhir, Ajay, Mel George, Haewon McJeon, Nigel W. Arnell, Daniel Bernie, Shivika Mittal, Alexandre C. Köberle, Jason Lowe, Joeri Rogelj, and Seth Monteith. 2021. 'Near-Term Transition and Longer-Term Physical Climate Risks of Greenhouse Gas Emissions Pathways'. *Nature Climate Change*, December. doi.org/10.1038/s41558-021-01236-x

GRI. 2021. 'GRI 3: Material Topics 2021'. GRI.

Harrington, Luke J., Carl-Friedrich Schleussner, and Friederike E. L. Otto. 2021. 'Quantifying Uncertainty in Aggregated Climate Change Risk Assessments'. *Nature Communications 12* (1): 7140. doi.org/10.1038/s41467-021-27491-2

Krishnan, Mekala, Hamid Samandari, Jonathan Woetzel, Sven Smit, Daniel Pacthod, Dickon Pinner, Tomas Nauclér, et al. 2022. 'The Net-Zero Transition: Its Cost and Benefits | Sustainability | McKinsey & Company'. mckinsey.com/business-functions/sustainability/our-insights/the-net-zero-transition-what-it-would-cost-what-it-could-bring

Landell-Mills, Natasha. 2021. 'Hold Auditors to Account for Climate Risks'. *Sarasin & Partners Global.* 20 September 2021. sarasinandpartners.com/row/think/hold-auditors-to-account-on-climate

Lee, Linda-Eling. 2021. '2022 ESG Trends to Watch'. MSCI. msci.com/documents/10199/9d2eeece-c2db-3d86-873f-faaac8cd62ef

Macfarlane, Laurie. 2019. 'Investor of First Resort'. *The Bartlett Review*, 2019. ucl.ac.uk/bartlett/about-us/bartlett-review/bartlett-review-2019/essays/investor-first-resort

Marbuah, George. 2020. 'Scoping the Sustainable Finance Landscape in Africa: The Case of Green Bonds'. Stockholm: Stockholm Environment Intitute. stockholmsustainablefinance.com/wp-content/uploads/2018/06/SSFC_green-bonds_africa_report.pdf

McCauley, Darren, Vasna Ramasar, Raphael J. Heffron, Benjamin K. Sovacool, Desta Mebratu, and Luis Mundaca. 2019. 'Energy Justice in the Transition to Low Carbon Energy Systems: Exploring Key Themes in Interdisciplinary Research'. *Applied Energy* 233–234 (January): 916–21. doi.org/10.1016/j.apenergy.2018.10.005

Mooney, Chris, Juliet Eliperin, Desmond Butler, John Muyskens, Anu Naraynswamy, and Naema Ahmed. 2021. 'Countries' Climate Pledges Built on Flawed Data Post Investigation Finds'. *The Washington Post*, 7 November 2021. washingtonpost.com/climate-environment/interactive/2021/greenhouse-gas-emissions-pledges-data/

Ndikumana, Léonce, James K. Boyce, and Ameth Saloum Ndiaye. 2014. 'Capital Flight from Africa'. In Capital Flight from Africa, edited by S. Ibi Ajayi and Léonce Ndikumana, 14–54. Oxford University Press. doi.org/10.1093/acprof:oso/9780198718550.003.0002

Newell, Peter, Shilpi Srivastava, Lars Otto Naess, Gerardo A. Torres Contreras, and Roz Price. 2021. 'Toward Transformative Climate Justice: An Emerging Research Agenda'. *WIREs Climate Change* 12 (6). doi.org/10.1002/wcc.733

Newell, Peter, Michelle Twena, and Freddie Daley. 2021. 'Scaling Behaviour Change for a 1.5-Degree World: Challenges and Opportunities'. Global Sustainability 4. doi.org/10.1017/sus.2021.23

Newell, Peter J., Frank W. Geels, and Benjamin K. Sovacool. 2022. 'Navigating Tensions between Rapid and Just Low-Carbon Transitions'. *Environmental Research Letters* 17 (4): 041006. doi.org/10.1088/1748-9326/ac622a

OECD. 2021. 'Ownership and Governance of State Owned Enterprises: A-Compendium of National Practices 2021'. OECD. oecd.org/corporate/Ownership-and-Governance-of-State-Owned-Enterprises-A-Compendium-of-National-Practices-2021.pdf

Paun, Ashim, Lucy Acton, and Wai-Shin Chan. 2018. 'Fragile Planet: Scoring Climate Risks around the World'. HSBC. sustainablefinance.hsbc.com/carbon-transition/fragile-planet

Savvidou, Georgia, Aaron Atteridge, Kulthoum Omari-Motsumi, and Christopher H. Trisos. 2021. 'Quantifying International Public Finance for Climate Change Adaptation in Africa'. *Climate Policy* 21 (8): 1020–36. doi.org/10.1080/14693062.2021.1978053

Schuwerk, Rob, and Barbara Davidson. 2021. 'Flying Blind: The Glaring Absence of Climate Risks in Financial Reporting'. Carbon Tracker. carbontracker.org/reports/flying-blind-the-glaring-absence-of-climate-risks-in-financial-reporting/

Simpson, Cam, Akshat Rathi, and Saijel Kishan. 2021. 'Sustainable Investing Is Mostly About Sustaining Corporations'. Bloomberg.Com, 2021. bloomberg.com/graphics/2021-what-is-esg-investing-msci-ratings-focus-on-corporate-bottom-line/

Smith, Paul. 2021. 'The Climate Risk Landscape'. *UN Environment Programme*. unepfi.org/wordpress/wp-content/uploads/2021/02/UNEP-FI-The-Climate-Risk-Landscape.pdf

Sovacool, Benjamin K., Mari Martiskainen, Andrew Hook, and Lucy Baker. 2019. 'Decarbonization and Its Discontents: A Critical Energy Justice Perspective on Four Low-Carbon Transitions'. *Climatic Change* 155 (4): 581–619. doi.org/10.1007/s10584-019-02521-7

Taleb, Nassim Nicholas. 2012. *Antifragile: Things That Gain from Disorder*. 1st ed. New York: Random House.

Tan, Celine. 2022. 'Audit as Accountability: Technical Authority and Expertise in the Governance of Private Financing for Development'. *Social & Legal Studies* 31 (1): 3–26. doi.org/10.1177/0964663921992100

TCFD. 2021. 'Climate-Related Disclosures Prototype'. IFRS. ifrs.org/content/dam/ifrs/groups/trwg/trwg-climate-related-disclosures-prototype.pdf?

Tollefson, Jeff. 2021. 'What Biden's $2-Trillion Spending Bill Could Mean for Climate Change'. *Nature*, December, d41586-021-03787–7. doi.org/10.1038/d41586-021-03787-7

UNCTAD 2020. Economic Development in Africa Report 2020: Tackling Illicit Financial Flows for Sustainable Development in Africa. unctad.org/system/files/official-document/aldcafrica2020_en.pdf

UNECA 2015. Illicit financial flows: report of the High Level Panel on illicit financial flows from Africa. Addis Ababa. hdl.handle.net/10855/22695

Yan, Chendan, Myles Tatlock, Tim Clare, Jakob Schenker, and Hanna Westling. 2021. 'Private Equity Sector Science-Based Target Guidance'. SBTi. sciencebasedtargets.org/resources/files/SBTi-Private-Equity-Sector-Guidance.pdf

By incorporating stories of action [...] educators can foster a sense of agency and optimism.

Chapter 6: COMMUNICATING CLIMATE RISK *IN* EDUCATION

INTRODUCTION

Climate and environmental communication research tends to be dominated by North American and Western European case studies. Similarly, a common challenge in climate change education is the prevalent **Global North bias** in educational resources. The majority of textbooks, learning materials, and research are produced and distributed by institutions in the Global North, perpetuating various narrow, Northern-centric perspectives on climate change. Even at best, this can limit students' understanding of the diverse experiences and impacts of climate change worldwide; at worst, it can be considered a form of soft power reinforcing old colonial hierarchies. Such bias can also render educational materials not just ineffective, but even harmful to students in the Global South, leaving them less resilient and demoralised.

Climate change can be profoundly distressing to learn and think about. Educators have a duty to communicate in ways that are sensitive to this distress. **Eco-anxiety** can be a common reaction to the scale of the problem, and can be exacerbated by misinterpretation of predictions and scientific uncertainty. By incorporating stories of action, and drawing students into debates on alternative solutions, or reminding students that the future remains unknown and undetermined, educators can foster a sense of agency and optimism. For example, teaching about renewable energy, nature restoration, agricultural and other technological innovations, climate activism, and other **positive steps being taken worldwide**, can help students to manage negative feelings, and inspire them to take action in their own lives. More subtly, students can be invited to encounter climate change as a space of open possibilities, where they can **assert their own values** and **express their own identities.**

Subsections

Introduction

Sidebar: Addressing eco-anxiety as an educator

Case study: Ugandan climate futures

ADDRESSING ECO-ANXIETY AS AN EDUCATOR

EDUCATORS PLAY A CRUCIAL ROLE in shaping the perceptions and attitudes of future generations. By being sensitive, adaptable, and empathetic, they can guide learners through the emotionally charged topic of climate change in a constructive and empowering way. Climate change is associated with eco-anxiety. Note that sometimes *eco-anxiety* is used as an umbrella term, similar to 'climate distress', referring to all emotional distress associated with climate and the environment. Sometimes *eco-anxiety* is used in a narrower way, to refer specifically to anxiety, and somewhat distinct from other emotions such as ecological grief, solastalgia, eco-angst. Here we use it in the broader sense.

▶▶ **Be (a real version of) yourself.** Every educator brings their own personality to their work. What works for one educator might not work for others. What are you good at? Educators might have particular strengths in active listening, or being a calming and soothing presence, or using humour, or mixing small doses of emotionally challenging material into larger learning activities, or leading mindfulness exercises, or making space for anger, or finding hopeful stories, or something else entirely. So probably the most important piece of guidance is to *do your best to be present as yourself,* and to find your own strengths. Of course, many educators feel like they develop a kind of teaching 'persona,' but that persona is still a part of the real you.

▶▶ **Reflect on your own positionality.** This means that you can (without 'making it all about you'!) acknowledge the ways that climate change is affecting you, psychologically and materially, and reflect on how your own identity and circumstances shape these impacts. Doing this well can foster an environment of inclusivity and respect, as educators who understand where they are speaking from can better appreciate and integrate diverse perspectives and backgrounds into their teaching. It can support a critical pedagogy that actively works against perpetuating systemic inequalities within education.

▶▶ **Consider the emotions you're bringing into the space, and try to bring good vibes.** Do what you need to in order to make your sessions uplifting and fun. It is possible to speak about even very dismaying topics in an engaging, upbeat, and even enjoyable way. In the long run, perhaps not *all* climate change education needs to cultivate this atmosphere, but given the negativity that predominantly surrounds the topic, it will probably be a welcome change for many learners. Maybe this approach doesn't suit your personal style as an educator, but we can at least all ensure that we aren't bringing more negative emotions into the space than necessary.

▶▶ **Think about where else students may be receiving education.** Education is not limited to formal institutions. Education might be interwoven with daily activities, like pastoral and agricultural work. This offers a unique chance for students to learn about climate impacts through direct experience.

▶▶ **Emphasise agency.** Share stories of climate action. It's essential to emphasise the capacity for change and resilience. Empower students by providing them with examples, and actionable steps they can take, whether at a personal, community, or global level. This can help counter feelings of helplessness. Discuss innovations, community actions, legal victories and global initiatives that are making a difference. Highlighting the young climate activists making waves internationally can inspire and provide relatable role models. You could explore incorporating actual climate actions into your curricula. Of course, emphasising agency isn't straightforward. When we focus on what is being done, and/or when we actually do it, we necessarily also encounter many barriers and snags. For example, one simple and effective form of project-based learning could be to investigate green claims using publicly available data, and wherever greenwashing is discovered, publicize it — this could be exciting, but also might be disheartening if nothing seems to change as a result. Some climate action can also be risky, so be extra conscious of your safeguarding duties and other legal and ethical responsibilities toward students' safety and wellbeing.

▶▶ **Be aware of students' existing coping mechanisms.** Students may already be aware of eco-anxiety (whether or not that's what they call it) and have practices around it. This is of course part of the big headline message: the best communication is always two-way (or at least two-way). Create spaces for dialogue, and practice active listening.

▶▶ **Normalise (some) climate change, and show you're not scared of it.** Don't play into the 'all or nothing' framing. Even in the best-case scenarios, the world is going to be hotter and sea levels will continue to rise for centuries. But we are doing things about it already, and if our efforts improve then the situation will improve too. Studies suggest that many young people have unwarrantedly extreme beliefs about levels of warming (and other impacts) currently being predicted for this century, and underestimate progress towards net zero. Instead, mitigation, adaptation, and justice considerations should be part of our everyday practices. You don't only have to teach climate change when the word 'climate' is in that week's lesson title. When climate impacts become relevant in the course of teaching other material, mention them, and emphasise agency, solutions, and climate justice.

▶▶ **Honour intergenerational dynamics.** When there are age differences between educators and students, acknowledge them. Given the evolving nature of the climate crisis, educators need to consider what information is relevant and how it's presented. Avoid 'passing on the torch,' or making it seem like climate change is a problem for the future. When relevant, let them know about the things you are doing right now, using the power and resources available to you. There's a balance to be struck between equipping students for the future, and ensuring young learners don't feel overwhelmed by the burden of responsibility.

▶▶ **Prepare in advance for sensitive subject matter.** Recognise that students may have a variety of quite personal connections with many different aspects of climate change. It can be helpful early on to explicitly set some **expectations** with learners about the kind of classroom conduct and learning atmosphere you want to cultivate. Some educators even find it useful to co-design a Classroom Contract with students to empower students and help them feel invested in these ambitions. Explore guidance and debates around the cultivation of safe spaces (also known as safer spaces or positive spaces), and think about how these might apply to divisive or emotionally challenging aspects of the material you are teaching. For example, conversations about loss and damages can be challenging: students in the Global North, already facing higher costs due to shouldering demographic transition and feeling dispossessed through appreciated real estate prices, might be resentful of some climate justice ideas such as being expected to pay climate reparations or climate debts to Global South for damage that occurred before their time. Other discussions that can be divisive or emotionally fraught include climate colonialism, degrowth and postgrowth, demographic change and population growth, the relative priority of adaptation and mitigation, development and postdevelopment[1], responsibility for climate refugees, nature conservation vs. land rights, etc.

▶▶ **Let students know it is OK to feel uncomfortable.** Generally speaking, safe spaces do *not* mean that uncomfortable subjects must be avoided or even minimised. Discomfort is often necessary for learning to take place. What it does mean is that the learning community should foster trust, so that students can encounter discomforts in a way that feels safe. This can be done by setting expectations and modelling best practice. Students should be given opportunities to express their feelings, and the reality of those feelings should be validated. It is possible to acknowledge that a feeling is normal and rational, without necessarily endorsing the direction it is taking a student's thought. A safe learning environment is one where every learner feels seen and respected, is invested in one another's learning experiences, and is prepared to give one another the

---

1   While experts in the Global North consider the failure of climate mitigation to be one of the top risks, experts from the Global South prioritise failure of climate adaptation as a risk (weforum.org/reports/global-risks-report-2023/)

benefit of the doubt whenever conflicts do emerge. Micro-affirmations, small gestures of inclusion and trust-building, can be consciously practiced. 'Calling in' can be preferred to 'calling out' wherever possible. Every context is different, and although there are many models out there which you can borrow, it is best if you personalise your approach, drawing on principles and values you really feel you believe in.

▶▶ **Acknowledge feelings.** You can begin discussions by acknowledging the emotional weight of the topic. It's okay to let students know that feelings of concern, fear, anger, or grief are valid and natural responses. Students also report feeling guilty, ashamed and disgusted by their own complicity and general lack of action. Foster an environment where students feel safe to express their feelings without judgment. This could be in the form of group discussions, one-on-one check-ins, or providing resources for counseling.

▶▶ **Connect the local and the global.** While discussing global challenges, also emphasize local solutions. Highlighting actions such as renewable energy adoption or nature restoration can inspire students to envision positive change and motivate them to participate. What is local for the educator might not be local for the student. In a classroom with many international students, distant impacts of national and regional policies (for example, the EU's Carbon Border Adjustment Mechanism) might be felt personally for some.

▶▶ **Empower students to express their identities and values.** Emphasise the choices that climate change offers. Explore topics where there may be more than one right answer. By fostering critical thinking, students can navigate present challenges and understand the broader societal implications. Allow students to approach climate change as a platform where they can voice their values and shape their identities. Engage them in debates on diverse solutions and encourage them to offer their own perspectives.

▶▶ **Provide historical context.** Climate change can be a way of learning about history, and vice-versa. Carefully positioning climate change within a historical context can help students relate to it. This can provide them with a deeper understanding of the impacts and solutions in the context of their daily lives and broader history.

▶▶ **Incorporate hands-on learning.** Explore ways of embedding learning within everyday tasks. about sustainable practices and the local impacts of climate change. Creating something tangible or participating in solution-driven projects can provide a sense of accomplishment and purpose.

▶▶ **Incorporate the arts.** Use creative practice as a way to explore the climate crisis. Introduce students to creative responses by artists. Give students opportunities to explore ideas and express feelings through their own creative practice. You could incorporate visual art, storytelling, drama, and games and play.

▶▶ **Celebrate youth voices.** While it's essential to prepare youth for the future, it's equally vital to engage them in the present discourse. Invite them to share their thoughts, concerns, and solutions, and ensure their voices are valued in broader discussions.

▶▶ **Lighten the mood.** Sometimes humour helps.

▶▶ **Rhythm and balance are important.** If things have gone gloomy for a while, ask questions and offer prompts to try to pivot to the positive. While presenting the challenges and threats of climate change, also highlight success stories, solutions, and positive actions that are being taken globally. This ensures that students do not feel overwhelmed by only negative information. Have some positive stories or talking points in your back pocket just in case.

▶▶ **Be aware of embodiment.** You may want to integrate mindfulness exercises, deep breathing, or even short meditation sessions before or after particularly heavy discussions.

▶▶ **Reframe and recenter uncertainty.** Uncertainty in itself can be intimidating and distressing, but uncertainty can also be exciting and freeing. In particular, emphasise the indeterminacy of the future and that most projections regarding climate change, already limited by data and scientific understandings, also do not account for innovation and social change, including social tipping points. Remind students of the full range of climate projections made by scientists, not just the most dire ones, and the fact that the social and economic implications of changing climate are generally much harder to predict than the physiological ones.

▶▶ **Talk to colleagues.** As an educator, sharing your experiences, and staying updated with the latest information and psychological guidance related to climate change can provide the necessary tools to address student concerns effectively.

▶▶ **Look to the wider world.** Provide additional resources, if there are any. Share resources where students can seek additional information or support. This might include counseling services, climate activist organizations, charities and NGOs, or resources like documentaries, websites, books, and so on.

▶▶ **Listen to students.** Of course this is just good pedagogy in any context! Feedback from students can be invaluable in understanding what is resonating with them and what might be causing undue stress.

CASE STUDY: UGANDAN CLIMATE FUTURES

Background

There is growing interest in speculative fiction and games to raise awareness of climate issues, to promote climate action, and to develop visions of liveable futures to steer decision-making. Much of this work has prioritised Global North contexts, as a recent review of literature on the use of games in climate education makes clear[2]. The Red Cross Red Crescent games collection is one exception, although it has little emphasis on climate futures.

Climate-related educational resources are currently scarce in Uganda. There is limited coverage of climate change within the school curriculum, and public awareness of climate change is relatively low. Misconceptions are common, especially with regard to connecting the global to the local—the view that climate change is caused by local actions such as cutting trees or pollution is prevalent. Damage to the ozone layer is often confused with the build-up of CO_2 in the atmosphere. Although there is a national plan to introduce climate education into a national curriculum, this has not happened yet, and young people (70% of Ugandans are under 30) mostly source their information from reporting in the media or Indigenous and traditional knowledge. In recent studies, these sources were widely found to be unreliable. Climate stories supported by accurate scientific reporting are currently rare in Ugandan media, while traditional knowledge tends to reinforce the misconception that the global problem is of local origin. Complicating the national climate education agenda is the anticipation that revenues from the oil extractions in Uganda will significantly bolster the government's future budget and are considered an essential source of finance for Uganda's development and climate adaptation by Ugandan politicians. Uganda's high vulnerability to the impacts of climate change has been compounded in recent decades by a rapid environmental decline. Wetlands and forests are disappearing as agriculture expands to feed a growing population, harvests are falling due to soil depletion, and food imports are rising. While some of this damage might be attributable to climate change (heat waves, possible rain pattern shifts), it is common for people not to distinguish the global problem from local drivers. There are specific issues around agency for young people in Uganda especially when it comes to 'positive actions', as many are forced by poverty to knowingly make local problems worse, for example, by cutting trees for charcoal (charcoal supplies 90% of people's energy needs). When we asked the students in Kampala with whom we collaborated in connection to this climate education case study, 'What climate action can you take in the future?' most mentioned 'planting trees.'

---

2 Fernández Galeote et al., 'Gamification for Climate Change Engagement'.

KAMPALA YÉNKYA PROJECT OVERVIEW

The aims of this project were to create resources suitable for afterschool clubs (rather than part of the school curriculum) that are fun, informative about climate change and, most importantly, co-produced with local students, creatives and educators.

Specifically, we engaged four secondary schools in the vicinity of Kampala (Ngogwe Baskerville, Victoria Ssi, Sacred Heart and Nyenga Secondary School) representing students from different socio-economic backgrounds. The age group ranged from 15 to 21-year-olds. Many of these students come from farming or fishing communities near Lake Victoria, which was reflected in the settings for the stories, the games and related activities in the project. The students were eager collaborators and inspired us to deliver a lot more engagement than originally planned or budgeted for.

Maurice Ssebisubi is an educator associated with these schools through his development work and is well-known to the students. He is also the founder of the Uganda Youth for the Environment club. Dilman Dila—Ugandan writer, filmmaker and activist—made a film with the students prior to the Kampala Yénkya project.

The project aimed to make a difference to students' understanding of climate change. Therefore, the first task was to assess what students already knew. Maurice Ssebisubi conducted this assessment through quizzes and informal, off-the-record, interviews with the students, teachers, and government officials responsible for climate education in Uganda, to ensure that the project would be responsive to local needs.

Figure 1. (left) Scene of a documentary made by Dilman Dila;
Figure 2. (right) Logo of the UYE Club, founded by Maurice Ssebisubi.

BASELINE ASSESSMENT

Ten students were chosen at random in each class, giving a minimum of 40 students per school. Maurice Ssebisubi explained to the students that the objective of the quiz was to assess their knowledge of climate and climate-related information without prior teaching. To set a more conversational mood, the students were asked about the most pressing issues, globally, that they were aware of. Most mentioned Covid-19 and other diseases, terrorism/war, drought, and famine.[3] They noted that they get this information from local news radios and TV channels. They discussed altogether that these are man-made problems to which solutions can be found. The students were then separated into groups according to their class year and each group was given 45 minutes to agree and write down the best answers. The answers were peer-assessed, and Maurice Ssebisubi led probing discussions in order to understand why students answered the questions the way they did.

---

3   This prioritisation of risks accords well with the opinions of experts in Africa, see Table B.2 in Global Risk Report 2023 (https://www3.weforum.org/docs/WEF_Global_Risks_Report_2023.pdf); environmental risks appear rarely among top 5 short term risks (2 years). When physical climate risks are mentioned, it is as extreme events or failures of adaptation—failure to mitigate climate change appears among the top five risks only for Zambia (and only Chad lists ecosystem collapse among its top 5 near future risks). Cost of living crisis, debts and inflation risks dominate risk tables and these are the main reasons that governments are pouring billions (trillions globally) into fossil subsidies (removing these subsidies would raise food prices and fuel costs for those already struggling to afford the basics, add to inflationary pressures, and risk public unrest). Terrorism, war and collapse of vital infrastructure (development) are top risks for both experts and students.

Most students have heard of climate change from the media, but many incorrectly considered the hole in the ozone as a major cause. Students realised that the USA and China had a large share of responsibility for the climate crisis, but linked it to pollution caused by Chinese projects locally in Uganda. No one linked precipitation in Uganda and the conditions in the Indian Ocean (the main driver of rain variability). Fewer than half linked the Paris Agreement to temperature as opposed to wine or the ozone layer (most only heard of the Paris Agreement and associated targets for the first time during the quiz). Students had not heard of climate tipping points, but appreciated that deforestation and biodiversity loss were threats. Most could not locate carbon (C) on the periodic table (many had not learned about it yet in school). No one guessed correctly that plants or animals (humans were pictured) contained carbon, but most knew that coal did. Students were unfamiliar with common graphical representations of probability and uncertainty, such as bar plots or probability density functions. Students had trouble reading heat maps, bar charts, and other common data visualisation formats. These difficulties were partially due to the fact that Uganda closed schools for longer than any other country during the Covid-19 pandemic—most students missed out on two years of education.

Most students have heard of climate change from the media, but many incorrectly considered the hole in the ozone as a major cause. Students realised that China and USA had a large share of responsibility for the climate crisis, but linked it to pollution caused by Chinese projects locally in Uganda. No one linked precipitation in Uganda and the conditions in the Indian Ocean (the main driver of rain variability). Fewer than half linked the Paris Agreement to temperature as opposed to wine or the ozone layer (most have heard of the Paris Agreement and associated targets for the first time during the quiz). Students have not heard of climate tipping points, but appreciated that deforestation and biodiversity were threats. Most could not locate carbon (C) on the periodic table (many have not learned about it yet in school). No one guessed correctly that plants or animals (humans were pictured) contained carbon, but most knew that coal did. Students were unfamiliar with common graphical representations of probability and uncertainty, such as bar plots or probability density functions. Students had trouble reading heat maps, bar charts, and other common data visualisation formats. These difficulties were partially due to the fact that Uganda closed schools for longer than any other country during the pandemic—most students missed out on two years of education.

PRIORITISING COMMUNICATION GOALS

The educators in Uganda were especially interested in bolstering students' ability to interpret data. In determining priorities for learning outcomes in our project, we also considered Uganda's government agenda for climate education—*National Climate Change Communication Strategy* (2018) developed by the Ministry for Water and Environment. The messages to enhance climate resilience are very practical, for example:

Agriculture: modernise farming by adopting new technologies and methods; use better seed varieties; introduce (drip) irrigation and rain harvesting; introduce climate and market smart decision-making (what to do, when to do it, e.g. how much to apply fertilisers or pesticides); switch to agroforestry; manage livestock to avoid overgrazing.

Energy: stop using charcoal, switch to solar and biogas.

STRENGTH (Internal)	WEAKNESS (Internal)
• Availability of climate change adaptation and mitigation information on better practices. • Numerous channels of communication. • Readiness of the masses to change attitudes, behaviors and practices if effective and efficient climate change communication is done. • Availability of technical personnel in climate change communication. • Political will to support climate change communication.	• Climate change action is usually unfunded priority. • Climate change issues are not mainstreamed in the government's plans and budgets. • Lack of enough technical personnel for climate change communication. • Diversion of resources meant for climate change adaptation and mitigation to other sectors. • Lack of convincing and cheap alternatives to those involved in activities that adversely affect the environment. • Limited internal capacity to mobilize resources for climate change action.
OPPORTUNITIES (External)	**THREATS (External)**
• Availability of climate funds that can be tapped in to support climate change communication in Uganda. • Ready technology from partners for replication in Uganda. • Development partners ready to support climate change related efforts in the country. • Trainable human resource for climate change communication action.	• Least appreciation of climate change issues by influencers and champions. • Misconception and misrepresentation of climate change by some politicians and religious leaders. • Climate change deniers. • Over reliance on indigenous and traditional knowledge by some sections of the society for climate action and prediction. • Negative perceptions by the public about the meteorologists in Uganda.

Figure 3. SWOT table reproduced from the Ugandan National Climate Change Communication Strategy (2018)

Specifically for youth, the strategy advises: 'be empowered, live safely with changing Environment' and 'voice your concerns, speak out.' For extension officers and planners, it advises putting more emphasis on Indigenous knowledge. For climate action, the report recommends tree planting, adopting green technologies, public transport, improving disaster warning systems, preserving biodiversity, wetlands, and enhancing forests, stopping the encroachment of agriculture on ecosystems and halting the practice of bush burning. It does not mention 'polyculture' specifically, though this is largely due to how language is used. In Uganda polyculture is a common practice, farmers mix subsistence and cash crops with plant varieties (such as legumes) to improve the fertility of the soil.

The *Strategy* advises on a number of ways to communicate key messages, from armbands to theatre, although it does not mention games (and neither does *The National Climate Change Act 2021*, a detailed, nearly 200-page long policy document). The appendix to the *Strategy* report offers a SWOT analysis for climate change communication in Uganda that was informative in the planning stages of the project, shaping discussions regarding activities and stories that might be effective. For example, in one of the stories written for the project, Dilman incorporated a joke about a meteorologist and in another, a corrupt local official who is trying to get rich from a poorly designed waste management policy.

DEVELOPING IDEAS

Having identified the gaps in the students' knowledge, and after consulting on national priorities, a series of long conversations over regular Zoom meetings and frequent WhatsApp exchanges ensued between Dilman (writer), Maurice (educator) and Polina (environmental scientist) that culminated in five stories by Dilman that addressed the key themes. On the basis of Dilman Dila's stories, Jo Lindsay Walton (game designer) led the creation of a TTRPG (tabletop roleplaying game) that encouraged exploring climate themes in a free-form manner.

The game was grounded in Dilman Dila's worldbuilding but not confined to it, enabling the players to expand and morph it according to their imagination. The game also incorporated some of the learning outcomes that local educators prioritised. Dilman Dila's stories formed a foundation not only for the game but also for other activities that we collectively developed that offered a more focused approach to specific climate topics, such as historical responsibility for climate change or balancing mitigation and food security. Nonetheless, we aimed to avoid creating 'lesson plans', crafting activities that albeit nerdy (e.g. math puzzles) were still playful, and if anything, felt subversive to their usual school learning because they hybridised through puns or metaphors subjects that are taught as distinct streams. This was not a systematic embedding or mainstreaming of sustainability across the curriculum, but cartoonish mashups that students, to our relief, found entertaining. Creating these side-dishes of activities took a long time, as many ideas were discarded before the first prototypes were presented to the students. We also worked on developing Tarsia-like puzzles to explore

Figure 4. Kampala Yénkya, TTRPG

ten specific climate issues in relation to each story, but eventually decided to set aside this approach in favour of a much more diverse and odd set of activities, and, of course, the TTRPG.

Dilman Dila created illustrations for the stories that are published by Ping Press, together with the games and activities. We built a website where educators are able to download games, activities and other resources, while students can anonymously create climate action plans.

Figures 5, 6, 7. Story illustrations by Dilman Dila

CHALLENGES

Although we have no good data on the prevalence of tabletop role-playing (TTRPG) in Uganda or in Africa more widely, there is evidence to suggest it is not well-established. For example, the Applied Hope Games Jam and Utopia on the Tabletop project in 2021, which included two open calls, attracted over eighty submissions from TTRPG designers, players, artists, and scholars, none of whom were from Africa. From amongst 200 students collaborating with us on the project, not a single one had played a TTRPG before. It was not easy to convince local educators to attempt to introduce it.

Storytelling and games are educational technologies widely used in the Global North and realising that Ugandan youth was missing out was one reason for attempting the project. But it was also a challenge, because TTRPG play can involve a high level of tacit knowledge. The written rules of TTRPGs work in concert with unwritten rules and competencies which are transmitted in a living tradition of performance and storytelling. Players also often adapt the official core game to their own preferences by adding or modifying rules (homebrew rules, table rules, safety tools). Without one or two experienced players to show how it is done, it can be tricky to get it started.

So this small project was attempting to make several leaps at once. We hoped to create a game suitable for players who might all be new to TTRPGs. We also hoped to create a game that would be both fun and educational. We were also interested in a certain type of TTRPG experience: cooperative, contemplative, non-hierarchical games such as *For the Queen* and *The Quiet Year*, rather than the more popular action-focused TTRPGs focused on violent resolution of conflict, and without collaborative worldbuilding. There was also some speculation as to how TTRPGs might interact with existing Ugandan cultures of oral storytelling, which often have their own interactive elements. We speculated that this might perhaps be an advantage, but we had no way to be sure.

Given more time and resources, there are obvious ways to address the challenge of tacit knowledge. Experienced TTRPG players could be sought, within Uganda as well as globally, to share game sessions with staff and students from the schools. These could be conducted in-person or online. These could include the climate-themed game we created for the project or — since the main purpose would be to show the possibilities of TTRPG play — other games could also be played. Some of these could also be recorded as "actual play" podcasts or videos. Internet connectivity can be challenging and expensive, however.

LEARNING OUTCOMES

What did we want to teach? Because the environmental clubs were new and existing materials were very scarce, we had a lot of leeway. This was also intimidating.

To develop a general sense of learning outcomes, we consulted sources including Uganda's national climate risk communication strategy (whose implementation was held back by Covid and other factors), the national curriculum (especially Geography), and materials associated with Youth for Future Africa. We also benefited from the direct experience of team member Maurice Ssebisubi. Later on, to develop specific questions and answers, we also relied on academic literature.

We wanted some balance of the following:

- An emphasis on adaptation to climate risk that could be actioned in practical ways right away.
- Supporting players to create their own speculative futures, well-informed about the uncertainties, and controversies. The aim was to build on "futures literacy" perspectives (UNESCO) by incorporating Africanfuturist and solarpunk speculative storytelling.
- An emphasis on climate justice.
- Foundational concepts in climate science and climate policy.
- Debunking of misconceptions around climate change.

Once more, there are some obvious approaches which we would ideally have liked to have used. Learning outcomes would benefit from more extensive co-production, especially in embedding and elaborating local and traditional knowledge useful for climate resilience.

WORLDBUILDING

One question was whether or not to set the game in a future Kampala, like the narratives, or to leave it more open. There were arguments on both sides. For a time, we explored the option of an imaginary city, Akasozi City, as potentially more freeing of the imagination. On balance we preferred imagining a future Kampala as a more relatable undertaking. For similar reasons the date moved around from 2060, to 2080, to 2100, then back to 2060.

Some reviewers who did not live in Uganda did express strong preferences for either a more abstract setting, or a choice of settings. We decided this was a good idea in principle, but out of scope for this particular project.

PLAYTESTING

Iteration is a core tenet of almost all game design. Games are (just like climates?) filled with non-linearity and tipping points. Small adjustments to mechanics can sometimes result in huge differences to game dynamics and the experience of players. Playtesting is also when tacit knowledge, invisible to the designers and writers, often floats to the surface — watching new players come up with entirely legitimate but unexpected interpretations of the written rules.

Because of the pilot nature of the project, we would not be able to carry out all the playtesting we would really like to. We could slightly mitigate the challenge of playtesting a totally new game by borrowing mechanics from an existing game (piggybacking on its playtesting). Avery Alder's elegant *The Quiet Year* formed the mechanical basis. However, there was still a lot of playtesting that went into creating a final prototype. The game was fully tested with several teams in the UK.

The game mechanics were explored without storytelling, and statistical modelling in R (open source software) was used to assess various point weights combinations. In Uganda, playtesting involved many teams, several game iterations and two physical prototypes. The feedback that was generously provided over the course of several school terms was incorporated and the game kept evolving until the students were satisfied.

Figure 8. UYE Club playtesters in Uganda.

In game design a few tweaks could still change everything, so even a modest hack of a well-tested game is likely to fail in many ways on its first few outings. But at least this wasn't the first time that our lead designer had hacked this particular game and playtested the results, so we did have some sense of which mechanics might be more sensitive to changes. Nonetheless, it was uncharted territory especially since the students were encountering TTRPGs for the first time. However, it was an instant hit. The demand exceeded the expectations, and we have already printed twice as many games as promised in the proposal. We are hoping to expand to more schools across Uganda and beyond, in the future.

Some of the major changes driven by playtesting included:

- The integration of a competition mechanic. The initial version had an end condition but no win condition.
- Clarifying the conditions under which the game can end, after exploring how the chance of ending the game in a particular way depends on the difficulty level of the game's climate questions.
- Adding a Facilitator role and addressing the rules more directly to this person.
- Making the Q&A text much shorter, by moving most of the text to a "Further Information" appendix.
- Creating two versions of the game where point weights differed, with custom cards having a more randomised set of values, in part to discourage paying attention to strategy and reorient the players towards storytelling. The free Oracle version, that

Figure 9. Group of playtesters in Uganda.

can be played with a regular set of cards, has by necessity a simpler point structure.

- Adding 'inspiration cards': this was done in part to achieve a balance between providing freedom to the players to tell their own stories, and giving them structure, support, and prompts not merely to reproduce dominant narratives about the future. The inspiration cards are optional, but add flexibility to the game, and could also be used for other purposes (e.g. creative writing or storytelling prompts). The inspiration cards were based largely on Dila's work, with some additions and adaptations from Levontin and Walton.

Some of the major changes driven by reviewing included:

- Many changes to the content of the worldbuilding and storytelling prompts. This included more customization to Uganda.

EVALUATION

We collected and made use of feedback throughout the development of the game, but once the final prototype was agreed upon, we followed up with a formal evaluation. Ssebisubi randomly invited 30 players to anonymously fill out a questionnaire. We asked students who recently played the KY game the following questions:

- What parts did you like best?
- How did it make you feel?
- Did you learn anything new?
- Did it create new questions?
- Was there a speculative idea or technology that you wish was real?
- What was your favourite idea?
- Can you think of actions you can take now for climate justice?

The responses were overwhelmingly positive in terms of enjoyment and affirmed that some of the learning outcomes were achieved. In particular, the questionnaire confirmed that key climate communication messages concerning charcoal, solar power, forests, sustainable transport and agriculture were successfully delivered via the game.

Figure 10. Kampala Yénkya, story, game, and activity book, freely downloadable at imagine-alternatives.com.

AUTHOR CONTRIBUTIONS:

Research: *JLW, PL, MS, and DD;* **Writing:** *JLW;* **Creative Input:** *JLW, DD, and JK.*

Chapter 7: HACKS, INSIGHTS, AND RESOURCES

INTRODUCTION

As climate risk communication grows more important in society, what tools and insights will be of use to communicators?

This final chapter is something of a grab-bag. It contains tips for **using visuals** in climate risk communication, tips for **communicating with policymakers,** some **provocations** collected from the COP26 Universities Network Climate Risk Summit workshop on climate risk communication (October 2021), some useful **definitions** about uncertainty and risk, and the beginnings of a **growing directory of climate risk communication resources,** also available here as a living document (bit.ly/ClimateCommsTools).

The authors of this Toolkit are hopeful that future iterations will be possible to expand this practice-oriented content, and we welcome feedback, recommendations, and offers of collaboration and co-production. In the years to come climate risk communication will be an increasingly important theme, and there is every chance that the field will diversify, mutate, and undergo fragmentation while also being shaped by projects of inventory, synthesis, simplification and curation.

What is the future of climate risk communication? Whatever it is, it's coming at us fast. There are already a wealth of available resources out there about communicating with policy and the general public, a small handful of which are signposted below. Many of these resources conceptualise climate risk communication in a fairly generic and high level way; creating such resources, exploring innovations, testing them empirically and refining them, and introducing them into new contexts will remain important work going forward. However, our experience of assembling this Toolkit has also suggested the need for more tools and resources doing the following seven things.

(a) Innovate on scope, including much more targeted and niche approaches aimed at a smaller number of users and applicable to a smaller number situations, but in more specific and concrete ways;

(b) Innovate on participation, including tools which embed the insights of international and historical global perspectives, and a real orientation to substantive equity and just transition;

(c) Innovate on standards and scores, including tools which seek to address the shortcomings and risks of league tables, reporting frameworks, and 'gamified' climate transition;

(d) Innovate on customisation, modularity, and recombinancy, exploring for example how more tailored tools (as in (a) above) can be created at scale, using robust procedural generation methods;

(e) Innovate on framing, exploring for example ways to spread climate change and climate action throughout culture and society, rather than letting it be boxed off as a specific topic or theme;

(f) Innovate on reflexivity, including tools which help users to reflect on the tools' own limitations, understand where those tools may need to be adapted, or where users might go to find a more appropriate tool (or where the material circumstances are not adequate to achieve the desired purposes, no matter what communications and/or decision support tool is used);

(g) Innovate on findability. It's already a crowded landscape, and it's likely to get more crowded. This may mean meta-resources (curated directories etc.), and other ways of getting resources to those who need them when they need them.

Subsections

Introduction

5 Tips for using data visualisation to communicate about climate change

5 Tips for using photo resources to communicate about climate change

10 tips for dialogue with policymakers

Conversations at the COP26 Universities Network's Climate Risk Summit

Definitions of risk, uncertainty, and related terms from the IPCC

Classifying uncertainty

Tools and resources

5 TIPS FOR USING DATA VISUALISATIONS
TO COMMUNICATE ABOUT CLIMATE CHANGE

THE PRINCIPLE OF EXPRESSIVENESS

» A data visualisation should encode all the relevant information, and no irrelevant information.

» Avoid unnecessary decoration and 'chart junk.'

» **HOWEVER:** there can be exceptions; for instance, a truly novel or clever presentation may be more eye-catching and memorable for some users.

THE PRINCIPLE OF APPROPRIATE KNOWLEDGE

» Make sure your user knows the conventions for extracting the relevant information.

» E.g. you can: provide a clear key and explanatory notes; use conventions that are well-established; provide training.

» **HOWEVER:** if a user is interpreting a visualisation 'wrongly' there may be a deeper reason. So be prepared to listen and adjust your own expectations about what is and is not relevant.

THE SEMANTIC PRINCIPLE

» Choose conventions that will support correct interpretation, even in the absence of appropriate knowledge.

» This can be thought of as making 'natural' or 'common sense' choices, aligned with common schemas such as 'bigger means more' or 'red or orange means conflict / danger / heat.'

» **HOWEVER:** visual elements come with baggage you can't wish away, and which will be different for different users.

COLLABORATE ACROSS DISCIPLINE

» For example, visualisation teams can bring together climate experts, end users, graphic designers, science communication practitioners, as well as researchers across the social sciences and arts and humanities (especially the digital humanities and the environmental humanities), and wider stakeholder communities.

» **HOWEVER:** reaching consensus across diverse roles is not a substitute for robust testing.

TEST YOUR VISUALISATION

» Ideally you should test comprehension and decision quality with the actual end users, in the actual use setting, using an objective methodology.

» Self-reporting is not reliable. A graphic designer's satisfied client is not the same as a user making good choices.

» **HOWEVER:** some testing is always better than none, even if it is informal.

5 TIPS FOR USING PHOTO RESOURCES
TO COMMUNICATE ABOUT CLIMATE CHANGE

MAKE IT SPECIFIC

- » Show real people's everyday lives. Avoid stock photography or scenes that look very staged.
- » Show human subjects. But be cautious when representing causes of climate change: it may be better to try to show the causes on larger scales, rather than 'blaming' individual consumers, for example.
- » Show specific, serious impacts at a local scale, and use captions and text to tell your audience what they're seeing.

EVERYBODY LOVES A CRYSTAL BALL

- » People want to see 'how we will live in the future.' Photos are not the most obvious way to do this ….
- » … however, showing low carbon behavior and other climate 'solutions' can at least prefigure the future. They can also produce more positive emotional responses, and they are usually less polarising.
- » Also take care not to imply that you are illustrating the future, if that's not what you're doing.

KNOW YOUR AUDIENCE (EVEN BETTER, LISTEN TO THEM)

- » As with any form of communication, it helps to know your audience or — even better! — to engage in dialogue with them.
- » Remember to listen openly, and be prepared to adjust your own perceptions.
- » Remember, what you see is not necessarily what they see.

EXPERIMENT

- » Don't rely exclusively on familiar climate images such as melting ice caps or smoke stacks.
- » Climate change affects everything. Make fresh connections and tell new stories.
- » Sometimes imaginative artistic and curatorial choices can make a usually cliched subjects feel fresh and new.

CONSIDER THE CONTEXT

- » How do your images relate to your text? To each other? What emergent story do they tell?
- » What other associations might your images have that you didn't intend? Deciding those associations aren't relevant doesn't mean they won't impact your audience. You can't wish them away, but you can be aware of them.
- » Working with arts and humanities researchers (e.g. environmental humanities) may help to understand the context.

10 TIPS FOR DIALOGUE WITH POLICYMAKERS

THESE TEN TIPS FOCUS ON THE UK CONTEXT, BUT THEY ARE APPLICABLE IN MANY PLACES ...

1. **Listen actively to create real dialogue.** The temptation to go into "lecture mode" is real. It can help to prepare structured interactive formats in advance. The presence of a trained and experienced facilitator can make a big difference. Keep in mind your policymaker(s) may have many kinds of expertise of their own. Later, when you follow up (e.g. a letter of thanks), show that you are listening to policymakers' expertise, agendas, priorities, and needs.

2. **Prepare key insights in advance.** Make your advice memorable; "make your advice concise" (Tyler 2013). Do communicate complexity and uncertainty around your key insights, don't obscure those insights. Come prepared, but be cautious of becoming too attached to any pre-prepared insights (or to specific ways of expressing them). A real commitment to dialogue implies adaptability.

3. **Give options and talk about the pros and cons of each.** You want to strike a balance between "I think you should do x" and "I'm here with the facts, what happens next is your problem." When you present options in a balanced way, policymakers can integrate their own insider expertise on policy trends, political acceptability, policy levers, and their own understandings of uncertainty. Be supportive and attentive, and ready to clarify, reframe, or update your options if necessary. "Policy making is iterative; the art of the possible" (Tyler 2013).

4. **Expect policymakers' time to be limited.** Do your homework about who you are speaking to, so you can make the most of whatever time you have together. A pragmatic science-policy co-production process may consist of several short sessions with different groups of policymakers (De Meyer et al. 2021).

5. **Try to meet policymakers where they are.** Remember that in many policy areas, "[s]tarting policies from scratch is very rarely an option" (Tyler 2013). Deep and rapid changes are necessary, but options always need to take into account what is already there. Connect your information with the structures, risks and opportunities that policymakers already intuitively understand. This may involve their specific area of responsibility, and/or broader concerns such as jobs or national security. Climate risk affects all aspects of society, so you should be able to find ways to connect with policymakers where they are already.

6. **If the mood is against you, try saying it another way.** At any given moment and policy context, there will be assumptions which are very hard for you to shift. When assumptions cannot go unchallenged, then of course you should have the courage to do so. But also be aware that you may be seen as unreasonable, even when the evidence is firmly on your side. Your other option is to remove the jarring elements of your message, and find some other way of expressing the same thing.

7. **Bring all your expertise, and bring your networks too.** Be prepared to speak beyond the specific research you are engaging in. Also look out for emergent opportunities to facilitate connections. You may not be speaking to exactly the right policymaker, or you may not be exactly the right expert for this policymaker to be speaking to.

8. **Celebrate positive and plural action.** Climate change is polarising but climate change is also urgent. Mitigation and resilience should not be unduly delayed by efforts to get everyone on the same page. If you are at an impasse with policymakers, try to support them to take some positive action in the short term (even when based on reasons you disagree with) and keep dialogue open in the longer term. Mutually exclusive frameworks can still give rise to policies that are mutually complementary.

9. **Be ambitious in shifting the bigger narratives around climate risk.** Consider how you might engage with less obvious departments and agencies. Explore both direct and indirect engagement with policymakers, e.g. through the media, grassroots organizations, community groups, think tanks, pressure groups, consultants, professional services networks, industry and third sector, social media and broader cultural production.

10. **Rapport changes the rules.** Where possible, seek to build longer-term relationships, especially at the more local level. "Policy makers are people" (Tyler 2013).

RECOMMENDED FURTHER READING:

De Meyer, Kris, Freya Roberts and Lucy Hubble-Rose, 'Risk for Elephants: Three insights from the sciences of brain and mind to understand and improve risk communication' and 'Golden nuggets: communicating with policymakers' (Climate Action Unit, 2021). https://www.doi.org/10.14324/000.rp.10137325

Sutherland, William J., David Spiegelhalter, and Mark Burgman. 2013. 'Policy: Twenty Tips for Interpreting Scientific Claims'. *Nature* 503 (7476): 335–37. https://www.doi.org/10.1038/503335a.

Tyler, Chris. 2013. 'Top 20 Things Scientists Need to Know about Policy-Making'. *The Guardian*, 2013. https://www.theguardian.com/science/2013/dec/02/scientists-policy-governments-science.

CONVERSATIONS *AT THE* COP26 UNIVERSITIES NETWORK'S CLIMATE RISK SUMMIT

SOME OF THE MOST RECENT CHATTER ABOUT CLIMATE RISK COMMUNICATION

COP26 Universities Network Climate Risk Summit took place over three days from the 29th September to the 1st October 2021. The last day was dedicated to an [interactive workshop](#) with just under a hundred participants (scientists, policymakers, consultants, engineers, lawyers, etc.) exploring the theme of communicating climate risks. Here are a few questions and insights shared on the day; this Toolkit is, in part, our response.

RESPONSES FROM A QUESTIONNAIRE

The question we asked was: *"Please give a specific example of a challenge you have faced around climate risk communication and decision-making. (For example, a challenge in communicating information, or a challenge in finding and interpreting the information you need. It could be a past challenge, or an ongoing challenge. Try to be as specific as possible)."*

See [Climate Risk Communication engagement](#) form.

Contributions may be incorporated into any future iteration of this Toolkit.

Some of the challenges that respondents mentioned:

- Desire for "sound bites" not contextual understanding
- Trust in the wrong even openly (science-)fictional sources of information
- Political bias
- Perceived lack of agency in response to risk
- Perceived irrelevance to lived experience
- Uncertainty over what values one holds
- Difficulty in grasping complex non-linear systemic risks
- Scientists assuming that everyone thinks like them
- Peer-review system denying scientists an opportunity to encounter diverse audiences
- Jargon and responsibility the scientists feel necessary to communicate details and caveats instead of a simplified narrative
- Tendency to emotionally reject information that entails large changes
- Tendency for people to interpret new information in support of prior beliefs regardless of its content
- Inaccessible styles of communication (long complex sentences)
- Uncertainty of what someone's baseline knowledge is
- Making unambiguous and intuitive visualisation that preserve the detail and uncertainty of science
- Communicating uncertainty effectively, ensuring that it is correctly understood
- Communicating modelling uncertainty while not miscommunicating a sense of urgency and credibility of results
- Finding up to date and relevant local information in the developing world
- Making information about the distant future feel pertinent
- Making information about risks in distant places feel pertinent
- Constructing 'what if?' future scenarios based on current knowledge across different timelines
- Connecting climate risks to actions in indirectly impacted domains, such as cardiology

HIGHLIGHTS FROM THE ZOOM CHAT

Here are a selection of thought-provoking comments from the climate risk communication workshop Zoom chat. They have been anonymised, and in one or two cases slightly tweaked for spelling and readability.

"We need to work together to bring together academia and practitioners in risk communication. Culture is a factor in assessing whether messages are relevant and effective in communication with different groups of stakeholders, notably the younger generation."

"We need to move towards a dialogue model — the people 'on the ground' have crucial knowledge and approaches to bring to the discussion, and should not purely be viewed as 'recipients' of 'beneficiaries' of climate information."

"Do we sufficiently understand the value of uncertainty in terms of informing robust decisions?"

"There are so many human difficulties in perception of risk, especially for low-frequency high-impact events."

"'Understanding the meaning behind the numbers' is very important for many disciplines, including my own (finance)."

"Society needs to engage so as to hold decision-makers to account for the impact of their decisions."

"Does 'risk communication' become more effective when it includes 'response communication' or 'solutions communication'?"

"The challenge with risk and uncertainty is that different people and different decisions (even for the same person) may have different risk appetites, and as a result can cope with different levels of uncertainty."

"I like engaging with end-users, but it really does take work to understand their needs, and their jargon, and your own, and bridge it."

"Actively engaging with the end-user is critical for understanding their perspectives, their pain points and their motivations. It has been essential to adapting the messages and the tools to their needs."

"On communicating with business leaders: generally they get the urgency of climate change, but persuading them that it's their responsibility, or that it's in their interests to act ambitiously (especially when the economic system doesn't incentivise them to lead change) is the most challenging thing."

"I think that's a really interesting point about identifying user needs but also working with users to transform how they understand their own needs…"

"A huge one is the assumption of the need for economic growth / GDP / cost-benefit analysis as key measures of success, therefore 'greenness' needing to sit alongside growth in the form of 'sustainable' 'green' 'inclusive' etc., rather than moving away from economic growth as a priority altogether."

"GDP is fundamentally flawed when talking about sustainability, but that is a topic most incumbent policymakers in many countries don't want to engage with."

"Degrowth also means deconsumption, which means fewer jobs."

"Of course, 'degrowth' is also one of those terms that can mean many things, e.g. some prefer to talk about 'post-growth' or 'growth agnostic' approaches, or just talk about 'decoupling,' or Beyond GDP metrics."

"I really like Lord Deben's argument that we should reclaim the word 'growth' as people's associations with it are positive (children grow, plants grow, we grow professionally etc.), but redefine what we're trying to grow."

"I definitely would NOT call this the capitalocene. The, 'rentalocene' yes. Remember the extra money is not made based on the capital good as such; the capital good is used as a facade to extract rents. So rentalism is a better term than capitalism. In a 'true capitalist' system there wouldn't even be the possibility to pollute, because the competitors wouldn't allow it."

"I think honesty on the part of scientists is important. When I attend small circle seminars scientists are more honest and humble about what they really know and what they conjecture about. Honesty can help one carry their message further. Scientists pretending they know things they don't know is not only dishonest, it also hurts the credibility of scientists."

WHEN WORDS MEAN DIFFERENT THINGS IN DIFFERENT CONTEXTS

We asked: "Anyone want to share a word that has different uses in different contexts?" Participants flagged up terms such as *adaptation; life cycle analysis* (meaning different things in biochemistry and engineering domains) *one-in-a-hundred-year flood; positive trends* (does it mean increasing or good?); *just transition; materiality* (material financial risks to the business, or material risks to people and planet (or both), or tangibility and physicality); *flexibility* (the same arrangements may be seen as flexible or inflexible from the perspective of employer or employee); and *ethics* (in business this often connotes a compliance and liability orientation, rather than a concern with what is right and wrong, which happens (if at all) in connection with terms like CSR and ESG). Of course there are many more. Can you think of some?

DEFINITIONS OF RISK, UNCERTAINTY, *AND* RELATED TERMS FROM THE IPCC

AR6 WGI strongly reinforces the need for rapid and deep reduction in CO2 and other GHG emissions (achieving at least net zero) alongside other forms of climate action. There is no room for reasonable doubt about this. Nonetheless, uncertainty and risk remain crucial concepts to mediate between climate science and appropriate climate action. For its recent AR6 WGI report, **the IPCC has outlined definitions of uncertainty and risk.** We have deliberately not aligned the Toolkit to these IPCC definitions. This is because we want to showcase a range of different understandings of these concepts, and how they may impact communication. A more flexible approach is therefore appropriate for this Toolkit. However, it is also useful to present the IPCC definitions here, since these are referred to in several places in the Toolkit, and form relevant background throughout.

On the subject of **risk** specifically, AR6 WGI states that it has

> *adopted a unified framework of climate risk, supported by an increased focus in WGI on low-likelihood, high-impact events. Systematic risk framing is intended to aid the formulation of effective responses to the challenges posed by current and future climatic changes and to better inform risk assessment and decision-making. AR6 also makes use of the 'storylines' approach, which contributes to building a robust and comprehensive picture of climate information, allows a more flexible consideration and communication of risk, and can explicitly address low-likelihood, high-impact events.*
>
> *(AR WGI, Ch 1, p. 6)*

The following definitions are from AR6 WGI 'Annex VII: Glossary' (2021).[1]

Risk: The potential for adverse consequences for human or ecological systems, recognising the diversity of values and objectives associated with such systems. In the context of *climate change,* risks can arise from potential impacts of climate change as well as human responses to climate change. Relevant adverse consequences include those on lives, *livelihoods,* health and *well-being,* economic, social and cultural assets and investments, infrastructure, services (including *ecosystem services*), *ecosystems* and species.

In the context of climate change impacts, risks result from dynamic interactions between climate-related *hazards* with the *exposure* and *vulnerability* of the affected human or ecological system to the hazards. Hazards, exposure and vulnerability may each be subject to uncertainty in terms of magnitude and *likelihood* of occurrence, and each may change over time and space due to socio-economic changes and human decision-making (see also *risk management, adaptation* and *mitigation*).

In the context of climate change responses, risks result from the potential for such responses not achieving the intended objective(s), or from potential trade-offs with, or negative side-effects on, other societal objectives, such as the *Sustainable Development Goals* (SDGs) (see also *risk trade-off*). Risks can arise for example from uncertainty in implementation, effectiveness or outcomes of climate policy, climate-related investments, technology development or adoption, and system transitions. See also *Hazard* and *Impacts* (*consequences, outcomes*).

Uncertainty: A state of incomplete knowledge that can result from a lack of information or from disagreement about what is known or even knowable. It may have many types of sources, from imprecision in the data to ambiguously defined concepts or terminology, incomplete understanding of critical processes, or uncertain projections of *human behaviour.* Uncertainty can therefore be represented by quantitative measures (e.g. a probability density function) or by qualitative statements (e.g. reflecting the judgment of a team of experts) (Burgman 2016). See also *Confidence* and *Likelihood*.

Note that the definitions of *risk* and *uncertainty* do not cross-reference each other. Further definitions directly related to **risk and uncertainty** from the IPCC AR6 WGI Glossary include:

Deep uncertainty: A situation of deep uncertainty exists when experts or stakeholders do not know or cannot agree on: (1) appropriate conceptual models that describe relationships among key driving forces in a system; (2) the probability distributions used to represent uncertainty about key variables and parameters; and/or (3) how to weigh and value desirable alternative outcomes (Lempert, Popper, and Bankes 2003).

---

1   Italics and other cross-citational information has been preserved as in the original, and two minor amendments ("trickle backs") listed at the top of the Annex have been implemented in the text. As with all citations to the AR6 WGI at the time of writing, these definitions remain subject to final IPCC edits.

Sampling uncertainty: Uncertainty arising from incomplete or uneven availability of measurements in either space or time or both.

Risk assessment: The qualitative and/or quantitative estimation of risks. See also *Risk management* and *Risk perception.*

Risk framework: A common framework for describing and assessing risk across all three working groups is adopted to promote clear and consistent communication of risks and to better inform risk assessment and decision making related to climate change.

Risk management: Plans, actions, strategies or policies to reduce the *likelihood* and/or magnitude of adverse potential consequences, based on assessed or perceived *risks*. See also *Risk assessment, Risk perception,* and *Risk transfer.*

Risk perception: The subjective judgment that people make about the characteristics and severity of a *risk*. See also *Risk assessment, Risk management,* and *Risk transfer.*

Risk trade-off: The change in the portfolio of risks that occurs when a countervailing *risk* is generated (knowingly or inadvertently) by an intervention to reduce the target risk (Graham and Wiener 1995).

Other definitions relevant to understanding the IPCC's approach to risk and uncertainty include:

Agreement: In this report, the degree of agreement within the scientific body of knowledge on a particular finding is assessed based on multiple lines of *evidence* (e.g. mechanistic understanding, theory, data, models, expert judgement) and expressed qualitatively (Mastrandrea et al. 2011). See also *Confidence, Likelihood, Uncertainty,* and *Evidence.*

Confidence: The robustness of a finding based on the type, amount, quality and consistency of *evidence* (e.g. mechanistic understanding, theory, data, models, expert judgment) and on the degree of *agreement* across multiple lines of evidence. In this report, confidence is expressed qualitatively (Mastrandrea et al. 2011).

Hazard: The potential occurrence of a natural or human-induced physical event or trend that may cause loss of life, injury, or other health impacts, as well as damage and loss to property, infrastructure, livelihoods, service provision, ecosystems and environmental resources.

Impacts: The consequences of realised risks on natural and human systems, where risks result from the interactions of climate-related hazards (including extreme weather / climate events), exposure, and vulnerability. Impacts generally refer to effects on lives, livelihoods, health and wellbeing, ecosystems and species, economic, social and cultural assets, services (including ecosystem services), and infrastructure. Impacts may be referred to as consequences or outcomes, and can be adverse or beneficial.

Low-likelihood, high impact events: Outcomes/events whose probability of occurrence is low or not well known (as in the context of deep uncertainty) but whose potential impacts on society and ecosystems could be high. To better inform risk assessment and decision-making, such low-likelihood outcomes are considered if they are associated with very large consequences and may therefore constitute material risks, even though those consequences do not necessarily represent the most likely outcome.

CLASSIFYING UNCERTAINTY

As the COVID-19 pandemic has made obvious, people's ways of making decisions under uncertainty vary greatly across individuals. For example, cultural and political beliefs shape what different individuals perceive as reasonable. Cognitive biases which are fairly uniform across cultures may manifest in different ways according to the circumstances of the individual. Differences can be present even in closely knit groups of scientists, who are likely to perceive some scientific uncertainties in divergent ways, or even have different mental pictures of what different uncertainties are and what their relative importance is. This is especially true in connection to tipping points or other 'deep uncertainties'.

Knowledge about climate risks comes from many sources: observations, experiments, theory, and models (embodied, conceptual, statistical, simulations, etc.). Each source of knowledge contains many different forms of uncertainty, and there is no universal system for classifying them. Here we offer a few fairly broad and commonly recognised categories of uncertainty. Some categories may overlap.

RECOMMENDED FURTHER READING:

Levontin, Polina et al. 2020. Visualising Uncertainty: A Short Introduction. AU4DM.
au4dmnetworks.co.uk/resources/

French, Simon (ed), 2019. Decision Support Tools for Complex Decisions Under Uncertainty. AU4DM.
au4dmnetworks.co.uk/resources/

- **Stochastic uncertainties:** Physical randomness of the physical, ecological, social, economic, or technical processes.
- **Epistemological uncertainties:** Limitations to our ability to describe/represent the world linguistically, mathematically, or statistically.
- **Observational uncertainties:** Limitations to our ability to record what is going on. Observational uncertainties might include limitations such as:
  › **Accuracy:** the difference between observation and reality;
  › **Precision:** the quality of the estimate or measurement;
  › **Completeness:** the extent to which information is comprehensive;
  › **Consistency:** the extent to which information elements agree (conflicts in data);
  › **Lineage:** the pathway through which information has been passed;
  › **Currency and temporality** more generally: the time span from occurrence to collection of data;
  › **Credibility:** the reliability of the information source;
  › **Subjectivity:** the extent to which the observer influences the observation;
  › **Interrelatedness:** the dependence on other information;
  › **Spatial coverage**.
- **Semantic uncertainties or ambiguities:** Terminology is often ill-defined and has conflicting meanings in different (scientific) contexts. Words can be ambiguous and lead to different interpretations of information. Interpretations can be influenced by how the communication is framed, the setting in which it takes place, perceptions about the communicator's intentions, as well as many other factors. Sometimes a word can have a very similar meaning but a different nuance or emotional charge across different communities, which can also lead to uncertainty.
- **Ethical uncertainties:** What makes a good decision? What is 'right' and for whom? What should be valued? What are acceptable risks, thresholds, and trade-offs? Who should have the right to decide and how?
- **Subjective (expert) judgements:** Experts are constantly making calls, from a decision that some uncertainty should be quantified, to setting parameter values, to processing data, selecting appropriate equations, deciding if the model is sufficiently plausible, and how different models should be weighted, to advising on trade-offs, constraints, and climate goals.
- **Computational uncertainty:** Increasingly, computers are integral to gaining insights into climate risk. The complexity of models and their code, run times and other computational demands, the nature of statistical algorithms (e.g. machine learning, if used) introduce their own uncertainties. Is the code error-free? Have models converged? Are they exploring the whole parameter space, have they been over-fitted to data, do they have predictive power or skill, and how should we assess whether the models are fit for purpose?
- **Deep uncertainty:** Decisions are made under deep uncertainty when key stakeholders cannot agree on appropriate models, probability distributions, and/or values.

TOOLS AND RESOURCES

Here are a small handful of resources related to communicating climate and environment information, including communicating climate science for decision-makers and stakeholders, climate and environmental storytelling, and facilitating participatory processes. This list has been crowdsourced, starting in October 2021, and will be maintained at least for the next year as the living document (located here) component of the Toolkit. Please feel free to recommend your own resources in the online document, and be as descriptive as possible about why you are recommending them.

NAME / LINK	TYPE OF RESOURCE	COMMENTS	KEYWORDS
COP26 Universities Network + Climate Action Unit Communicating Climate Risk Handbook	Toolkit and presentation slides	A variety of tips and insights, mostly from Climate Action Unit, primarily aimed at scientists engaging with policymakers. Includes insights for understanding and engaging end users, writing hacks	comms; end users; writing; decision support
IPCC WGI Interactive Atlas	Interactive atlas	"A novel tool for flexible spatial and temporal analyses of much of the observed and projected climate change information underpinning the Working Group I contribution to the Sixth Assessment Report, including regional synthesis for Climatic Impact-Drivers (CIDs)."	maps; interactive maps; IPCC; uncertainty;
#TalkingClimateChange Handbook	Guide	"We are deeply influenced by the conversations we have with our peers. Talking about climate change with our family and friends is a crucial part of making change. Explore our guidance for how to have climate conversations that will leave you feeling inspired and connected."	public; popular discourse; conversations; guides; deliberation; participation
#TalkingClimateChange workshop package	Workshop resources	"These resources provide practical evidence-based guidance on how you can help friends, family, colleagues, neighbours and members of your community feel more confident about talking about climate change in their daily lives. The idea is to spread the word and upskill our communities to have better climate conversations — conversations that leave them feeling inspired and connected."	public; popular discourse; conversations; guides; education; workshops, training
FlowingData	Blog	"I'm Nathan Yau. I run FlowingData. [...] I have a PhD in statistics from UCLA, with a focus on visualization for presenting data to everyone. I want as many people as possible to understand data, and I think visualization — from statistical charts to infographics to data art — is the best way to get there."	data visualisation; data art; aesthetics
Kate Raworth, Doughnut Economics www.kateraworth.com/doughnut/	Book	Raworth's book seeks to imagine the economics of the future, and is also notable for its discussion of the role of charts and diagrams in the history of economics and its social and political impact	data visualisation; economics; de-growth; growth agnosticism; Beyond GDP; metrics
CambridgeZero www.zero.cam.ac.uk/	Organisation	The university's hub for all things related to climate crisis and transition to a zero-carbon world, connecting up many different research centres and groups, and with a strong strand of climate communication	net zero; research; climate science
IPCC Photo Library www.ipcc.ch/sr15/mulitimedia/photo-library/	Website	A small collection of photographs together with guidance on how to use visuals to communicate about climate change	documentary; visuals; photographs; aesthetics
10 Tips on Visualising Climate Risk	Tool	Ten tips for using visuals to communicate (both data visualisation and photography) from AU4DM	design principles; visuals; photographs; aesthetics

NAME / LINK	TYPE OF RESOURCE	COMMENTS	KEYWORDS
Communicating Climate Risk Toolkit—a survey	Survey	Help the COP26 Universities Network and AU4DM to develop tools focused on communicating complex and uncertain information.	survey
weADAPT www.weadapt.org/	Platform	"weADAPT is a collaborative platform on climate change adaptation issues. It allows practitioners, researchers and policymakers to access credible, high-quality information and connect with one another."	infographics; research; comms
National Trust Climate Hazard Maps	Dashboard	An ArcGIS based platform to explore climate hazards in the UK	maps; interactive maps; hazards; GIS
MCC Carbon Clock www.mcc-berlin.net/en/research/co2-budget.html	Communication	Live countdown of 'remaining carbon budget.'	case studies; visuals; speculative design
Visualising Uncertainty: A short introduction	Toolkit	This primer, published by the Analysis under Uncertainty for Decision-Making network (AU4DM), summarises the current state of the art of uncertainty visualisation research. It brings together a wealth of relevant studies, concepts, and practical tools and recommendations.	design principles; data visualisation; deep uncertainty
WeDoData	Company	Specialises in all kinds of data visualisation, great examples (in French).	data visualisation; dashboards; narratives; infographics
Worldwide Climate Policy	Dashboard	'How could the burden of GHG emissions reductions be shared among countries? We address this arguably basic question by purely statistical methods that do not rely on any normative judgment about the criteria according to which it should be answered.' Although, assuming that statistical methods are not 'normative' is, in our opinion, incorrect, there are valuable insights in this visualisation. See also Climate Equity Reference Calculator.	data visualisation; dashboards; mitigation policies
RealClimate.Org	Scientists' Blog	"We're often asked to provide a one stop link for resources that people can use to get up to speed on the issue of climate change, and so here is a selection. Unlike our other postings, we'll amend this as we discover or are pointed to new resources. Different people have different needs and so we will group resources according to the level people start at."	climate science communication; visualisation; modelling
Carbon Brief	Website	"Carbon Brief is a UK-based website covering the latest developments in climate science, climate policy and energy policy. We specialise in clear, data-driven articles and graphics to help improve the understanding of climate change, both in terms of the science and the policy response. We publish a wide range of content, including science explainers, interviews, analysis and fact checks, as well as daily and weekly email summaries of newspaper and online coverage."	graphics; climate science communication; fact checks
Climate Equity Reference Project	Website and Dashboard	"The Climate Equity Reference Calculator is a general online equity reference tool and database that systematically applies a generalized and transparent equity reference framework with the goal of quantitatively examining the problem of national fair shares in a global effort to rapidly reduce greenhouse gas emissions. It can be applied using a range of possible assumptions, and whatever values are chosen, they are applied to all countries, in a dynamic fashion that reflects the changing global economy."	data visualisation; dashboards; mitigation policies; equity
Chapman, Daniel A., Adam Corner, Robin Webster, and Ezra M. Markowitz. 2016	Article	'Climate Visuals: A Mixed Methods Investigation of Public Perceptions of Climate Images in Three Countries'. Global Environmental Change 41 (November): 172–82. https://doi.org/10.1016/j.gloenvcha.2016.10.003.	climate imagery; visual communication, imagery public engagement; mixed-methods

AUTHORS, CONTRIBUTING EXPERTS & ACKNOWLEDGEMENTS

Jo Lindsay Walton, Corresponding Author
Sussex Humanities Lab, University of Sussex, UK.
J.C.Walton@sussex.ac.uk.

Polina Levontin, Author
Centre for Environmental Policy, Imperial College London, UK.

Martine J. Barons, Contributor
Applied Statistics & Risk Unit, University of Warwick, UK.

Dilman Dila, Contributor
Writer, filmmaker and storyteller, Kampala, Uganda.

Jana Kleineberg, Contributor
Kleineberg Illustration & Design, Liverpool, UK.

Erik Mackie, Contributor
Cambridge Zero, University of Cambridge.

Maurice Ssebisubi, Contributor
Embassy of Iceland, Kampala, Uganda.

Mark Workman, Contributor
Grantham Institute for Climate Change, Imperial College, London, UK.

This publication is part of a series, that also includes:
- *Visualising Uncertainty: A Short Introduction*
- *Decision Support Tools for Complex Decisions Under Uncertainty*

The first edition of the Toolkit received funding and support from the UK Universities Climate Network (UUCN), formerly known as COP26 Universities Network. The UUCN is a network of over 85 universities and research centres working together to promote a resilient and zero carbon future. The UUCN enables collaboration within the UK academic sector to advance climate action nationally and internationally.

The **Analysis Under Uncertainty for Decision-Makers Network** (AU4DM) is a community of researchers and professionals from policy, academia, and industry, who are seeking to develop a better understanding of decision-making to build capacity and improve the way decisions are made across diverse sectors and domains.

THE STORY BEHIND THE COVER

"Fighting for Climate Justice,"
temperature quilt by Fran Sharp.

The cover, and some other aspects of design in this Toolkit, have been inspired by this temperature quilt by Fran Sharp. Quilters are helping to visualise and communicate climate risks to the public through their work.

We learned about Fran Sharp's work from an article by Rebecca Onion (2020) in Slate.com, which put this work into the context of not just communication but resistance: "These projects also play with the idea of 'steganography'—the concealment of secret information in plain sight. The Tempestry Project's Emily McNeil told the Philadelphia Inquirer in 2019 that the group formed after hearing about scientists and archivists who were preserving climate-related research data before the Trump inauguration in early 2017. "We were just sort of joking one night about how we should return to more concrete forms of data storage, like tapestries, because you can't just get rid of them on the Internet," McNeil said. The history and mythology of fiber and textile art is full of steganography, real, fictional, and apocryphal—the Belgian resistance during World War II, recruiting women whose windows were located over train yards to knit patterns of the trains' arrivals and departures; Madame Defarge of Dickens' A Tale of Two Cities, knitting a list of people to be guillotined; enslaved women sewing codes into quilts that helped people navigate the Underground Railroad." Onion remarks, "Climate change is a classic open secret: a thing that we all know is happening, but that our officials (by and large) choose to ignore when they are making the decisions that matter. The temperature blanket is a very 2020 way to call attention to the reality of this data. There it is, warming your legs."

Onion, Rebecca. *'The Quilters and Knitters Who Are Mapping Climate Change'.* Slate, 8 February 2020. slate.com/technology/2020/02/quilts-knitting-cross-stitch-climate-change.html.

A NOTE FROM THE ARTIST:

Fran Sharp has been quilting for 20 years, and has made over 100 quilts. She especially likes quilted pieces with a message, be it political, spiritual or about nature. She hopes that viewers will make meaning from the images and add their own interpretations.

This quilt, "Fighting for Climate Justice" depicts temperature data for Boston from the year 2019; each rectangle (one day) has two shapes representing the high and low temps of the day. Each month is one column, with January on the left.

This page was intentionally left blank.

This page was intentionally left blank.

This page was intentionally left blank.